Walter Benjamin and
Cultural Translation

Bloomsbury Advances in Translation Series

Series Editor: Jeremy Munday, Centre for Translation Studies, University of Leeds, UK

Bloomsbury Advances in Translation publishes cutting-edge research in the fields of translation studies. This field has grown in importance in the modern, globalized world, with international translation between languages a daily occurrence. Research into the practices, processes and theory of translation is essential and this series aims to showcase the best in international academic and professional output.

A full list of titles in the series can be found at:
www.bloomsbury.com/series/bloomsbury-advances-in-translation

Titles in the series include:

Celebrity Translation in British Theatre, Robert Stock
Collaborative Translation, edited by Anthony Cordingley and Céline Frigau Manning
Community Translation, Mustapha Taibi and Uldis Ozolins
Corpus-Based Translation Studies, edited by Alet Kruger, Kim Wallmach and Jeremy Munday
Extending the Scope of Corpus-Based Translation Studies, edited by Sylviane Granger and Marie-Aude Lefer
Genetic Translation Studies, edited by Ariadne Nunes, Joana Moura and Marta Pacheco Pinto
Global Trends in Translator and Interpreter Training, edited by Séverine Hubscher-Davidson & Michał Borodo
Institutional Translation for International Governance, Fernando Prieto Ramos
Intercultural Crisis Communication, edited by Federico M. Federici and Christophe Declercq
Islamic State in Translation, Balsam Mustafa
Music, Text and Translation, edited by Helen Julia Minors
The Pragmatic Translator, Massimiliano Morini
Quality in Professional Translation, Joanna Drugan
Retranslation, Sharon Deane-Cox
Sociologies of Poetry Translation, Jacob Blakesley
Systemic Functional Linguistics and Translation Studies, edited by Mira Kim, Jeremy Munday and Zhenhua Wang
Theatre Translation, Massimiliano Morini

Translating For Singing, Ronnie Apter and Mark Herman
Translating Holocaust Lives, edited by Jean Boase-Beier, Peter Davies, Andrea Hammel and Marion Winters
Translating the Poetry of the Holocaust, Jean Boase-Beier
Translating in Town, edited by Lieven D'hulst and Kaisa Koskinen
Translation Solutions for Many Languages, Anthony Pym
Telling the Story of Translation, Judith Woodsworth
Vladimir Nabokov as an Author-Translator, Julie Loison-Charles
What Is Cultural Translation? Sarah Maitland

Walter Benjamin and Cultural Translation

Examining a Controversial Legacy

Birgit Haberpeuntner

BLOOMSBURY ACADEMIC
LONDON • NEW YORK • OXFORD • NEW DELHI • SYDNEY

BLOOMSBURY ACADEMIC
Bloomsbury Publishing Plc, 50 Bedford Square, London, WC1B 3DP, UK
Bloomsbury Publishing Inc, 1359 Broadway, New York, NY 10018, USA
Bloomsbury Publishing Ireland, 29 Earlsfort Terrace, Dublin 2, D02 AY28, Ireland

BLOOMSBURY, BLOOMSBURY ACADEMIC and the Diana logo are trademarks of Bloomsbury Publishing Plc

First published in Great Britain 2024
Paperback edition published 2026

Copyright © Birgit Haberpeuntner, 2024

Birgit Haberpeuntner has asserted her right under the Copyright, Designs and Patents Act, 1988, to be identified as Author of this work.

Cover design: Elena Durey

All rights reserved. No part of this publication may be: i) reproduced or transmitted in any form, electronic or mechanical, including photocopying, recording or by means of any information storage or retrieval system without prior permission in writing from the publishers; or ii) used or reproduced in any way for the training, development or operation of artificial intelligence (AI) technologies, including generative AI technologies. The rights holders expressly reserve this publication from the text and data mining exception as per Article 4(3) of the Digital Single Market Directive (EU) 2019/790.

Bloomsbury Publishing Plc does not have any control over, or responsibility for, any third-party websites referred to or in this book. All internet addresses given in this book were correct at the time of going to press. The author and publisher regret any inconvenience caused if addresses have changed or sites have ceased to exist, but can accept no responsibility for any such changes.

A catalogue record for this book is available from the British Library.

Library of Congress Cataloging-in-Publication Data

Names: Haberpeuntner, Birgit, author.
Title: Walter Benjamin and cultural translation : examining a controversial legacy / Birgit Haberpeuntner.
Description: London; New York: Bloomsbury Academic, 2024. | Series: Bloomsbury advances in translation | Includes bibliographical references and index. | Summary: "Dissecting the radical impact of Walter Benjamin on contemporary cultural, postcolonial and translation theory, this book investigates the translation and reception of Benjamin's most famous text about translation, "The Task of the Translator", in English language debates around 'cultural translation'. It offers a clearer picture of the translation and reception processes that have generated the immense impact of Benjamin on contemporary cultural theory, as well as new perspectives for a way of reading that re-shapes the canonized texts themselves and holds the potential of disturbing, shifting and enriching their more 'traditional' readings"– Provided by publisher.
Identifiers: LCCN 2023046673 (print) | LCCN 2023046674 (ebook) | ISBN 9781350387188 (hardback) | ISBN 9781350387218 (paperback) | ISBN 9781350387201 (eBook) | ISBN 9781350387195 (ePDF)
Subjects: LCSH: Translating and interpreting–Philosophy. | Benjamin, Walter, 1892-1940–Influence. | Benjamin, Walter, 1892-1940. Aufgabe des Übersetzers. | Benjamin, Walter, 1892-1940–Translations–History and criticism.
Classification: LCC P306 .H33 2024 (print) | LCC P306 (ebook) | DDC 418.02–dc23/eng/20231206
LC record available at https://lccn.loc.gov/2023046673
LC ebook record available at https://lccn.loc.gov/2023046674

ISBN: HB: 978-1-3503-8718-8
PB: 978-1-3503-8721-8
ePDF: 978-1-3503-8719-5
eBook: 978-1-3503-8720-1

Series: Bloomsbury Advances in Translation

Typeset by Deanta Global Publishing Services, Chennai, India

For product safety related questions contact productsafety@bloomsbury.com.

To find out more about our authors and books visit www.bloomsbury.com and sign up for our newsletters.

Contents

List of Figures viii
List of Abbreviations ix

Introduction: Obscurity and Tension 1

Part I Walter Benjamin

1 The Iconic Text in Context 25
2 The Conceptual Relevance of Translation in Benjamin's Early Writings 30
3 Terminological Gaps, Translation Practice, and Literary Criticism 46
4 *Umschmelzungsprozesse*, and a Late Return to Translation 58

Part II . . . Meets Cultural Translation

5 Benjamin's Arcade 75
6 Benjamin's Afterlife 102
7 Benjamin's Untranslatability 128

Conclusion: Unforeseen Constellations 151

Notes 159
References 182
Index 193

Figures

1	Passage de l'Opéra, galerie de l'Horloge, Paris	78
2	Drawing of the spatial structure of an arcade	83
3 and 4	Drawings of a cave-like arcade, as well as a light and airy arcade	83
5	Salle Labrouste, Bibliothèque Nationale, Paris	89

Abbreviations

GS I–VII Benjamin, W. (1972–1999), *Gesammelte Schriften*, eds. R. Tiedemann and H. Schweppenhäuser, Frankfurt a.M.: Suhrkamp. VII vols., II supplements.

GB 1–6 Benjamin, W. (1995–2000), *Gesammelte Briefe*, eds. C. Gödde and H. Lonitz, Frankfurt a.M.: Suhrkamp, 6 vols.

SW 1–4 Benjamin, W. (1996–2003), *Selected Writings*, eds. M. Jennings and M. Bullock, Cambridge, MA: Harvard University Press, 4 vols.

Introduction
Obscurity and Tension

Walter Benjamin and Cultural Translation

Without my being aware of it, the two focal points of this study began to crystallize about fifteen years ago.[1] I was enrolled in a double master's program in English and American studies, and theater, film, and media studies. It did not take long for me to encounter Walter Benjamin—at the English department, nonetheless. Benjamin seemed to be omnipresent there, at least in the form of reference. I vividly remember becoming aware of the fact that Benjamin was constantly being quoted—in a seminar class on cultural translation. It was telling, I know now, that our professor never explained to us what cultural translation was; instead, she asked us to tell her what we thought it was. We had to write a response paper in which we were to develop our own understandings of cultural translation and relate these to the prose texts we had read in class. But in our library, I only found two books in which the term was actually used, namely Homi Bhabha's *The Location of Culture* (1994) and Ashok Bery's *Cultural Translation and Postcolonial Poetry* (2007). I soon realized that under the usual time constraints, I was in over my head with Homi Bhabha, so I quietly shut *The Location of Culture* and opened *Cultural Translation and Postcolonial Poetry*, where I found a helpfully concise formula, and I ran with that. From then on, the term, to me, denoted the "different ways in which one language or culture can be related to, or transferred into, another" (2007: 7). It was as easy as that. As I realize now, this is simultaneously a very limited and a very broad understanding of cultural translation, and it may be criticized from various angles. Still, something opened up for me, and I found ways of bringing it up in seminar papers for years to come.

This was not only my first encounter with cultural translation, but it also awarded me the insight that Walter Benjamin was, indeed, omnipresent. Shortly before I gave up on *The Location of Culture*, I found Benjamin's name mentioned in there, as I found it also in Ashok Bery's study on *Cultural Translation and*

Postcolonial Poetry. So, eventually, I decided that I wanted to read the actual texts that Walter Benjamin had written, and I began attending all the close-reading seminars about Walter Benjamin I could find. That way, my perspectives on Benjamin multiplied. I read his German texts and the English translations. I read about his texts in contemporary English-language studies about cultural and postcolonial theory, and I read German philological studies about the complexities of Benjamin's thinking and writing. Thus, an intriguing field of tension opened up, not only between different disciplines, but also between the English and German Benjamins, and my own different ways of approaching the two. On the one hand, I encountered pearls of stunning and powerful linguistic imagery, which had been taken from Benjamin's German texts and incorporated into the studies of contemporary English-language commentators, who have tried to use Benjamin to think beyond Benjamin. On the other hand, I was delving ever deeper into the convoluted philosophical German texts that were usually—and often only—discussed within the context of Benjamin's own works, and within the context of European modernity. From this field of tension developed the idea of this book.

The main reason, beyond my initial encounter, why I chose to zoom in on the field of cultural translation was a continued observation, over the years, that there seemed to be an ever-growing interest in translation throughout the humanities and social sciences. The abovementioned class I took was, in many ways, a foreshadowing—in its own uncertainty about the term, for one, but also with regard to the increasing attention being paid to translation in general, and to concepts in particular that were increasingly detached from linguistic and literary parameters. In different disciplinary contexts, translation had become an analytical tool for the study of a wide range of different phenomena. In order to capture this move beyond the literary and the linguistic, the notion of "cultural" had seemingly become irresistible, and it was added to "translation." That way, the concept of cultural translation quickly worked its way into many aspects of the contemporary humanities and social sciences, and it remains there to this day. The concept has clearly hit a nerve, as evidenced not only in its popularity, but also in the fact that there continues to be a heated academic debate about its use and viability. A major issue seems to be that it resists a unified definition: the "cultural" is deceivingly world-conjuring, referring to nothing in particular and everything at once, just as the intrinsic ambiguity of "translation" does not allow for much more clarification. Thus, the concept of cultural translation is exceptionally hard to pin down. It is constantly being re-invented. New meanings are inscribed. New frames of reference are set and expanded. And still, in almost all of the concept's various manifestations, there is a familiar reference: Walter Benjamin. That is why I decided to take a closer look at this constellation, in which Walter Benjamin and cultural translation meet—over and over again, and in very different, often contested contexts.

As I began reading into the varied theories of cultural translation, it quickly became clear to me that I would at least have to try and trace its discursive and conceptual history, in order to find out more about the theoretical, disciplinary, and historical constellation that actually put the "cultural" next to "translation." From the beginning, then, I have encountered frequent attempts at (re-)constructing the "origins" of the term, and most of them led down two particular tracks. The first one—tracing a cultural anthropological line, which is often credited with having coined the term—takes Talal Asad's 1986 text on "The Concept of Cultural Translation in British Social Anthropology" as its main benchmark.[2] What many of the publications linked with this first genealogical line, if you will, have in common is a critical engagement with the idea of cultural translation as a "translation of cultures." In talking about "translating cultures," a strictly linguistic, interlingual concept of translation is necessarily expanded—in a move that goes hand in hand with Clifford Geertz' famous idea of culture-as-text: for if cultures are "readable," then why should they not be "translatable"? Thus, it is not surprising that Asad's critique of the "translation of cultures"-concept, its status within anthropology, and the position of the ethnographer-author-translator, is part of the seminal 1986 publication *Writing Culture: The Poetics and Politics of Ethnography*. While Asad refers to the idea of "translating culture" as cultural translation, he also says that under different names, it has "since the 1950s . . . become an almost banal description of the distinctive task of social anthropology" (1986: 140). In doing so, Asad refers, among others, to Godfrey Lienhardt and Ernest Gellner, both of whom configure and critically engage with the task of the anthropologist as a task of translation—in an expanded sense, but without yet using the term "cultural translation."

A second genealogical line, then, latches onto a later benchmark: Bhabha's 1994 publication *The Location of Culture*, which has become regarded as almost singularly responsible for the widespread popularization of the term, cultural translation.[3] Bhabha actually uses the term for the first time in 1989, in a magazine article for the *New Statesman*,[4] which he wrote in reaction to the fatwa issued to kill Salman Rushdie after the publication of his *The Satanic Verses* (1988).[5] This is also the context he picks up again in "How Newness Enters the World," that is, Chapter 11 of *The Location of Culture* (1994). From the liminal position of the migration experience, which he configures as translational and transitional, he develops a decidedly postcolonial notion of cultural translation. Due to the theories Bhabha draws on, and the references he makes,[6] this second genealogical line leads back to poststructuralist perspectives on translation—mainly De Man and Derrida—and to a German Romantic tradition, which is said to have favored a "foreignizing" approach to translation.[7]

As I outline in more detail later on in this introduction, the second genealogical line is the one within which Walter Benjamin is most often embedded, firmly nestled in-between that German Romantic tradition and the poststructuralist readings by De Man and Derrida. Yet this discursive role attributed to Benjamin is, of course, reductive. In order to move beyond this limiting narration in favor of a better integrated perspective, and to engage productively with the dynamics of cultural translation at present, it seems crucial to complicate and contextualize these two lines—one tied to Bhabha, and the other to Asad (who, by the way, also significantly relies on Walter Benjamin)—by indicating, at least, other contexts and historical indices that cultural translation inevitably carries with it still. For that reason, let me briefly outline the way I see the varied historical and theoretical travels of cultural translation as still reaching into its present dynamic.

Emerging Interdisciplines, Entangling Genealogies

For one, it seems crucial to stress that, when the term was eventually used by Bhabha in the late 1980s, the concept "behind" the term had already "silently," without its label, traveled extensively, especially around the young discipline of Translation Studies: during the late 1970s and the 1980s, Translation Studies tried to define its own disciplinary space apart from linguistics and literary studies, and this space was decidedly cultural. From that space emerged an understanding that would integrate the linguistic, literary, *and* cultural aspects of translation, yet these reflections from within the discipline have often become bracketed out in the widespread reception of Bhabha's formulation of cultural translation outside of Translation Studies. There, the term is often read as *only* embedded in Bhabha's context, and is thus—rightfully so—criticized as limited.

Especially for readers unfamiliar with this disciplinary discourse, it may be interesting to note that an influential first attempt at providing a comprehensive theory of translation that could form the basis for a scientifically founded discipline was undertaken in the 1960s by Eugene A. Nida, a US-American linguist, Bible scholar, and translator, who distinctly aimed at developing a "science of translating."⁸ Nida's translation theory is embedded in a framework similar to Noam Chomsky's generative grammar,⁹ and it seems firmly anchored within a paradigm of equivalence: assuming that expressions in one language can have the same "value" in another language, the relation between "original" and "translation" is substantially configured as one of equivalence (Pym 2010: 42–6). Like most theories operating within this paradigm, Nida's is based on a set of oppositions, mainly, between formal and functional (or dynamic) equivalence. Roughly, the former remains close to the source and to the form and content of the message, where the latter shifts toward the receptor and attempts to reproduce the function of the message, which lies primarily in the relationship between text and reader (e.g., Nida 1964: 159). Nida's work taps into what Susan Bassnett calls an early culturalist phase of engagement with translation, in that he argues for a well-founded understanding of the particularities of cultural context in order to be able to adequately assess functional equivalence. However, his understanding of and relationship with the study of culture is largely influenced by his own work as a missionary and Bible translator, which he recounts in his 1954 book *Customs and Cultures*. So, while "a whole line of thinking in translation emerges out of the cultural work of Bible translators like Eugene Nida" (Bassnett 1998: 129), it is crucial to stress, as Bassnett does, that his concept of culture was highly situated, with his linguistic and cultural work firmly anchored within a fundamentally Eurocentric, Christian-missionary framework.

In a subsequent structuralist phase, then, additional approaches emerged to systematically give shape and definition to Translation Studies' own space for the study and practice of translation. What all of them had in common was that they promoted and took part in a shift from the authority of the source text toward its life in the target culture. The two that are discussed most frequently were developed almost simultaneously, but, at least at the beginning, independently from each another, though in response to similar stimuli.¹⁰ The two projects are the Vermeer/Reiss skopos theory and the manipulation school—a denomination based on the seminal publication *The Manipulation of Literature: Studies in Literary Translation* (1985), edited by Theo Hermans, with contributions by Susan Bassnett, André Lefevere, and Gideon Toury. Starting out from different disciplines—Vermeer/Reiss in linguistics and the manipulation school largely in literary studies—they both attempted to define a distinct project of Translation Studies. And besides a shared target-orientedness, they both regarded translation as a process of "cultural transfer" (i.e., the title of Vermeer's 1986 paper)¹¹ and/or a "crucial instance of what happens at the interface between different linguistic, literary and *cultural* codes" (Hermans 1985: 11). In a publication entitled

Translation, History and Culture, Susan Bassnett and André Lefevere described this turn toward the cultural as follows: "Now, the questions have changed. The object of study has been redefined; what is studied is the text embedded in its network of both source and target cultural signs and in this way Translation Studies has been able to both utilize the linguistic approach and to move out beyond it" (2002: 12). With this statement, Bassnett and Lefevere stress their own focus in emphasizing the texts' double-embeddedness in target *and* source culture, as well as their deliberate move beyond linguistics; yet, in doing so, they also pinpoint processes that took place throughout the young field. Translation Studies carved out its own disciplinary space—as an interdiscipline, some would argue[12]—by developing and promoting an integrated understanding of translation that would include linguistic, literary, *and* cultural facets, methods and areas of research.

All this raises an interesting question: If these "cultural" understandings of translation were so instrumental for the development of Translation Studies, and have continued to be throughout its phase of consolidation and up until today, why has there still been a need to make the "cultural" explicit as such? Why use the term "*cultural* translation" at all? Following up on this question has led me into the field of anthropology—and back again, into its neighboring disciplines. Arguably, anthropology is the one discipline concerned with culture as its main object of research,[13] at least until the 1970s, and the one that set off the sparks to ignite cultural turns in other disciplines. During the 1960s and 1970s, cultural anthropology saw a return to Franz Boas'[14] hermeneutic approach to studying culture, as the discipline went through developments that may be read through the lens of a broader linguistic turn. This was especially due to Clifford Geertz' conception of culture-as-text,[15] which had profound effects on the concepts both of text *and* culture: on the one hand, the usage of text as an analog allows Geertz to talk about readability, and to apply hermeneutic as well as semiotic methods; on the other hand, text (as culture) can no longer be limited to written words, but has to include practices, performances, and lived experiences.

Soon, other disciplines began to express their interest in this emerging field of cultural anthropology: historian William H. Sewell, for instance, recounts that he decided to borrow methods for his own work, to better

> understand the meaning of workers' practices that I had been unable to get at by using quantitative and positivist methods—my standard tool kit of what was then called "the new social history." I experienced the encounter with cultural anthropology as a turn from hardheaded, utilitarian, and empiricist materialism

... to a wider appreciation of the range of human possibilities, both in the past and in the present. (1999: 35–6)

He was not alone in this. Many "outside" scholars tried to render productive the borderlands between anthropology and their own disciplines. At the same time, however, these developments have resulted in a hot debate within the discipline about the constructed nature of culture and the role of the ethnographer. These discussions have carried the discipline into a reflexive turn, which was associated with the so-called *Writing Culture*-debate. In 1986, the US-American historian James Clifford and the anthropologist George E. Marcus edited the abovementioned collection of essays, *Writing Culture. The Poetics and Politics of Ethnography*, which is where Asad's text about cultural translation was first published. The book was widely read and discussed, beyond the field of anthropology. In many ways, *Writing Culture* constituted a continuation of the hermeneutic understanding of culture-as-text, and simultaneously offered its critique: If cultures are (ensembles of) texts, who is writing and constructing them? In bringing this question to the forefront, the author-ethnographers' positions, as well as their imagining, constructing and writing acts, are exposed and questioned.

The unveiling of ethnographers as narrators biased by their own historical and sociocultural embeddedness—as mostly male, European-American academics—did not only unsettle the ethnographers themselves but the whole discipline, which led to a "severe identity crisis" (Sewell 1999: 37) and to a destabilization of the discipline's concept of culture.[16] Sewell says:

> anthropology's most central and distinctive concept . . . has become a suspect term among critical anthropologists—who claim that both in academia and in public discourse, talk about culture tends to essentialize, exoticize, and stereotype those whose ways of life are being described and to naturalize their differences from white middle-class Euro-Americans. (1999: 37–8)

Culture had become suspect. On the one hand, it was seen as carrying an ontological burden; on the other hand, the conception of culture-as-text began to emphasize cultures' constructedness, and questions were now being asked about those who construct (the other) culture-as-text in the ethnographic process. Such challenges have, as Brightman remarks in his text, "Forget Culture," resulted in "lexical avoidance behavior" (1995: 510): in the face of crisis, anthropology put the noun "culture" in quotation marks, or simply avoided it altogether.[17]

As Clifford stresses, twenty-five years later, in a comment on the *Writing Culture*-debate, all that had happened at a very particular historical moment:

"I see *Writing Culture* as occupying a transitional moment—late 1960s–early 1990s—in the larger history of the last half-century. And I understand this postwar history as the interaction of two distinct but entwined historical processes: decolonization and globalization" (Clifford 2012: 423). Global expansion, reactive regionalization, and localization, as well as new modes of distributing media, popular culture, and populations—these are all polycentric as well as hegemonic processes that have gone hand in hand with continued and renewed imperial domination. At the same time, as national liberation movements were successful in breaking away from colonial rule, especially between 1945 and the 1960s, there have also been ongoing anti-colonial cultural processes connected with a decentering of power and cultural representation, a self-conscious reinscription of repressed or forgotten histories, minorities, and literatures, as well as a deconstruction of colonial gestures and Western norms and forms of knowledge.

Engaging with both globalization and decolonization, postcolonial perspectives have thus emerged to form a complex discourse that not only refers to a critical historical category denoting the ways in which the global situation is shaped by such historical forces of colonization, decolonization, and neo-colonization but also moves beyond this historical dimension as a discourse-critical cultural theory directed against Eurocentric orders of knowledge. The latter manifested in publications like Edward Said's *Orientalism*, published in 1978. A "holy trinity" of postcolonial studies thus emerged with Edward Said, Gayatri Chakravorty Spivak, and Homi Bhabha (Young 1996: 163f), accompanied during the 1980s by a growing number of studies that focused on former colonial literatures. These critics looked at how colonial experiences were processed in symbolic forms, how discourses reinforced processes of colonization, and if and how (literary) counter-discourses could become spaces of resistance, subversion, and self-empowerment.

In these endeavors, postcolonialism drew critical energies from post structuralism, and at this crucial intersection, postcolonialism and structuralism meet translation. For a concrete example of what poststructuralism came to criticize in this regard, let me briefly go back to 1959, when the Russian philologist and linguist Roman Jakobson wrote his well-known article, "The Linguistic Aspects of Translation." Jakobson argues that there is no non-linguistic meaning and states, with Charles Sanders Peirce, that meaning lies not within the sign itself, but in its "translation into some further, alternative sign, especially a sign 'in which it is more fully developed'" (Peirce, in Jakobson 1959: 233). Jakobson then distinguishes three types of translation:

1. Intralingual translation or *rewording* is an interpretation of verbal signs by means of other signs of the same language.
2. Interlingual translation or *translation proper* is an interpretation of verbal signs by means of some other language.
3. Intersemiotic translation or *transmutation* is an interpretation of verbal signs by means of signs of nonverbal sign systems. (1959: 233)

He thus expands the term "translation" to include an intralingual movement, which raises epistemological questions, as well as an intersemiotic movement, which sparks questions about the relation between different arts and media. However, to him, interlingual translation remains the core sense of translation, that is, "translation proper." This is where Jacques Derrida begins his criticism:

> when it is a question of translation "proper," the other uses of the word "translation" would be in a position of intralingual and inadequate translation, like metaphors, in short, like twists or turns of translation in the proper sense. There would thus be translation in the proper sense and translation in the figurative sense. And in order to translate the one into the other, within the same tongue or from one tongue to another, in the figurative or in the proper sense, one starts down a road that quickly reveals how this reassuring tripartition can be problematic. (Derrida 1985a: 199)

Derrida is relentless in his rejection of logocentrism, which he identifies "as an exigent, powerful, systematic, and irrepressible desire for such a [transcendental] signified" (1976: 49). To him, there is no such thing as a transcendental signified: "every signified is also in the position of a signifier," "the thing itself is a sign" (1976: 49). With this perspective, Derrida seems to be very close to Jakobson, yet he regards the latter's writing, his formulations and rewordings, as inconsistent. Not only does it enforce a notion of "proper" vs. secondary meanings, but it also assumes that languages, and sign systems, are segmentizable entities between or within which translation operates: "This obviously presupposes that one can know in the final analysis how to determine rigorously the unity and identity of a language, the decidable form of its limits" (1985a: 171). It is a presupposition Derrida does not want to share.

Obviously, such a perspective has significant repercussions, especially for translation theories rooted in the abovementioned paradigm of equivalence, within which the translation process is supposed to align the translated text with its source in terms of equivalence, measured against the meaning enclosed within the original. From a poststructuralist perspective, this pattern aches to be deconstructed. In his book *Contemporary Translation Theories*,

Edwin Gentzler outlines some of the questions that deconstruction asks of translation:

> What if one suggested that, without translation, the original text ceased to exist, that the very survival of the original depends not on any particular quality it contains . . . ? What if the "original" has no fixed identity that can be aesthetically or scientifically determined but rather changes each time it passes into translation? (1993: 145)

From a deconstructive perspective on translation, the source text can no longer be the authority that dictates its translation in terms of equivalence. Tellingly, when Derrida comments on translation in his writings, the role of the source text is often described by means of entities that are present and absent at the same time. In *Specters of Marx*, the source text, too, takes on the characteristics of a specter, it "always moves, by definition, in the manner of a ghost. The thing haunts, for example, it causes, it inhabits without residing, without ever confining itself to the numerous versions" (1994: 20–1). The source text as a ghost: this image calls forth associations with a threshold, an in-between, in this case between life and death, between spatio-temporal moments. In various respects, this threshold/in-between, where it is possible for things to be "at once present and absent," is like a siren's call to poststructuralist critics. Particularly in regards to translation, Gentzler points out that poststructuralists "have found thinking in that space between languages that occurs in the process of translation exceedingly fruitful—that space that occurs before the right word has crystallized—for the pursuit of such [deconstructive] activities" (2002: 199).

This space is also where one of the most productive convergences between poststructuralism and postcolonialism manifests. In colonial enterprises, the geographical border that separates "us" from "them" is drawn and redrawn to invent, just as much as it is drawn to record: "the spatial was always and only a loose image for a perceived or desired racial, cultural and gendered divide" (Ashcroft, Griffiths and Tiffin 1998: 88). Postcolonial critics thus attempt to re-think the spatial, particularly the border, and ascribe to it a subversive, creative, and transformative potential for the process of unveiling, complicating, and deconstructing binaries. Two of the most well-known, though very different, reconfigurations of the border are Gloria Anzaldúa's borderlands, and Homi Bhabha's third space. While the former is explicitly connected to a particular geographical space, the borderlands between the United States and Mexico, the latter denotes an epistemological category, as well as a conceptual space in which his understandings of hybridization, processuality, and temporality meet.

It emerges when Bhabha talks about the difference between cultural diversity and cultural difference. The former, he argues, suggests a set of distinct and separate cultures existing besides each other, a perspective that forms the basis for conceptions such as multiculturalism, cultural exchange, and so on, which presupposes and propagates a sense of closure and pregiven conditions (1994: 30f). Bhabha challenges this perspective by means of his notion of cultural difference. In doing so, he draws attention to a term that may be seen as located between *langue,* as a system, and *parole,* as an utterance being generated from the system, namely *enunciation,* that is, the process of articulation that shapes the relation between the two. This shift in focus, roughly, entails a shift from the statement—its content, meaning, reference, or judgment—toward the performance, practice, or experience of speaking (Phillips and Tan 2005). To Bhabha, the undecided space of *enunciation* becomes an epistemological passage: "The production of meaning requires . . . the passage through a Third Space, which represents both the general conditions of language and the specific implications of the utterance in a performative and institutional strategy" (1994: 36). Culture, to Bhabha, is thus "a signifying or symbolic activity" (Rutherford and Bhabha 1990: 210) in the third space of enunciation, where relations between system and articulation are created and re-created, unvaryingly producing cultural difference. Thus, culture can never refer to an origin or a single meaning, and there can never be hierarchical claims to originality or "purity."

Especially when analyzed as an activity, culture thus needs to be situated in time and space. This is a crucial aspect of the overall approach that Bhabha promotes in his seminal book on *The Location of Culture,* and it ties in with something that is often not taken seriously with regard to his work, namely, its materialist undergirding (Young 2017; Marchart 2007). This becomes especially clear when looking at the time and place of Bhabha formulation of culture, and of cultural translation: "In Britain, in the 1980s . . ." (qtd. in Young 2017: 186). At that time, when Bhabha was a lecturer at the University of Sussex, cultural studies and its leading figures were still a dominant influence for the British intellectual scene, and especially the 1980s saw a firm orientation toward a cultural materialism inspired by, above all, Antonio Gramsci and Louis Althusser. In Bhabha's own words, which he writes about one of his most influential contemporaries, Stuart Hall, after his death: "The contours of Thatcherite discourse were custom-built to raise the ire of an early *New Left Review* intellectual from Jamaica, who had deftly recast Antonio Gramsci in the spirit of poststructuralism and was by the mid-80s increasingly coming to regard Britain as a postcolonial society of diasporic cultures and migrant communities"

(Bhabha 2015: 1). Much of this, it might be argued—from the migration-activist background, to the contemporary intellectual milieu and its influences—is also applicable to Homi Bhabha himself.

More than that, though, it is notable how the institutionalization of yet another interdiscipline (e.g., Bassnett 1998: 138), namely, British cultural studies, reaches into the contemporary dynamics negotiating the cultural dimensions of translation. It is no coincidence, I would argue, that the credo of early Translation Studies was to find a descriptive practice of looking at all aspects of translation theory, history, and practice, while keeping in mind "the indissoluble connection between language and way of life" (Bassnett 2014: 2)—echoing Raymond Williams' famous formulation of culture, groundbreaking for cultural studies in particular, as "a whole way of life" (1958: XIV). For cultural studies, this broadened understanding of culture has enabled a substantial re-valuation of popular culture, and it has yielded a sharpened focus on its conflictual dimensions: its proponents aim at bringing to light ambivalences, as well as the political motivation of seemingly unpolitical cultural practices and phenomena, in order to productively complicate and problematize them (Marchart 2008: 13). Consequently, there is a strong mutual interrelation between British cultural studies' political and theoretical trajectory, which finds expression, for instance, in its investment with working-class culture and adult education. In a very tangible sense, then, cultural studies promote the necessity of fostering the political intervention of theory, a project that is, at that time in Britain, closely aligned with the contemporary *New Left*, its intellectual leading figures, and their readings of the abovementioned Gramsci and Althusser. To be sure, it is hotly debated whether the promise of a fruitful cooperation between translation and cultural studies in these matters, or even the promise of the abovementioned project of cultural studies as such, has ever been productively honored; this is immanently clear from the debate around the concept of "cultural translation," to which I return later on in this chapter. Yet there is, for all the similarities outlined earlier,[18] an undeniable kinship between the two interdisciplines and their institutional histories.

All of these cross-disciplinary developments, which took place in the 1960s–1980s, are paradoxical and fascinating to trace. They have not only yielded various interdisciplines, such as translation and cultural studies, but they have clearly provided the breeding ground for both Asad's and Bhabha's understandings of cultural translation. In fact, Bhabha would have heard a version of Asad's paper on cultural translation at a 1984 conference in Essex, and it seems as if—in a move that is very much indicative of his dealing with sources in general[19]—Bhabha has decided to revive "the idea of cultural translation just as Asad was pronouncing its death in anthropology" (Young 2017: 191). Clearly, the genealogies of cultural translation are thus much more muddled and entangled than it might seem at first sight. And, what is more, it must also be noted that the term "cultural translation" turns up much earlier than all of the outlined developments: most notably, it has been used in the fields of linguistics and linguistic anthropology since the early decades of the twentieth century, for instance, in the writings of Edward Sapir.[20] Later, it is also picked up by Eugene Nida, the early pioneer of Translation Studies, in the 1960s.[21] And only then, it eventually reaches a phase of relative popularity in cultural anthropology during the mid-1980s, when it finds its way into the *titles* of notable scientific publications—most prominently, of course,[22] through Asad's contribution to the *Writing Culture*-publication of 1986. It is at that point in time, too, that the idea of culture-as-text(s) begins its travels, with the result that anthropology's project of reading, writing, and translating cultures triggers various cultural turns in other disciplines. Yet, at the same time, these developments have left culture's "home discipline" destabilized. It may thus be argued that the field gave up some of its critical energies to other, newly emerging disciplines—to the young discipline of Translation Studies, for instance, which took translation back, relieving it of its anthropological burden, and inscribing it instead with a cultural component of its own; without, however, feeling the need to make the "cultural" explicit by referring to the process as "cultural translation."

Debating Turns and Terms

While the outlined developments have, initially, largely taken place within—and in the contact zones between—linguistics, (comparative) literary studies, anthropology, translation, and cultural studies, "cultural translation" today, it seems, is increasingly applied as an analytical tool in multiple other disciplines such as legal studies (e.g., Foster 2014), medicine (e.g., De Pue et al. 2010), public relations or economics (e.g., Grunig et al. 1995), art history (e.g., Milner and Campbell 2004), gender studies (e.g., Macedo and Pereira 2006), history (e.g., Burke and Hsia 2007; Gamsa 2011), social studies (e.g., Mariette de Haan 2012), or language teaching (e.g., Farahzad, Parviz and Razmjou 2011)—largely with the objective of examining the travels of cultural artifacts, expressions, and practices within and between cultures, or in order to try and make sense of cultural exchange in a broader sense.

Against this background, it may be argued that the travels of the concept of cultural translation have facilitated a turn toward translation throughout the humanities and social sciences. Already in 2006, Bachmann-Medick proclaimed that we were experiencing a translational turn. In her study *Cultural Turns: Neuorientierungen in den Kulturwissenschaften*, she proposes we resist the temptation to identify one cultural turn and look instead at the interdisciplinary developments during the late twentieth to early twenty-first century in terms of multiple cultural turns. She identifies various impulses, and traces them throughout different disciplines in order to illustrate that these smaller stories can subvert the narrative of a singular cultural turn, and that they may also contribute to a "disempowerment" of the prior, the linguistic turn's claim to validity as a singular "mega-turn." Thus, she argues that the series of cultural turns that she has identified—interpretive, performative, reflexive/literary, postcolonial, translational, spatial, and iconic—provides a reservoir of focalizations that open up new horizons for research in the wake of the linguistic turn (2006: 19).

Whereas, in general, I am skeptical of the way in which Bachmann-Medick outlines this "turn-dynamic,"[23] I cannot help but find it alluring to think in terms of a translational turn. As I have mentioned before, there has been this demonstrably growing interest in translation throughout the humanities and social sciences, which does not seem to be slowing down.[24] To me, the movement through which translation had its focus shifted away from linguistic and literary parameters, and has instead (been) turned toward the world-conjuring "cultural" in its travels through various neighboring disciplines, is indeed reminiscent of how the concept of culture-as-text traveled around, through the 1980 to the 1990s, triggering cultural turns in other disciplines. Back then, cracking open the concept of culture has undeniably allowed for "something else," something productive, to evolve from the borderlands around anthropology, which has led to a re-focalization in other disciplines, "gradually invoking those dimensions of culture, lifeworld, history and, above all, action that had been masked out—suppressed, even—by the language-narrowness of the linguistic turn" (Bachmann-Medick 2012b: 36).[25] This makes it all the more alluring, I find, maybe for lack of a better term, to similarly think of the travels of cultural translation as a catalyst for a turn toward translation in other disciplines.

At the same time, it may well be that this reminiscence is what has contributed to an express uneasiness from within the field of Translation Studies, about how translation has increasingly been used as an analytical tool in various other disciplinary contexts, in which the qualifier "cultural" makes (a new and different) sense. For, as productive as culture-as-text may have proved to be for other disciplines, it led to a destabilization of the concept of culture within its "home discipline," to the degree that cultural anthropologists literally stopped talking about culture. Back then, this disciplinary uneasiness has turned into a breeding ground for heated, interdisciplinary debate—and it did so, too, with regard to the concept of cultural translation. There was, for instance, a discussion platform series hosted by the journal *Translation Studies* in 2009 and 2010, entitled *Forum: Cultural Translation* (2009–10), in which multiple responses by renowned scholars, who had published on cultural translation and related topics before, follow up on an impulse text by Boris Buden and Stefan Nowotny. Translation studies scholar Anthony Pym also contributed to this debate in a separate article, "On Empiricism and Bad Philosophy in Translation Studies" (2009), in which he writes that he was asked to comment on the impulse text but declined, because he had "no idea what the text was about" (2009: 34). Eventually, there is also a crucial earlier text, which leads the way for several recurring points of criticism, namely, Harish Trivedi's "Translating Culture vs. Cultural translation" (2005), as well as a recent article by Brian James Baer, "From Cultural Translation to Untranslatability" (2020), which constitutes a critical update.

To briefly recapitulate on the broad strokes of the debate,[26] one of its central issues is what is considered an uncontrolled metaphorical extension, which is linked to a fundamental concern for the practice of interlingual translation and bilingual engagement in a broader sense (esp. Trivedi 2005, also Baer 2020). A prevalent Eurocentrism in theorizing translation is also repeatedly pointed out (Chesterman 2010; Young 2010), as well as, related to the first concern, a fear of "unregulated" interdisciplinary dissemination (esp. Tymoczko 2010, Wagner)—and the "disciplinarily proprietorial air" (Young 2010) of Translation Studies. Two more interrelated issues are an ethical point, on the one hand, and the struggle for cultural translation's methodological validity, on the other. The former is tied to the criticism that cultural translation has lost touch with social and political realities, and that it discursively perpetuates and reinforces the inequality of power relations in its predominantly Western academic discourse (Baer 2020; Pym 2009; Bery 2009; Chesterman 2010; Ha 2010). As for the latter, there is loud criticism directed at the uncritical transfer of theory of interlingual translation to the field of cultural translation (Tymoczko 2010; Pratt 2010).[27]

There are several aspects of this debate that have hit a nerve with me, especially with regard to the particular issues I examine in this book. For one, there is this repeated "charge" of metaphorization, as well as Robert J. C. Young's response, that translation quite literally *is* metaphor, and that to argue against the metaphorical extension of translation implies that there is an "original" meaning that is linguistic—which it never was, as it has always had different but equally relevant layers of meanings. This entire argument, it seems to me, points toward a deeper-seated discord within the debate. For one, it relies, in either of its various forms, on an "original" meaning or context of translation—which is often meticulously but one-dimensionally constructed for the sole purpose of being deconstructed, re-conceptualized, exceeded, gone beyond. At the same time, though, there are plenty formulations of cultural translation, often based on postcolonial and/or poststructuralist premises, that aim at subverting, or at least challenging, the very notion that this argument is based on, the very notion of the "original" as such. This is to say that conceptual foundations in this debate vary to such a degree that it almost seems as if "cultural translation" has become an arena for these conflicting philosophical partisanships much rather than an instrument for productive interdisciplinary debate. Buden/Nowotny, for instance, do not hide the fact that their concept of translation, and thus their approach of cultural translation, comes with a clear historical and theoretical index that refers to deconstructive and poststructuralist critiques of anthropology and cultural theory. And this is what much of the respondents' criticism is ultimately directed at. Consequently, parts of the discussion feel like a surrogate debate about two more deep-seated issues in particular: the direction of Translation Studies as a discipline and the direction of the humanities at large. In the context of the latter, shots are fired at poststructuralism and deconstruction, and there are loud calls for a return to empiricism. At the same time, the humanities, and cultural studies in particular, are accused of having become stuck in an ivory tower, dominated by a Western *Bildungsbürgertum* playing chic intellectual games in a hegemonic, global form of English, while neglecting complicated political realities, lifeworlds, and practices. And the discourse around cultural translation is taken to be representative of, if not jointly responsible for all of these concerns. On the other hand, as I have alluded to before, there are aspects of the discussion that point toward a general uneasiness within and about the field of Translation Studies. The continuous questioning of the term and the need to make the "cultural" explicit there, quickly leads to the conclusion that both, the term and the concept of cultural translation hardly hold any merit. This argument goes hand in hand with a prevalent skepticism toward the "metaphorical extension" of translation, the use of translation as an analytical tool, or the import of translation theories to other disciplinary contexts. Thus, this debate about making that "cultural" explicit mirrors a sense of protectionism, as well as concerns about losing grasp of translation.[28]

Examining a Controversial Legacy

Now, with the stakes raised, I return to the question regarding the discursive role attributed to Walter Benjamin in this context. In their characterization of cultural translation's conceptual development, Buden/Nowotny assign a particular place to Benjamin: as a continuation, yet at the same time "radical criticism" of German Romantic translation theory, his concept of translation is seen as a starting point for a development that leads to Derrida and Bhabha. In their responses to the impulse text, then, ten out of the fifteen respondents also explicitly refer to Walter Benjamin. Most of them substantiate Benjamin's positioning within the outlined genealogical line:[29] Simon, for instance, reinforces the iconic place of Benjamin as the starting point of a powerful counter tradition (and she stresses that Translation Studies have long been aware of this tradition). Cortés curtails, but further adheres to the genealogical line: he reduces it to two names, Benjamin and Bhabha, as he credits the two for being the minds behind a perspective that he calls "Benjamin and Bhabha's heterogeneous fluidity" (2010: 101). To Kien Nghi Ha, Benjamin is one of only three names to stand out from Buden/Nowotny's travel through the conceptual history of cultural translation. Lieven D'Hulst adds a historian's perspective, claiming that while a thoroughly historical view has largely been absent in looking at cultural translation, what does take place is "rational reconstructions" (Rorty, in D'Hulst 2010: 353), that is, genealogy-based approaches that result from direct lines being drawn between single scholars—and one of these direct lines he identifies as the one from Schleiermacher to Benjamin, Derrida, and Bhabha. These scholars are attributed a paradigmatic role, he argues, while the discursive and institutional transfer processes are neglected.

Walter Benjamin thus clearly becomes one such central hub on an often-drawn genealogical line of cultural translation. In this role, he is often invoked in various attempts at constructing and/or legitimizing one or another genealogy of cultural translation, rather than examined in a process of detailed, productive, and creative engagement with *what* he said. And indeed, it is this way of (not really) engaging with what Walter Benjamin actually said that turns into a label of "bad philosophy," as Pym argues in his article on "Bad Philosophy in Translation Studies." As I illustrate throughout this book, a quotation of, or reference to, Walter Benjamin seems to be enough to either assume philosophical partisanship, usually with the genealogical line that eventually leads to deconstruction and poststructuralism, and/or to elicit said accusation of bad philosophy. To me, though, this kind of criticism is strikingly similar to the way in which the *entire reception* of Benjamin's texts in English is often—particularly from the side of German native speakers—stereotypically criticized as overall de-contextualizing and superficial. Or, it is argued, Benjamin has simply been misunderstood, misinterpreted, and mistranslated. In what follows, I therefore attempt to circumvent this entire dynamic by looking at the relation between Walter Benjamin and cultural translation from a different perspective.

So, here we are again, back at what I had wanted to do from the beginning: find a productive way of examining this intricate constellation, marked by obscurity and tension, in which Walter Benjamin and cultural translation meet, over and over again. To find said productive way, however: that was another story. When I talked to people about it, some told me that this was going to be a straightforward study in reception. Yes, that was partly what I wanted to do. I had heard that I was going to need discourse analysis. Yes, certainly, partly. Conceptual history, comparative literary analysis, Translation Studies. Partly. I had a clear idea of where I wanted to go, but no signposted way of getting there. At some point, however, time constraints and economic necessity dictated that I hurry, so I stopped reading about methodology and started to work (while finding creative ways of dodging methodological questions). And, in the end, it was precisely the labyrinth of detours that I have outlined earlier which has brought me to a point from which I am able to see what I have been doing. As I am writing this introduction, I see this book as an unorthodox study in reception, which relies on translation as its main methodological principle. I take the translation of Benjamin's German texts into English as a starting point, or, more precisely: I start with moments of conflict, disturbance, and displacement, and then look toward possible new spaces that open up in the process. I investigate how the English-language reception makes these creatively productive in discussions of "cultural translation," and how they re-shape, or complement, Benjamin's texts.

This methodology was most effective in the second part of this study. The first part, however, seemed to require a different approach. It was crucial for various reasons, I decided, to illustrate the way in which Benjamin thought about, theorized, and practiced translation throughout his writings. As I have indicated, the English-language reception of Walter Benjamin is often judged for being, in different ways and degrees, "too far away" from the German texts. And as much as I go on to challenge the underlying position that these judgments are based on, I do see the value of mediating a sense of closeness to Benjamin's writings, while also emphasizing its multifaceted nature. That is the quality I aim for in the first part of this study, beginning with, but going way beyond the one essay that is usually referred to, namely "Die Aufgabe des Übersetzers." While I anchor the iconic essay firmly within its biographical, theoretical, and historical background, which is often disregarded in its reception, I quickly move beyond this central essay, in order to illustrate the multifaceted relevance of translation in Benjamin's other writings. This includes the immense relevance of Benjamin's translation practice throughout his life. In the end, this chapter constitutes what I call a biographical semantics of translation, which offers a contextually more complete picture of the intersections between Benjamin's translation theory and practice. In doing so, I follow the methodological guidelines provided by a German publication entitled *Benjamins Begriffe* (Opitz and Wizisla 2000), which assembles essays that look at the unfolding of Benjamin's terms, in order to trace his way of thinking in the dynamic and transformative development of the terms themselves. I thus look for transformations, expansions, disturbances, and vacancies in the development of Benjamin's thinking about, and practice of, translation—throughout his works, and beyond "Die Aufgabe des Übersetzers."

The second part of this study, then, follows the methodology outlined earlier. It constitutes three case studies that illuminate the different ways in which Walter Benjamin and cultural translation actually meet in the texts of contemporary English-language commentators. I look at this constellation from an interlingual perspective, which means that I look for concrete shifts and disturbances, and then follow where they lead. In the first case study, I examine a translational conflict that has, as far as I am aware, so far gone unnoticed when it comes to the reception of Walter Benjamin: namely, the translation of two distinct German words denoting two distinct archeological structures, *Arkade* and *Passage*, as "arcade." Due to the theoretical and biographical importance of the Parisian *Passage* for Benjamin and his readers, it is almost exclusively this *Passage* from his later works that is read into the English word "arcade," while the image of the archway, the *Arkade*, is almost entirely lost. In following up on this shift in translation, I illustrate how this "conflict" has been rendered productive in the theorizing of cultural translation: it has opened up a space of possibilities in which English-language commentators, like Tejaswini Niranjana and Rey Chow, have inscribed potentials that go way beyond Benjamin's texts, as the "arcade" creates a terminological bridge that allows them to seamlessly bring together his early thoughts on translation with his later writings on history and mass media. These readings thus also demonstrate the way in which new perspectives on Benjamin are opened up in this process that illuminate correspondences in Benjamin's writings that have otherwise gone largely unnoticed.

In the second case study, I use the same method to look at another conflict in translation, in this case, one that has already been identified as a "mistranslation," namely, Benjamin's concept of *Fortleben* being translated as "afterlife." In the end, however, I demonstrate that Benjamin's concept in itself is sold short if it is only limited to the term *"Fortleben"*: it is much rather a figure of thought that surmises different Benjaminian terms and concepts (*Über-, Fort-*, as well as *Nachleben*)—and in its "translational journey," it actually unfolds and evolves in a transformative way that is similar to how terms tend to evolve throughout Benjamin's own writings. At the same time, this case study illustrates in detail how Benjamin's texts are deployed on strikingly different philosophical fronts: Benjamin's *Fortleben* indeed moves into Bhabha's postcolonial context through Derrida's poststructuralist "translation" of it, while Sarah Maitland firmly places Benjamin in a hermeneutic tradition. In her study, Benjamin is thus attributed a stunning discursive role: in an attempt to demarcate from what has become a habitual set of references in discussions of "cultural translation," and thus to soften hardened fronts of criticism, Maitland takes Benjamin—who Bhabha, as well as Niranjana and Chow, either position as a precursor of, or as an anachronistic corrective to, poststructuralist theory building—and re-positions him in the hermeneutic tradition she is perpetuating.

This latter issue, then, moves to the forefront of concern in the third and final case study. I proceeded from another "translational conflict," which has led many commentators to read the Translator-Essay in the light of "the untranslatable": Benjamin's most-read translator, Harry Zohn, renders "whatever in a translation is not retranslatable" (1968c: 302) as "the element that does not lend itself to translation" (1968b: 75)—which, in Bhabha's infamous reading, turns into the "untranslatable" element of cultural translation, its "element of resistance." This final case study has the same methodological structure as the previous ones, and yet there is an additional layer to it: for after looking into Benjamin's concepts of un/translatability, in the Translator-Essay and beyond, and after investigating Bhabha's infamous reading of them, I analyze how this reading was "operationalized" in discussions about the "questionable practice" of working with Benjamin in the context of cultural translation. Bhabha is charged with instrumentalizing, decontextualizing, and unreservedly metaphorizing Benjamin's concepts; but for the sake of these arguments, a "correct," fully contextualized and "literal" understanding of Benjamin is mobilized. In this process, Benjamin is, ironically, appropriated in attempts at denouncing the appropriation of Benjamin. While this kind of criticism looks to demonstrate both the pitfalls of Bhabha's formulation of cultural translation, and the pitfalls of cultural translation theorization as such, it also reveals how cultural translation turns into an arena for conflicting philosophical partisanship. This third case study thus serves to illustrate how Benjamin is simultaneously summoned in support of a particular theoretical or philosophical position, and to criticize entire discursive formations for a lack of intellectual diligence or empiricism.

In the end, I argue in a brief epilogue that the abovementioned criticisms reveal an anxiety of openness that runs counter to the trajectory of Benjamin's philosophy and method. It begins with Benjamin's dictum predicting an "apocryphal" influence for his (and Adorno's) writings, yet it would seem as if the Apocrypha have become canonized: they are frequently ascribed absolute authority; which is to say that the prevalent way of approaching them, by proclaiming or promoting a "literal," "verbatim," or "true" understanding, has led to a perpetual (re-)production of doctrine. To address the subcutaneous dogmatism and conservatism in many of the pronounced findings of loss, this book demonstrates an alternative approach, centering instead Benjamin's *Fortleben*, the dynamic, testing, expansive, transformative trajectories of Benjamin's writings that lead *beyond* themselves. In doing so, this final chapter mobilizes two resistant qualities of *Fortleben*: its anthropophagic nature, which leads into a complex transatlantic history of re-/appropriation; and a resistant quality of the apocryphal, the demand of remote and disruptive things to be recognized. In the end, I hope that readers will not only come away from this book with a clearer picture of the translation and reception processes that have generated the immense impact of Benjamin on contemporary cultural theory (and their sharp criticism), but that the new perspectives that the book engenders also demonstrate a way of reading that re-shapes the canonized texts themselves and holds the potential of disturbing, shifting, and enriching their more "traditional" readings. At the same time, I hope that these perspectives provide readers interested in cultural translation with new stimuli to engage productively with the dynamics of the term at present.

Part I

Walter Benjamin

1

The Iconic Text in Context

Berlin, 1920. A 28-year-old Benjamin had just moved back to Germany after spending two years in Switzerland earning his doctorate. Back in Berlin, Dr. Benjamin received an offer to publish his translations of Baudelaire's *Tableaux Parisiens*. This offer did not come out of nowhere: Benjamin had been working on these translations since 1914, and he had long been on the lookout for publishing options. Eventually, Richard Weißbach, who owned a small publishing house in Heidelberg, approached him with the prospect of publishing the Baudelaire translations as a monograph. This came as a relief to Benjamin: it was going to be his first book-length publication in Germany, his doctoral thesis having only been published in Switzerland.[1]

In December of 1920, Benjamin decided to add a theoretical preface to his translations. "Die Aufgabe des Übersetzers," as it was to be called, would allow him, he thought, to kill two birds with one stone: it would introduce him to a broader public as both a translator and a philosopher. The preface manifests, among many other things, a cleverly designed plan to achieve this twofold goal. While the text may often have been referred to as obscure and hermetic, it would be deceptive to leave it at that. Taking Benjamin's very concrete goals into consideration (i.e., to be taken seriously as a translator and as a philosopher), Benjamin must have been well aware that he would have to present not only notable translations but also resolute critical positions, relating to the goings-on within intellectual circles at the time. Thus it may be worth asking whom exactly he wanted to address. It has been argued (Abel 2014: 190ff; Barck 2012: 121f) that it was the circle around Stefan George, which is very reasonable, tactically speaking. They constituted an intellectual elite of almost ominous sovereignty, and George himself had translated Baudelaire's *Tableaux Parisiens*. A new translation would undoubtedly be noticed, if not by him, then at least by his followers. For Benjamin, this was an opportunity: through the publication of his own Baudelaire translations, he might be able to catch the attention of these important intellectual figures and, through the preface, could let them know what he stood for. To reach this intellectual elite, he chose a form and mode of operation that seems entirely appropriate, namely that of an esoteric essay only the initiated would understand.

The high expectations that Benjamin had set for himself did not make for an easy task. To produce the impressive piece that he had in mind, Benjamin intended to mobilize the intellectual force of all that he had been thinking about up until that point. In a letter to his friend Gershom Scholem in March 1921, Benjamin complains that the subject matter of the preface was

> so zentral für mich ..., daß ich noch nicht weiß, ob ich ihn, im jetzigen Stadium meines Denkens, mit der ausreichenden Freiheit entwickeln kann, vorausgesetzt, daß mir seine Aufklärung überhaupt gelingt. (GB 2: 145)
>
> so crucial to me that I still do not know whether I can develop it with sufficient freedom, given the current stage of my thinking and provided that I can succeed in elucidating it at all. (1994: 177)

This letter testifies to Benjamin's uncertainty with regard to the preface, as well as the troubles he had finding adequate philosophical literature on translation. He felt that not much had been written about this "crucial subject" and that he was ill-equipped to present it synthetically. Thus, he was looking for relevant literature to ground his thoughts through a process of thorough criticism. He asked Scholem for bibliographical references. But, in the end, it does not seem to have been necessary: in May, not even two months after the letter, he finished a first draft of the essay, which seems to rely much more on his own body of thought than on any secondary literature. Notably, though, many of the cursory mentions or references to other texts are in one way or another connected with the George circle (Pannwitz, Mallarmé, Hölderlin).

By the time Benjamin had finished a first draft of the preface, all questions regarding the contract for his Baudelaire translations had been resolved. Weißbach and Benjamin had come to agree that it would be a bilingual edition, as Benjamin had suggested. It would include Baudelaire's poems in French as well as Benjamin's German translation. There would be a luxury edition, as well as a "popular" version, which Benjamin had insisted on. For the latter, Benjamin would receive 15 percent of the profit from every book sold. Altogether, Benjamin deemed these conditions favorable, which they certainly were. This general agreement, however, was followed by a long back and forth, much of which was based on questions of aesthetics: when discussing print typography, for example, Benjamin insisted on experimenting with minimal punctuation and he showed a keen awareness of the different requirements regarding the setting of French and German texts.² At the same time, Benjamin continued to rework his translations, requiring drafts to be sent back and forth by the post.

With all these delays, it soon became clear that the planned publication date, October 1921, was not going to hold. Nonetheless, Benjamin and Weißbach made more plans together. Over the summer, Benjamin visited the publisher in Heidelberg, and while he declined Weißbach's offer to take over the editorship of his magazine, *Argonauten*, Benjamin took the opportunity to suggest the possibility of founding a new magazine. Weißbach agreed. Benjamin called his new project *Angelus Novus*, in reference to the Paul Klee drawing of the same title, which he had recently acquired.³ Benjamin was delighted and, as the publication of his Baudelaire translations seemed to be in limbo, he decided to develop a plan B in order, at the very least, to publish the preface: "The Task of the Translator" would be printed in the first issue of *Angelus Novus* as an independent essay.

However, Benjamin may not have taken the economic limitations of Weißbach's small publishing house into consideration. Soon, the first issue of the newly founded magazine was also overdue. And eventually, by 1923, the *Angelus Novus* project had died without yielding a single issue. Nonetheless, throughout 1922, Benjamin worked on both the *Angelus Novus* and his Baudelaire. In March, he held a lecture about Baudelaire and a reading from his translations at a bookstore in Berlin, which was received favorably, but not widely. Until the end of 1922, the back and forth between Weißbach and Benjamin continued. It was a difficult process and their correspondence reveals that much of it was of Benjamin's doing. While he was relieved that his translations would be published, he had not only high hopes but also great demands. And while he was not easily pleased, he was easily offended, and even thought, at times, that Weißbach was conspiring against him. At the same time, Benjamin himself was not very reliable. Sometimes, he seemed excited and eager, then he complained about a lack of attention, lamenting that he was unable to work because he had not received the corrections. Then again, he complained about too much attention and too many corrections.

Nonetheless, his translation project, unlike the *Angelus Novus*, did eventually come together. Benjamin held the final print sheets in his hands in May 1923. He had them corrected by September and, by October 1923, Benjamin's translation of *Tableaux Parisiens* was published. But things did not get any easier from there. In spite of all his endeavors, the book collected dust on the shelves. The popular version was not printed, to which Benjamin had to concede due to the dire economic situation at that time. Nonetheless, Benjamin tried his best to boost sales and visibility. He organized readings and sent out gratuitous copies to newspapers and important literary figures. The fate of this book remained important to him even ten years after it was first published. In 1933, Benjamin, exiled in Paris, approached booksellers on his own inquiring whether they would be interested in selling his bilingual Baudelaire translations.

Not only did his book not sell—neither did it draw much attention. Benjamin had such high hopes, in particular because he had friends in one of the leading newspapers, the *Frankfurter Zeitung*; he thought that he would receive favorable reviews. In January 1924, Benjamin received a note that Siegfried Kracauer would write a review for his book. But it did not go as planned: Kracauer gave the job to Stefan Zweig, who had translated Baudelaire, too. And again, Benjamin thought there was a conspiracy against him: Zweig's review was published in June 1924, on the first page of the *Frankfurter Zeitung*'s Sunday edition, and it was devastating. Benjamin found the review condescending to and patronizing of his translations. Moreover, Zweig did not even comment on the preface. A second, well-meaning review by Paul Wertheimer was published in the Viennese newspaper *Neue Freie Presse*, but the latter could not make up for the former in Benjamin's mind.

There is only one reaction by which Benjamin was demonstrably pleased, and that was a letter from the Austrian writer Hugo von Hofmannsthal. Benjamin highly admired Hofmannsthal's writing and criticism, and had even come to think of him as a "new patron" (1994: 227). Benjamin referred to Hofmannsthal's comments regarding his preface as an *Augurenlächeln*, an augurs' smile. The use of this term is intriguing. In German, it refers to the knowing smile of the initiate, suggesting understanding and comprehension. This is particularly interesting in light of the difficult relationship between Hofmannsthal and Stefan George, a possible addressee of Benjamin's Baudelaire-translation. The two had met in Vienna in 1891. George was six years older and had already established a reputation; Hofmannsthal was a little star-struck. Nonetheless, they forged a relationship. Hofmannsthal's poetry and essays were published in George's magazine, *Blätter für die Kunst*, and the two maintained a regular exchange of letters, until 1899. However, their contact eventually broke off after a few years of sporadic exchange, due to considerable differences in their views on art and due to Hofmannsthal's persistent criticism. Similarly, but from a different standpoint, Benjamin had also set out to criticize George from within. Thus, the term *Augurenlächeln* captures what Benjamin thought he had accomplished, at least with regards to Hofmannsthal: to give a knowing nudge to one of the knowing few, exposing where George's divinations had gone wrong.

As meaningful as Hofmannsthal's *Augurenlächeln* was to Benjamin, it was not enough to meet his high expectations regarding the reception of the Baudelaire-translation. Thus, all things considered, it represents a first big disappointment for Benjamin. It did not sell, and it did not seem to do much for Benjamin's reputation, neither as a translator nor a philosopher. The worst, however, was what remained unsaid: apart from Hofmannsthal's *Augurenlächeln*, the Translator-Essay was met with silence. From today's perspective, this is astounding, as it seems that there is no longer anyone "in the profession" (De Man 1985: 26) who has *not* said something about this text.

2

The Conceptual Relevance of Translation in Benjamin's Early Writings

Today, this famous preface is usually the first and often the only text discussed in relation to the topic of Walter Benjamin and translation. Without a doubt, this essay has been of great importance, not only for the many scholars who have commented on it during the twentieth century but also within the context of Benjamin's own work. As I argue in this section, the published translations, *Tableaux Parisiens*, remained dear to him throughout his life: it was his first monograph on the German book market; for the first time, his translation work had born tangible fruits; and it constituted his first public attempt to crystallize his intellectual endeavors around a subject that was immensely crucial to his thinking.

This "subject so crucial" had long occupied Benjamin's mind—and it would continue to do so, in theory and practice. Yet in thinking about this crucial subject, the Translator-Essay represents only a crystallized snapshot within the ever-changing net of relations that is Benjamin's work. It seems to raise more questions than it answers, particularly when it is left to stand on its own. In a peculiar way, this image-laden text reveals and hides something at the same time. Its textual imagery is dense and its gestures are simultaneously showing and pointing—in many different directions at once. Thus, I take it as a starting point for a tour through Benjamin's oeuvre. In doing so, I do not provide close readings, neither of the Translator-Essay nor of any other text. A whole shelf-full of books is dedicated to that objective. Instead, I trace here the way in which Benjamin theorizes and practices translation throughout his works, looking for superimpositions, correspondences, constellations, shifts, deferrals, and blind spots—and I attempt to be as concrete as possible in illustrating them in a biographical semantics of translation.

Benjamin first mentions *Übersetzung* in 1912, in a diary he kept during his *Bildungsreise* (Brodersen 1990: 44), an educational journey to Italy, which he took together with schoolmates after finishing high school. One of Benjamin's mates had to leave early, he tells us, and he left by boat: he was ferried over, *übersetzt* (GS VI: 287), to the big steamboat leaving for Trieste. This is the earliest text I found in which Benjamin uses the verb *übersetzen*—and he uses it to denote a spatial movement, referring to the process of bringing someone from point A to point B by boat. While this does not seem to bring us any closer to the "subject so crucial," it is a reminder of the broad spectrum of meaning that translation covers—both in common language use and in Benjamin's writings.

The next context in which Benjamin talks about *Übersetzung* is, unsurprisingly, very different. It comes up in another early text entitled "Teaching and Valuation,"[1] which Benjamin wrote in 1912-13 for a magazine entitled *Der Anfang*, which was edited by Gustav Wyneken and associated with the German Youth Movement. Under the pseudonym Ardor, Benjamin harshly criticized the institutional way of teaching history and German. In doing so, he does not rely on metaphor or vivid imagery in any way; there are hardly any descriptive or evaluative adjectives or adverbs at all, and his terminology stays within the field of prescriptive pedagogy. He sketches how lessons are usually structured, and two of his examples outline how translation is used as a tool to convey texts from the thirteenth century that were deemed important. Students read these texts at home, a few stanzas at a time, in its contemporary German translation as well as in their *Ursprache*, that is, Middle High German. The content is then retold at school, and stanzas are

> vom Lehrer in der Ursprache vorgelesen und teilweise übersetzt, teils durch Übersetzungsanleitungen kommentiert. (GS II: 35)
>
> read aloud by the teacher in their *Ursprache* and then partly translated, partly commented on through translation instructions. (My translation.)

This approach may take up to half a year, yet the inner *Gehalt*, the actual substance or content of the text, is never touched upon.

Here, translation opens up a very different, dense, and intriguing field of reference: in this institutional context, Benjamin considers it as an empty, didactic tool. He uses translation as an example of what he thinks is wrong with the prevalent contemporary way of teaching, which settles for *Stilübungen*,[2] exercises in style, instead of aiming for critical engagement with the inner value of literary works. With this argument, Benjamin anticipates a concept of criticism that would occupy his thoughts for a long time. The title of this text ambiguously hints at it, too: on the one hand, *Wertung* includes a notion that Benjamin harshly criticizes, namely a kind of judgment that leads to an assumed, canonic selection of literary works perpetuated by teachers and reproduced by students. But, on the other hand, *Wertung* also holds *Wert*, or value. And this notion of value is linked with what Benjamin wants to reclaim with regard to education, namely to engage with the inner value of a literary work through a process of criticism: "valuation . . . for the sake of knowledge" (2011: 94).[3]

Opposed to this, *Stilübung* only serves the mechanic function of transmitting the style of works that have been authoritatively selected to represent the assumed view of a certain epoch. Crucially, it is a temporal, a historical function of translation that is brought to the forefront of concern here: translation refers to a movement that primarily takes place between distinct historical moments, between different stages of development *within* the German language, not between what would traditionally be considered as distinct languages. Benjamin's early concept of translation holds the seeds of two interrelated aspects that will become increasingly important to Benjamin: translation as a temporal movement, in its particular connection with the growth of language(s), and its relation with criticism.

When Benjamin wrote this early essay, he was studying philosophy, German philology and art history in Berlin and Freiburg. During his studies in Freiburg, he met the young poet Fritz Heinle. A friendship developed between the two that was going to impact Benjamin for the rest of his life, not only because of what he describes as a magnetic and enigmatic bond between them, but also because of the way in which this bond was violently broken. When the First World War broke out in August of 1914, Heinle and Rika Seligson, his girlfriend, committed suicide. This was devastating to Benjamin. Until the end of his life, he would mention Fritz Heinle in his letters; he would write poems and essays dedicated to him; and he tried to publish Heinle's literary remains. But in spite of his ongoing endeavors, Benjamin never managed to do so. During the winter of 1914–15, Benjamin composed his first essay after Heinle's death and he later said that it was written in memory of his friend: "Two Poems by Friedrich Hölderlin."[4] The immediate impulse that prompted him to write this essay was a study by Norbert von Hellingrath about Hölderlin's Pindar-translations, which Hellingrath had recovered, analyzed, and published in 1910.[5] Benjamin's intensive reflections on Hölderlin, as a poet as well as a translator, went hand in hand with his own first attempts at translating: indeed, right around that time, in 1914–15, he began translating Baudelaire.

In 1915, Benjamin moved to Munich, where he continued his studies. He focused more on French literature now, and he also became interested upon the incentive of Rainer Maria Rilke in Mexican studies. This interest in different languages and literatures, he wrote in a later curriculum vitae, was due to his substantial "interest in the philosophy of language,"[6] which—together with his interest in the theoretical aspects of art—set the intellectual agenda for him at the time. In 1916, this constellation found expression in an essay entitled "On Language as Such and on the Language of Man."[7] It began as a letter to Scholem, in which Benjamin intended to comment on a discussion that the two had led about the relation between language and mathematics. But, after having written eighteen pages of that letter, Benjamin came to realize that this was a topic that needed a different kind of attention. Thus, he stopped writing the letter and began composing an essay. Later, he would describe his Language-Essay as a first step toward the "integration of [his] thought" (1994: 108).[8] This first step was the intensive study of the "essence of language," which Benjamin considered an essential basis for understanding "the essence of knowledge, justice and art" (1994: 108).[9]

The Language-Essay had never been intended for publication. It was written in a process of self-understanding and given only to a small circle of close acquaintances. Benjamin did not consider it complete, either. He had not been able to fully develop his thoughts yet; he was not even far enough, he said, to tackle the questions that triggered the essay in the first place (GB 1: 343). Nonetheless, he considered it to be an important first attempt, to which he would continue to return. And quite literally at the center of the essay, there is *Übersetzung*. About halfway through, Benjamin writes:

> Es ist notwendig, den Begriff der Übersetzung in der tiefsten Schicht der Sprachtheorie zu begründen, denn er ist viel zu weittragend und gewaltig, um in irgendeiner Hinsicht nachträglich, wie bis-weilen gemeint wird, abgehandelt werden zu können. (GS II: 151)

> It is necessary to found the concept of translation at the deepest level of linguistic theory, for it is much too far-reaching and powerful to be treated in any way as an afterthought, as has happened occasionally. (SW 1: 69)

In this text, Benjamin draws heavily on biblical topoi. He wrote to Scholem that his goal was to approach the essence of language "in its immanent relationship to Judaism and in reference to the first chapter of Genesis" (1994: 81).[10] References to Genesis indeed dominate the second part of the essay; in the first part, however, Benjamin develops an encompassing understanding of language without any reference to the Bible. It comes as no surprise that this concept of language is immensely difficult to grasp, but I give at least an impression of its magnitude, in order to contextualize the importance of translation within the frame of this concept of language. Benjamin begins with the argument that "every expression of human mental life can be understood as a kind of language" (SW 1: 62).[11] Then he goes one step further, expanding the scope of language from human mental life toward the entire scope of animate as well as inanimate nature:

> es gibt kein Geschehen oder Ding weder in der belebten noch in der unbelebten Natur, das nicht in gewisser Weise an der Sprache teilhätte. (GS II: 140)
>
> there is no event or thing in either animate or inanimate nature that does not in some way partake in language. (SW 1: 62)

Throughout the essay, though, Benjamin's concept of language is flexible and boundless. It takes different shapes, scopes, and frames of reference. He talks about a language of music, poetry, and sculpture; a language of justice and technology. To prevent the conclusion that this makes perfect sense, though, because every field has its own jargon, Benjamin adds the following half sentence: "a language of technology that is not the specialized language of technicians" (SW 1: 62)[12]—it is *not* a collection of distinct linguistic expressions exclusive to a certain field.[13] Instead, language refers to a *Prinzip*, a principle or "tendency" (SW 1: 62) *within* these field, directed at the communication of these fields' *geistige Inhalte*, their "mental contents" (SW 1: 62).[14] But this tendency is not all that language is: every form of expression that communicates these mental contents is language, too. Expression in the form of words, though, is a very particular case, namely the human one.

Then Benjamin introduces yet another pair of terms, namely *geistiges Wesen* and *sprachliches Wesen*. And with these, things get really tricky, particularly in English. The main issue is the term "*Wesen*." It comes with a long terminological history, not only in German philosophy but also in Benjamin's works, as the term is central in many of Benjamin's writings, particularly in the early ones. He also uses it in the letter to Schoen, quoted earlier, in which he states that he wants to approach the *Wesen* of language, in order to eventually find out more about the *Wesen* of knowledge, justice, and art. In this context, *Wesen* was translated as "essence"; throughout the Language-Essay, however, the English version shifts between "entity" and "being" as translations of *Wesen*. This illustrates some of the at times conflicting notions that this difficult term holds.

In the Language-Essay, Benjamin uses the term to differentiate between a linguistic or language-*Wesen* and a mental, spiritual, or immaterial *Wesen*. Both appertain to all events or things in animate or inanimate nature. With his discussion of the relation between the two, Benjamin adds his own perspective to a discussion about the relation between language and reality outside of language.

As expected, the relation that Benjamin outlines is a complex one, as there is no longer a clear border between language and reality outside of language. In all events or things, linguistic being and mental being overlap. That which *can* be communicated of the mental being is the linguistic being. However, that which *can* be communicated is *not* communicated *through* language, but *in* language—in the non-instrumental realm of language. This is true for all events or things, so there must be a language of events or things, too; the language of a lamp, for instance. The linguistic being of the lamp communicates its mental being *in* its language—but its language does not have words, or sounds, to do so. The linguistic being of mankind, on the other hand, is of a higher order: it is *benennend*, it is name-giving. Thus, there are different orders of language, such as the language of things or the language of man, which relate with each other like "media that are distinguished as it were by their density—that is, gradually" (SW 1: 66).[15]

Now, *Übersetzung* is not part of this encompassing concept of language that Benjamin outlines in the first section of the essay. Instead, the term surfaces in the *second* part, in reference to the book of Genesis. And it is assigned a truly fundamental status: the biblical act of naming is conceptualized as an act of translation. It is the translation of the language of things into the language of man, in which a receiving and a creating force—*Empfängnis* and *Spontaneität*, "reception and conception" (SW 1: 69)—come together. But that is not all that translation is. Referring back to his assertion that the different orders of language are like media of different densities, Benjamin states that translation unfolds its full meaning only if we see the relation between these media of different densities as a relation of translation, founded in translatability:

> jede höhere Sprache [kann] als Übersetzung aller anderen betrachtet werden . . . Mit dem erwähnten Verhältnis der Sprachen als dem von Medien verschiedener Dichte ist die Übersetzbarkeit der Sprachen ineinander gegeben. Die Übersetzung ist die Überführung der einen Sprache in die andere durch ein Kontinuum von Ver-wandlungen. Kontinua der Verwandlung, nicht abstrakte Gleichheits-und Ähnlichkeitsbezirke durchmißt die Übersetzung. (GS II: 151)

> every evolved language . . . can be considered a translation of all the others. By the fact that, as mentioned earlier, languages relate to one another as do media of varying densities, the translatability of languages into one another is established. Translation is removal from [*of*!] one language into another through a continuum of transformations. Translation passes through continua of transformation, not abstract areas of identity and similarity. (SW 1: 70; my annotation)

While the English rendition paints translation as the removal of *something* from one language into another, this relation is different in the German version, where the object *is* language, or rather, a particular order of language: translation is *Überführung*, transference, *of* one language into another. The different languages, or media of different densities, represent various gradations of incompleteness, and the more incomplete language can enter into the less incomplete only though transformative translation.

Toward the end of the essay, Benjamin describes this movement in its totality as a stream of translation, an "uninterrupted flow . . . through the whole of nature, from the lowest forms of existence to man and from man to God" (SW 1: 74).[16] And he continues with two additional, expressive metaphors to describe this movement; one secular, the other sacred: in the first one, the uninterrupted flow of translation is likened to the passing-on of a secret password:

> Die Sprache der Natur ist einer geheimen Losung zu vergleichen, die jeder Posten dem nächsten in seiner eigenen Sprache weitergibt, der Inhalt der Losung aber ist die Sprache des Postens selbst. (GS II: 157)

> The language of nature is comparable to a secret password that each sentry passes to the next in his own language, but the meaning of the password is the sentry's language itself. (SW 1: 74)

And with the second description, Benjamin returns to his familiar, biblical register:

> Alle höhere Sprache ist Übersetzung der niederen, bis in der letzten Klarheit sich das Wort Gottes entfaltet, das die Einheit dieser Sprachbewegung ist. (GS II: 157)

> All higher language is a translation of lower ones, until in ultimate clarity the word of God unfolds, which is the unity of this movement made up of language. (SW 1: 74)

Translation thus is *Sprachbewegung*, a movement made up of language, which finds its unity in God. Within the flow, the biblical act of naming translates the more incomplete language of things into the less incomplete language of man—and in the translational act of naming, Adam—still in paradise—communicates his being to God. His *Namensprache*, his name-language, is still unimpaired; it is the one language of man. But with the Fall of Man, plurality creeps in. Humankind loses grasp of name-language, which was "one of perfect knowledge" (SW 1: 72).[17] Instead, we gain the knowledge of good and evil. But this knowledge acquired is a knowledge from outside the name; good and evil, they stand "outside the language of names, unnameable and nameless" (SW 1: 72).[18] By referring to something outside the name, language becomes a means, an instrument: "the word must communicate *something* (other than [*außer*] itself)" (SW 1: 71; my annotation).[19] As soon as there is something "outside of" name-language, there are different ways of relating to it, understanding it. There is no longer *the* translation into *the* language of man, but instead there are,

> soviel Übersetzungen, soviel Sprachen, sobald nämlich der Mensch einmal aus dem paradiesischen Zustand, der nur eine Sprache kannte, gefallen ist. (GS II: 152)

> so many translations, so many languages—once man has fallen from the paradisiacal state that only knew one language. (SW 1: 71)

With the Fall, the language of man dissipates, it moves from one to many. And with this dissipation, man took a big step toward the fall of the tower of Babel.

As complex as all of this is, one observation is safe to make: within the scope of this essay, the concept of language is not at all based on the everyday use or dictionary definition of the term. This essay thus illustrates something crucial to many of Benjamin's texts: while he uses familiar terms and topoi, the concepts, references, and scopes of meaning attributed to them shift and take new turns. In this case, not only seemingly familiar concepts of language but also our commonsensical understanding of translation between separate language-systems are disjointed. Languages are not posited as enclosed systems sitting next to each other all across the world. Instead, language is principle and expression; all things and events partake in the principle of language and they all have their own ways of expression *in* language; and, eventually, there are different orders of language, such as the language of things, or the language of man. In describing translation as a gradual movement between these orders of language, a *Sprachbewegung*, Benjamin largely relies on spatial, physical, and topographical terms (e.g., *Dichte, Masse, Medium, Bezirke, Kontinua*, i.e., density, mass, medium, district, or area, continua), in order to grasp the sacred function of translating the language of things into the name-language of man, of communicating his own mental being to God.

Encapsulated in this conception of the gradual incompleteness of languages, their relation in translation, and their translatability established through a kinship in God lies a coincidence of language philosophy and epistemology: through the translational act that transfers an imperfect into a less imperfect gradation of language—from the language of things into the language of man, from the silent into the sound, and the nameless into the name—something is invariably added. And this something is knowledge: translation "cannot but add something to it, namely knowledge" (SW 1: 70).[20] The task that God gives to man is to name things, this act of name-giving is an act of translation, and this act of translation is an act of knowing.

The entanglement of language philosophy and epistemology also runs through Benjamin's dissertation, which he began working on in 1918, two years after the Language-Essay. In 1917, Benjamin had moved to Switzerland for his doctorate. The First World War had still not come to an end, and after several conscription orders—and several ploys to avoid them—he was deemed unfit, and eventually received a medical certificate as well as a visa to enter neutral Switzerland. He moved there together with his wife, Dora, whom he had married in April of 1917. In October, Benjamin began his PhD studies in Bern, where he enrolled at the department of philosophy. Looking for a dissertation topic, he thought at first he may write about Kant and history (1994: 98), but by the end of March 1918, he had changed his mind and decided that he would write his dissertation on the German Romantics' conception of criticism. For the following year, Benjamin's main focus was his dissertation, a draft of which was finished by April of 1919. While he felt that he had to compromise in some respects, in order to fulfill contemporary academic standards, he still thought that he had managed to accomplish what he had set out to do. He considered his dissertation to be pointing toward the "true nature of Romanticism" (1994: 139)[21] by way of the Romantic concept of criticism. And in it, the German Romantic concepts of knowledge and criticism meet with *Übersetzung*, in a reference that is reminiscent of his early Language-Essay from 1916. Benjamin outlines the idea that artworks, per se, are incomplete; criticism, in turn, becomes a method of making them less incomplete:

> für die Romantiker ist Kritik viel weniger die Beurteilung eines Werkes als die Methode seiner Vollendung. (GS I: 69)

> for the Romantics, criticism is far less the judgment of a work than the method of its consummation. (SW 1: 153)

At this point, where criticism is seen as a method of making an artwork less incomplete, it meets translation—which, Benjamin says in the Language-Essay, is a way for *languages* to become less incomplete. Benjamin quotes a statement by the German Romantic Novalis, who likens criticism to translation due to their shared aim toward consummation. Benjamin comments on Novalis:

> Vielleicht denkt Novalis, indem er Kritik und Übersetzung einander nahe rückt, an eine mediale stetige Überführung des Werkes aus einer Sprache in die andere,

eine Auffassung, die bei der unendlich rätselhaften Natur der Übersetzung so statthaft ist, wie eine andere. (GS I: 70)

It may be that, in bringing criticism and translation close to each other, Novalis was thinking of a medial, continuous transposition [*Überführung*] of the work from one language into another—a conception which, given the infinitely riddling nature of translation, is from the start as admissible as any other. (SW 1: 154; my annotation)

With this formulation, Benjamin echoes his ideas about languages as media of different densities, and translation as *Überführung*,[22] transference, through *continua* of transformation. However, there is also a significant shift: this time, Benjamin does not talk about the transference of one *language* into another, but about the transference of *Werke*, works or writings. What translation and criticism seem to have in common, however, is the fact that they add a certain quality to these works, making them less incomplete through a transformative process.

This shift in focus anticipates a central theme in the Translator-Essay, which Benjamin began working on about two years after finishing his dissertation. In the spring of 1919, Benjamin handed it in, and his final exams took place at the end of June. As Scholem notes in his diary, Benjamin lived in "dissolute and indecent angst" (2007: 304) regarding his exams; but in the end, he was awarded a summa cum laude. That year, his dissertation supervisor, Richard Herbertz, offered him a position in Bern. But Benjamin and his family were dependent on allowances from Benjamin's parents, and inflation was rising in postwar Germany, which devalued these allowances that came in from Berlin. Thus, Switzerland became too expensive for the young family and they moved back to Germany.

And here we are: in Berlin, 1920. It was a difficult year for Benjamin, marked by depression, financial difficulties, and problems with his family. Nonetheless, he began thinking about a second dissertation, or *Habilitationsschrift*, as it is called in German, which was a prerequisite for a university career in Germany. At that time, he thought he would choose a topic from the field of language philosophy, maybe about the relation between language and logos, between word and concept (1994: 156). This phase of reading and thinking about linguistics and linguistic philosophy fell together with the most intensive phase of translation practice yet, as he had just received the offer to publish his translations of Baudelaire's *Tableaux Parisiens*. And he continued his theoretical reflections on translation with the Translator-Essay, which he began working on in 1921.

In tracing the term "*Übersetzung*" through Benjamin's writings, the Translator-Essay has been the obvious go-to for many commentators—which is why I cut my comments as short as possible, and focus on how the term, *Übersetzung*, is used there and how it relates to the way in which it is used in other texts. There is, for one, a significant kinship between the Language- and the Translator-Essay: as the former circles around translation, and the latter gives center stage to it, Benjamin seems to deliver on the declaration he made in the Language-Essay that translation is too powerful a concept to be treated in any way as marginal. What is more, Benjamin's CV from 1940 attests to the fact that he thought of the Translator-Essay as "the first precipitate of my reflections on the theory of language" (SW 4: 381);[23] keep in mind that the Language-Essay, which may be considered as the actual first explication of his reflections on the theory of language, had not been published during his lifetime.

While the Language-Essay from 1916 and the Translator-Essay from 1921 are indeed closely related, crucial parameters are nonetheless shifted. In the Language-Essay, Benjamin tries to approach the essence of language in its relation to Genesis, he outlines Adam's act of naming as a translational act and ends the essay, arguably, with the Fall of Man. The Translator-Essay, in a way, marks a continuation, as it deals with the task of the translator—after Adam. Benjamin shifts his focus from a stream of translations between deferred orders of language, such as the language of things or the language of man, toward the integration of relations and translations between post-Adamite human languages, as well as their historical growth and development. From the outset, this seems to make for a more conventional concept of interlingual translation. Nonetheless, the framework developed in 1916 remains intact and shines through in the Translator-Essay.

After Babel, translation is a particular form, or mode,[24] which operates on *Werke*, works or writings. The relation between an original and a translation, like that between languages of different orders, is one of translatability, which is founded in the kinship of all languages. As a distinct form, translation comes with a unique *Darstellungsmodus*, a mode of (re-)presentation or enactment, which is different in constitution from other linguistic relations, such as signs or analogies. This particular mode is described as "intensive" realization: it realizes, in an intensive, anticipatory way, the relation between languages among each other, as well as their historical growth and development. Conventional theories of translation, Benjamin says, locate the relation between languages in similarities of meaning or form. But within a paradigm based on similarity, translation cannot realize growth and development, because these dynamics are fueled by renewal and transformation; neither can a translation that strives for equivalence realize the relation between languages, because it is a relation of kinship, not of similarity.

Within this framework, the task of the translator far exceeds common understandings of interlingual translation. For one, three languages are involved: source, target, and *Reine Sprache*, Pure Language—a vanishing point that all languages indicate, which makes translation possible in the first place. It is a point of complementing intents. Crucially, Benjamin differentiates between *Gemeintes* and *Arten des Meinens*, between the "what" and the way of meaning. That which is meant, however, does not fully correspond to that which in the semiotic structure of the sign would be referred to as the signified, the mental concept. Benjamin turns to the example of *pain* and *Brot*: the words, the signifiers, differ; and the signified, the images we have in mind, differ as well. However, there is "something else" to which both point. Benjamin does not specify what this "something else" would be in his *Brot/pain* example, but it does become clear that the relation between languages can never be discovered in a single one of them, so much as only in the differential relation between them. Translation, in turn, is the only form that can make the differing intents, the differing directionalities toward a vanishing point, perceivable.

In this context, Benjamin also refers to the topic of his dissertation: he argues that Romantic critics had unprecedented insight into the lives of works, but they failed to find an adequate place for translation within the framework of their theories. They attributed their attention to criticism, which, Benjamin says, marks a particular moment in the *Fortleben*, the continued life, survival, or afterlife of writings, but a much lesser one than translation. Like translation, criticism may add something to the lives of writings; but criticism cannot realize the growth and development of languages, and it cannot realize the relation between languages among each other. At this point, Benjamin goes on to distinguish between translation and poetry, between the task of the poet and the task of the translator. Poets, Benjamin says, look at language itself from inside one particular language; translators stand outside, looking at the entirety of their mother tongue from the perspective of a foreign text. Where poetry is "naïve, primary, concrete" intention, translation is "derivative, final, conceptual" intention (1968c: 303).[25]

Benjamin then re-evaluates a set of terms which, he says, are used in conventional theories of translation that aim at the reproduction of *Sinn*, sense or meaning: *Freiheit* and *Treue*, freedom and fidelity. He holds that the freedom of sense is usually dominant, while fidelity to the word is only relevant as it serves this freedom of sense. This approach, however, serves the instrumental side of language; whether in form or function, this instrumental sense is that which is conveyed *through* language, not *in* language (GS II: 142; SW 1: 63). Thus, Benjamin re-configures the concepts of freedom and fidelity for a theory of translation that is not focused on the reproduction of instrumental sense. In doing so, he sticks with the terms, but re-arranges their frames of reference. First, he turns things around: he deploys a law of *Treue*, of fidelity, to stop the freedom of sense from being *gesetzgebend*, from being the legislative power. It is a particular kind of fidelity, though, namely one that does not aim at *Wiedergabe*, reproduction, but instead at *Harmonie*, harmony. It lets the foreign language's desire for completeness speak from the translated work and makes perceivable a differential relation between the two. Based on this kind of fidelity, Benjamin re-establishes the importance of freedom in translation: in the service of fidelity, freedom is exercised on one's own language, freeing the foreign language's desire for completeness into one's own.

So, here is what Benjamin's translators must do in order to comply with the true form of translation: they must follow the law of fidelity in order to avoid the reproduction of sense; they must strive for that which goes beyond instrumental sense, for "something final, decisive" (1968c: 305);[26] and, eventually, they must exercise freedom in their own languages, freeing the elements of Pure Language, found in the relation with the foreign, into their own. The key strategy of non-equivalent fidelity, which destroys the reign of the reproduction of sense, is *Wörtlichkeit*, word-for-word-ness (or word-ness). In this context, Benjamin places another reference to the biblical Genesis: he reminds us, first in Greek, then in German that "in the beginning was the Word" (1968c: 304).[27] Thus, unsurprisingly, the word is also the *urelement* for Benjamin's translator. This reference to the Language-Essay, however, hints at the fact that *Wörtlichkeit*, in its word-ness, means more to Benjamin than a "simple" word-for-word translation.[28]

Overall, this text once again illustrates how common understandings of translation and language are attributed different scopes and frames of reference. On the one hand, Benjamin builds on a commonsensical understanding of translation, whereby the translators are humans (e.g., he mentions Hölderlin, George, Borchardt) who translate texts (e.g., *Werke, Texte*; works, texts). Yet the imagery with regard to the sites and dynamics of the movement diversifies. Benjamin does talk about post-Babelian languages, for example, French and German, as in his example of *pain* and *Brot*, and in the text itself, three languages are present—German, of course, but also French and Greek. But much of the imagery used to refer to the translation process is built upon the all-encompassing linguisticality articulated in the Language-Essay, which manifests in recurring terminological links (*Sprachbewegung, strömende Sprache, Medium,* i.e., movement made up of language, flowing language, medium). At the same time, some of the earlier images of dynamic and transformative translation are molded into generative life-metaphors of seeds, ripening, continued, or unfolding life. These are particularly prevalent when Benjamin talks about the relation between source and target text, as well as the relation between languages, both of which are realized in translation.

When it comes to Benjamin's criticism of what he calls traditional theories of translation, he increasingly uses inorganic metaphors, such as the architectural metaphor of *Wörtlichkeit* as an arcade, or the geometrical metaphor of sense as the point where a tangent touches the circle. And then, there are images with particularly rich historical and philosophical indices, such as the broken parts of a vessel; an Aeolian harp touched by the wind; or, that of a growing fruit tree composed of several images strewn across the same paragraph—from seeds, to *Stumpf und Stiel,* root stock and stem, and the unity of *Frucht und Schale,* fruit and skin.[29] Another crucial set of images are spatial, such as when language itself is seen as a mountain forest in relation to which translation stands outside and poetry within. Translation shouts the "original," in its source language, into the forest, which creates an echo and a reverberation in the target language. This image plays with closeness and distance, which is a recurring theme throughout this and many other Benjamin texts. In particular, there is the idea of something that is "quite close and yet infinitely remote" (SW 1: 261),[30] which returns, in a very similar shape, in Benjamin's description of *aura*.[31] Similarly, there is an omnipresent interplay between darkness and light, a game of in/visibility, and of heights and depths. The latter, then, leads back to the Language-Essay from 1916: if, as Benjamin would have it, sense is only fleetingly touched in translation, it falls ceaselessly from abyss to abyss, he says; only the holy text can halt such a falling, because in it, meaning ceases to be the *Wasserscheide,* or watershed, between the flow of language and the flow of revelation. Notions of revelation and the messianic end of history are explicitly and implicitly prevalent in this text, going hand in hand with a redemptive, harmonic, freeing, complementary notion of translation, expressed, for example, in phrases such as "harmony of languages" (1997: 164), "to liberate the language" (1997: 163), "languages [are] complemented and reconciled" (1997: 159).

Besides the Translator-Essay, there is another text that Benjamin wrote around the same time in which *Übersetzung* takes a similar role. It is the

"Announcement of the Journal *Angelus Novus*,"[32] which Benjamin wrote shortly after the Translator-Essay, in 1921–22. It is all that remained from the announced journal, and it begins with a plea for what Benjamin calls positive criticism, for which his magazine was supposed to be a platform—for that, and for translation. Benjamin describes how German writing had been in a state of crisis since the turn of the century. In this context, Benjamin invoked the healing power of translation, as he describes it as "a form that has always, healingly, accompanied its [German writing's] great crises."[33] This understanding dovetails with the Translator-Essay, as it re-formulates the redemptive, harmonic notion of translation in the more secular register. In this context, the healing power of translation lies in its capacity to realize the growth of language, which involves not only translation "within" one language, from one historical stage to another, but requires the help of other languages to realize its own growth:

> Wo nämlich dieser [der werdenden Sprache, B.H.] noch der eigene Inhalt nicht gegenwärtig ist, an dem sie sich aufbaut, bietet der ihrer würdige verwandte anderer zugleich mit der Aufgabe sich dar, um seinetwillen abgestorbenes Sprachgut aufzugeben und das frische zu entfalten. (GS II: 243)
>
> A language-in-the-making may not in itself be able to grasp the substance on which it grows, but the substance of another related and worthy language may offer its assistance, by abandoning for its sake a superannuated linguistic heritage and unfolding a fresh one. (My translation.)[34]

At the same time, this understanding of a healing translation relates to Benjamin's early essay, "Teaching and Valuation": he sets these healing translations apart from "conventional" translations that aim only at the *Vermittlung*, the transmission or communication, of paragons—which is what he so harshly criticized in the context of institutional education. Staying with the terminology of this announcement, Benjamin sees the healing kind of translation not as a schooling of readers in translated works from the past, but as a schooling of language itself "a strict and irreplaceable school of language-in-the-making" (SW 1: 294).[35]

During the time when Benjamin was working on the Translator-Essay, the journal *Angelus Novus*, and on his own Baudelaire translations, he was also thinking about a topic for his second dissertation. But his financial situation remained difficult and his academic future uncertain, which resulted in his plans constantly changing. In 1923, Benjamin eventually set his mind to pursuing a position at the University of Frankfurt, even though he did not have any ties, patrons, or colleagues to back his *Habilitation*. Nonetheless, he developed a concept for an encompassing project: it was to be a study on the German Baroque dramatic form known as *Trauerspiel*. This topic was suggested by someone Benjamin considered a possible sponsor for his habilitation, Franz Schultz, who held the chair of German literary history in Frankfurt. But Benjamin had previously expressed an interest in this topic, as well: already in 1916, he wrote essays on "*Trauerspiel* and Tragedy" and one on "The Role of Language in *Trauerspiel* and Tragedy."[36]

In the course of this project, Benjamin entered what he, in a letter to Scholem, described as "a kind of second stage of my early work on language . . ., dressed up as a theory of ideas" (1994: 261).[37] In his first phase of thinking about language, translation moves from being used as an empty didactic tool in education to eventually reaching almost overwhelming proportions: in the Language-Essay, everything between heaven and earth is translation (Wohlfarth 2001: 92).[38] The obscurity, rich imagery, and terminological instability of his Language-Essay continue into the Translator-Essay; and yet, the latter is set to explore an underlying translation perspective that is closer to a commonsensical understanding of translation. All this shines through in the "The Epistemo-critical Prologue"[39] of his second dissertation, but while in his earlier texts he tries to approach the essence of language, he now approaches toward the essence of knowledge. I have hinted at the correlation between Benjamin's thinking about language, translation, criticism, and knowledge in his earlier texts. This correlation becomes even more pronounced in his *Habilitation*, and as knowledge shifts into the center of this constellation, *Übersetzung* disappears.

3

Terminological Gaps, Translation Practice, and Literary Criticism

Benjamin finished his *Trauerspiel*-book at the beginning of 1925. At first, he handed excerpts of it to Franz Schultz, who flat-out declined to back him. Nonetheless, Benjamin officially submitted the manuscript in March. Hans Cornelius, the chair of aesthetics and art history at the faculty of philosophy, appointed a committee and drafted a preliminary evaluation—which was devastatingly negative. Benjamin was advised to withdraw, which he did. His academic career had ended before it even began.[1] Yet Benjamin had already started to entertain the idea that it may be life outside of academia that he was looking at. After all, the process of writing his *Habilitation* had been difficult, the outcome uncertain and his financial situation dire. Benjamin had begun focusing on writing articles, essays, and reviews for magazines and newspapers, he became a frequent radio contributor—and he produced and published a wide variety of translations. Notably, with the withdrawn habilitation, the concept of translation disappears from Benjamin's texts; and translation, as a practice, takes center stage.

At this point, Benjamin's text production is marked by a journalistic opening toward the public that went hand in hand with a more explicitly materialist critique of the public sphere. Yet this opening was certainly also fueled by economic considerations. By the end of 1925, Benjamin had become dependent on these avenues of income, and in particular on translation work. Between 1924 and 1932, Benjamin translated, from French to German, an introduction for Man Ray's collection of rayographs written by Tristan Tzara, a novel by Honoré de Balzac, poems by Saint-John Perse, an essay and novels by Marcel Proust, fragments of a novel by Louis Aragon, novellas by Marcel Jouhandeau, a selection of phrasebook exegeses by Léon Bloy, a story by Adrienne Monnier and an introduction for an anthology by Felix Bertaux; from Italian to German, he translated a poem by Gabriele d'Annunzio.

His most extensive project was the translation of Proust's novels. First, he took the offer to translate *Sodome et Gomorrhe* in 1925, but it soon became a more encompassing project than Benjamin had imagined: the previous Proust translations by Rudolf Schottlaender had "resulted in a lot of bad publicity and a great critical fiasco" (1994: 304). So, Benjamin was asked to re-translate the works of Proust, together with his friend and colleague Franz Hessel. Of the seven novels of *À la recherche du temps perdu*, Benjamin translated the fourth, *Sodome et Gomorrhe*, and together with Hessel he translated the second as well as the third, *À l'Guermanteombre des jeunes filles en fleurs* and *Le Côté de Guermantes*. For various reasons, *Sodome et Gomorrhe* was never published—and Benjamin's translation of it got lost; the second and third novels, however, were published as *Im Schatten der jungen Mädchen* (1927) and *Die Herzogin von Guermantes* (1930).

Benjamin's relation with translation as a source of income was riddled with tension. In a letter from 1926, Benjamin described his translation regimen to Jula Radt in an intriguingly pointed way:

> Ich bin hier übrigens fleißig, zum mindesten beim Übersetzen und was das Erstaunlichste ist, es wird mir ganz leicht. Dazu habe ich freilich ein Regime entdeckt, das zauberhaft die Kobolde zum Helfen lockt und darin besteht, daß wenn ich morgens aufstehe ich ohne mich anzukleiden, ohne Hände oder Körper auch nur mit einem Tropfen Wasser zu benetzen, ja ohne auch nur zu trinken, mich an die Arbeit setzte und nichts tue, ehe das Pensum des ganzen Tages beendet ist – geschweige denn frühstücken. (1966: 431)

> By the way, I am being very diligent, at least as far as translating is concerned, and the most amazing thing is that it is becoming very easy for me. Of course, I have discovered a regimen that magically entices the goblins to help out. It consists of my sitting down to work as soon as I get up in the morning, without getting dressed, without moistening my hands or body with a single drop of water, indeed without even drinking any. And I do nothing, much less eat breakfast, before finishing the task I set myself for the day. (1994: 297)

This regimen is magical and obsessive, fragile and ethereal. It may tilt at any moment. And behind it looms the cold fact of economic necessity. Benjamin had to work under conditions well known to all translators: time constraints and scarce payment. In January of 1926, while translating Proust, Benjamin complained to Scholem:

> Die Sache ist grenzenlos schwierig, und Zeit kann ich ihr aus vielen Gründen, vor allem der knappen Bezahlung wegen, nur sehr gemessen zur Verfügung stellen. (1966: 410)

it is immensely difficult and there are many reasons why I can devote very little time to it, the primary reason being how poorly I am paid. (1994: 289)

A year later, Benjamin mused about his professional development and he categorically ruled out further translation work. It had become clear to him that he needed "some sort of solid framework for the immediate future. Translation can obviously not provide this" (1986: 72).[2]

At the same time, there was a reciprocal relationship between Benjamin's translation practice and his intellectual endeavors, most notably when it came to Proust. Though this relationship, too, was always ambiguous: Benjamin considered this particular task of translation to be almost impossible and immensely ungrateful, but at least at the beginning, he seemed confident that it would also be stimulating (1966: 403, 1994: 284). To Rilke, a fellow translator, Benjamin wrote that the gains from "having been so deeply involved with this great masterpiece will in time become very tangible" (1994: 285).[3] And indeed, his engagement with Proust through translation found expression in an essay: in 1929, he finished "The Image of Proust"[4]—which bore the French working title "En traduisant Proust." The transformation of the essay's title is compelling: *en traduisant*, the gérondif of the verb *to translate* represents a grammatical form that does not exist in German; it describes the process and condition that Benjamin goes through in order to arrive at *Zum Bilde Prousts*, "The Image of Proust." The working title, however, was translated into German and all reference to translation removed. The same thing happens in the essay itself: it is cleared of all explicit references to the concept of *Übersetzung*.

While translating *À la recherche du temps perdu*, however, his involvement with Proust *en traduisant* became increasingly agonizing; Benjamin began describing it as dangerous and poisonous. Already in 1926, he complained that it made him sick. The intense closeness that Benjamin felt called forth "something like symptoms of intestinal poisoning" (1994: 305).[5] In 1928, Benjamin again likened the task of translating Proust with a sickness: it was a task of "monstrously absorbing nature, intensively and virally influencing [my] own writings."[6] Interestingly, however, it was not only the closeness that felt poisonous to Benjamin. More precisely, it was what he called the "the unproductive involvement with a writer" (1994: 305)[7] that called forth the symptoms. The magical task had turned sour; it had turned into poisonous, unproductive involvement. Yet Benjamin still wanted to establish a reputation as a translator. He first expressed this intention when his Baudelaire-translation was published, and he reiterated it when he translated Proust—with reference to the one person who slated his Baudelaire-translations: "I can count on being securely accredited as a translator, like, for example, Stefan Zweig" (1994: 278).[8]

And yet he writes in his 1929/1930: "Hessel and I had to put up with being introduced by D. as translators of Proust" (SW 2: 343).[9] Maybe he was simply fed up with Proust. And maybe another "accreditation" had become more worth aspiring to: the years following his failed *Habilitation* were, as mentioned, marked by extremely varied and frequent journalistic contributions in magazines, journals, newspapers, and on the radio. The breadth and quality of these contributions made it possible for him to build a reputation, and he increasingly grew into the role of a public critic and intellectual. In any case, Benjamin's attitude toward his own translation work was difficult and fraught with tension. Keeping this in mind, it is not surprising, yet still remarkable, how much space translation was allotted in his journalistic contributions. Once again, however, the frame of references has shifted: often, reference is made to translation out of pragmatic and bibliographic accuracy, for example, when Benjamin designates the translators of the texts he reviews. But there are several other instances, in which he does add to his theorization of translation, displaying his well-known linguistic fervor while leaving traces that point toward his earlier texts.

Between 1926 and 1932, for instance, Benjamin published a number of articles in which he reviewed translated writings. There is a review entitled "Translations" (1926),[10] in which he almost exclusively focused on the way in which two recently published books of poetry had been translated: Paul Verlaine's "Le pauvre Lelian," translated by Alfred Wolfenstein, and a collection of Arthur Rimbaud's poems, translated by Franz von Rexroth. These reviews illustrate the way in which even Benjamin's public contributions retain a quality that is reminiscent of his early texts. When translating Verlaine, Benjamin says, it would be in vain to reach out "very far to introduce these poems into German."[11] Instead, the dominant idea is closeness, which meets the image of the echo. In the Translator-Essay, Benjamin used this image to illustrate part of the translator's task: to find the exact point from which the reverberation of a foreign work's language can be heard in one's own. When it comes to Verlaine, this point of reverberation lies very close:

> So greift der deutsche Sprachgeist wirklich nur in seiner nächsten Nähe die Worte, aus denen Verlaines zögernder Stimmfall zurücktönt. (GS III: 40)

> Only in its immediate surrounding, the German language-spirit reaches the words from which Verlaine's tentative tone of voice resounds. (My translation.)

This closeness creates a narrow space for the translators to navigate in; they can only succeed if they "safeguard the certainty and serenity of the gesture within the most limited of spaces."[12] This limitation of space is what dictates the concrete translation strategies that must be used. In this case, it means getting rid of unnecessary additions, which would otherwise devastate the verse "like an infernal machine [devastates] the palace."[13] Thus, what Benjamin identifies as critical for this particular translation to work is austerity, ease, and close proximity. These guiding principles find expression in the image of a dreamer, who ever so slightly and faintly moves the hand searching for treasures; this, to Benjamin, is the German *Sprachgeist*, its language-spirit, looking in its immediate surrounding for the words that echo Verlaine.

The introductory metaphor of the text stands out, too: the translator's "material—or rather: his organ—is, besides his mother tongue, not the foreign text, but its language."[14] From this material, that is, of source and target language, the translators build their houses of cards. The image between hyphens literally falls out of alignment: while the term "material" fits with the imagery of constructing houses (of cards) and devastated palaces, the organic metaphor of two languages as the translator's organ does not.[15] To Benjamin, the most crucial element for the translation process is not the source text, but source and target language. This shift marks, once more, a challenge to the "original" as translation's sacred authority, which is already notable in the Translator-Essay. By referring to the two languages as one organ, this image also continues Benjamin's refusal to think of languages as distinct and clearly de-limitable entities sitting next to each other. All of these illuminating, image-laden deliberations, however, which seize upon Benjamin's early theories of language and translation, are only developed in reference to the Wolfenstein-translation, which Benjamin at least appreciates. In spite of its shortcomings, Benjamin calls it "full of reverence and love."[16] The Rexroth-translation, however, Benjamin almost brushes off. He showcases Rexroth's literary immaturity, his presumptuousness, and insufficient (language) abilities. In the end, he summarizes Rexroth's efforts as *dichterisch*, poetic: Rexroth did not stay true to the form of translation; instead, he wrote (poor) poetry.

In other reviews, Benjamin comments on whether he considers the task of translation to be completed successfully or not, and it is interesting to look at the reasons he gives. As particularly successful translations, he describes Halpern's rendering of Gladkov's *Zement*, and Zech's translation of Deubel: Halpern's translation allows the readers to experience Gladkow's novel "in the medium of a rarely consummate translation";[17] and Léon Deubel is given *Heimatrecht*, the right of residence, "in the best of all German republics, the old free state of their [the verses'] translations."[18] When he does *not* consider the translations to be successful, Benjamin repeatedly points out one fatal "deficiency," which returns in various shapes and forms: the translator does not stay true to the peculiar form of translation. Rexroth is charged with practicing poetry instead of translation, and in other instances, Benjamin remarks that the translation does not transform the source text, or it does not manage to make it "more than" the source text. This is the case, for instance, in Benjamin's review of the Ficino letters from 1927. A successful translation, he says, is not out of reach:

> mittelalterliches Latein [läßt] sich treu in eine deutsche Fassung übertragen, deren Schönheit gerade darin besteht, daß die Syntax des Urtexts hindurchschimmert. (GS III: 54)

> medieval Latin may indeed be faithfully transferred into a German version, the beauty of which is constituted precisely by the fact that the syntax of the *urtext* shines through. (My translation.)

This is not the case, though, with the German Ficino letters, and Benjamin is not shy about pointing that out: to him, the German version is an empty shell. Its German is *dürr* and *schikanös*, barren and vexatious, a language-surface without inner value.

This is reminiscent of how translation was supposedly used as an empty tool in the context of institutionalized education, which Benjamin so harshly criticized in "Teaching and Valuation." In line with his early criticism, he calls this empty, German language-surface *Ostermann-Deutsch*, in reference to Dr. Christian Ostermann, who, in the late 1800s, published popular translation exercise books to practice the translation from German into Latin, that is, to practice *Stilübungen*. Ostermann's German texts were widely criticized as artificial, non-German language-surfaces constructed to be translated into Latin by beginners (Liebsch 2013: 196–7). This may also help to further illuminate Benjamin's understanding of fidelity and *Wörtlichkeit*: one may be inclined to think that the translation of only the language-surface, with utter disregard for sense and meaning may be exactly what Benjamin is calling for. But it is not. This is also where, I would suggest, Benjamin's concept of translation holds within an intriguingly complex entanglement of both theory and practice. Due to its complex nature, Benjamin's thinking about translation is often considered as purely theoretical. And, at first sight, *Wörtlichkeit* may indeed appear to be an utterly impractical translation strategy. Conceptually, however, it does provide a set of parameters according to which practical translation strategies may be chosen. It stands for a commitment to a kind of fidelity that strives for harmony instead of equivalence: a commitment to the word, and to the whole of language; and a commitment to stay true to the thoughtful, critical, nature of translation. For each act of translation, translation strategies that strive to correspond with this understanding of *Wörtlichkeit* may be chosen and adapted accordingly. Fidelity to the word does *not* result in a life-less, barren language-frame. Instead, it requires an intense engagement with the inner value of the writings, with the languages involved, and with the process of translation as such, if the translator intends to follow the "true" form of translation, that is, transforming while *adding* something, a new and foreign quality, in the process.

With respect to the "additive quality" of translation, Benjamin has pointed out repeatedly that it shares a kinship with criticism. Both manifest the lives and continued lives of writings, as they allow for transformation, as well as the development of an added quality. This is one more reason why these reviews are remarkable: Benjamin indeed applies criticism to translation. There is even a very peculiar text, published in 1928 in the magazine *Die literarische Welt*, in which he explicitly reflects on this topic. It is entitled "A Fundamental Exchange of Letters about the Criticism of Translated Works."[19] There is a brief back story to this publication. In May of 1928, Benjamin wrote a review for the magazine *Die literarische Welt* in which he discussed Giacomo Leopardi's *Pensieri*, translated into German as *Gedanken* by Dr. Richard Peters. Benjamin did not comment on the process of translation at all. He only mentioned Peters' afterword. In his review, Benjamin pointed out that Peters forgot to mention the first ever published translation of Leopardi's *Pensieri*. In response, Peters sent an objection letter to the magazine, in which he claimed that he had started translating Leopardi before the first translation was published, which, he thought, explained, if not excused this misstep. In July of 1928, Benjamin had Peters' objection letter published in *Die literarische Welt*, together with his response. Apart from his explanation, Peters' letter also contained a complaint. He lamented that Benjamin dedicated seventeen lines to such a small misstep, yet he found not one word of commentary or criticism regarding his translation: "I cannot take this to be a loyal way of discussing a book."[20] This turns into an incentive for Benjamin to publicly muse upon the process of criticizing translated works. He poses two questions: the first one refers to Peters forgetting to mention the first published translation, and thus to the relation between the practice of translation and bibliography; the second concerns the actual process of criticizing translated works and/or the process of their translation.

What takes shape here is an unusual system of categorizations, as well as a sensitivity toward the different structures, desires, and demands of a text. To Benjamin, the question of bibliography is a question of scientificity. Within the logic of an argument that intends to question whether translation was a scientific task, Benjamin would argue that the translation of verse does *not* meet the criteria required to be considered scientific, but the translation of prose does, and in particular of philosophical texts. He points out, however, that he does not *want* to follow this line of argumentation. He would put it (slightly) differently: translation, he says, is

> eine Arbeit, die neben gewissen anderen Maßstäben auch denen der Wissenschaft genügen muß. Sie ist eine der gar nicht wenigen Disziplinen, die Wissenschaft auf die Kunst anwenden, genau so wie andere sie für die Industrie und die Architektur verwerten. (GS III: 120–1)
>
> work that must, besides certain other criteria, also meet the criteria of science. It is one of the several disciplines that apply science to art, in the same way in which others use science for industry or architecture. (My translation.)

While it is not scientific as such, translation must, among other things, fulfill scientific criteria. As a discipline, it applies science to art and in so doing the discipline of translation develops a philological *Technik* which is liable to "strict scientific laws in order to serve extra-scientific formations."[21] This *Technik* comes with its own *Hilfswissenschaften*, auxiliary sciences, one of which is bibliography. A very philologically strict Benjamin emerges,[22] who insists on the importance of bibliography and laments its decline: it may not be "the cerebral [*geistig*] part of a science,"[23] but it does play a central role in its physiology. It is "not its neuroplexus, but the system of its vessels."[24]

Regarding the second question about the process of criticizing translated writings, Benjamin identifies three kinds of writings, or rather, gradations of *Wert* or *Interesse*, of value or interest, which evoke and require different responses from translation and criticism. First, he mentions writings of "low value." For the most part, these are picked by translators whose only intention is to make foreign works accessible to German readers (which is the majority of translators, Benjamin adds). The critic's task is to point that out, and nothing else. Then, there are valuable writings the translation of which is "a balanced and unproblematic task."[25] In these cases, the reviewers' critical energies must be directed at the work itself, not at its translation. This, says Benjamin, was the case with Peters' *Gedanken*, which was why he essentially reviewed Leopardi's *Pensieri* in German, and not the process of its translation. But there is a third category of works: for certain writings of value, the translation turns out to be "a hazard, a daring feat."[26] As an example of this class of works, Benjamin invokes Proust. And when it comes to these hazardous acts of translation, translation-criticism is essential. In these instances, the silence of critics becomes problematic, but it does happen—with his own Proust-translation, for instance—and it will keep happening as long as there are no professional magazines that assemble criticism exclusively directed at translation. Benjamin calls for the establishment of such professional magazines, but until then: *qui tacet consentire videtur*, he who is silent is taken to agree.

In later reviews, Benjamin returns to the historical task of translation, and he investigates translation's role as a form within the framework of literary history and criticism. In doing so, he returns to the idea of writings' *Fortleben*, in different forms, as a process of transformation that comes with an added quality of difference. In a review from 1930, Benjamin criticizes Kirchhoff's translation, *Licht vom Licht: Hymnen*, written by Symeon the New Theologian.[27] Like in the previous review, the first concern Benjamin raises is one of distance: where Verlaine's poems were so close, Benjamin argues that Symeon's hymns are immensely far removed. So far, it may not even be possible to find an adequate perspective to look at them. All the additional space would need to be filled, but that does not happen. What is missing is the thoughtful and insightful quality that criticism and translation are supposed to provide, which would hint at the place of these hymns within the literature of their époque; whether they are typical or singular; what they stand for or against. Instead, what comes across in these translations Benjamin calls *das Floskelhafte* and *das Leerverstiegene*, "clichés and empty phrases" (my translation). The latter noun holds all that has gone wrong in this case: *das Leerverstiegene* is one of these German compounds, not commonly used but perfectly acceptably constructed. It contains *leer*, which means empty, and *verstiegen*, which holds notions such as overdone, excessive, exaggerated, wayward, or unrealistic. The text at hand is both at once empty and overdone. Apart from that, however, Benjamin does not philologically criticize the translation, but instead seems to argue that the text's desire and requirements have not been recognized and met. It would have required contextualization and intensive critical engagement, which the entire publication fails to provide, be it through editors' commentary, criticism, or the added quality of translation.

In 1927 and 1928, then, Benjamin reviews two anthologies. The first is about contemporary European poetry, *Europäische Lyrik der Gegenwart* (GS III: 65–6), collected and translated by Josef Kalmer, that Benjamin does not seem to appreciate at all; and the other is Borchardt's anthology of German travel literature, *Der Deutsche in der Landschaft* (GS III: 91–4), a collection of prose that Benjamin seems to highly appreciate. In his Kalmer-review, Benjamin criticizes two things: the translations, on the one hand, and the way of anthologizing, on the other. As for the translations, he claims that the translator has treated poetry like functional texts. To translate texts like these, nothing more is expected than a sufficient command of source and target language. Benjamin continues, though, that "verses are not information."[28] Thus readers of poetry in translation are entitled to demand "deeper sources of familiarity."[29] Here, a register of erotic conquest vs. deep familiarity comes into play. The translator turns into "a linguistic Don Juan."[30] Instead of deep familiarity with Turkish, English, Russian poetry—that is, a love of a particular language—Kalmer, the linguistic Don Juan, makes his conquests under the illusion of a universal poetry, without any attempt at intensively and intimately knowing the individual languages and poetries. This reveals an illuminating idea of poetic-linguistic relativity: just as there is no human universal language, Benjamin seems to say, there is no universal poetry; poetries are bound to the particular parameters, structures, procedures, and mysteries of particular languages. Benjamin's critique of Kalmer's way of anthologizing is, on the other hand, reminiscent of his early text "Teaching and Valuation": the use of translation as an empty tool to communicate a canon of selected paragons through time is connected with the arbitrary, uncritical selection, and canonization of certain texts as representations of certain époques or schools of thought. Kalmer's anthology, to Benjamin, is an example of such uncritical selection. It forgoes all critical engagement with the inner value of its writings. In this anthology, "a poem is, above all, a representative"[31]—the poem represents its poet, its poet a school, the school a nation. And among each other, in Kalmer's vision, they talk "poetry."

In his review of Borchardt's anthology, *Der Deutsche in der Landschaft*, Benjamin continues a sexually connoted imagery in order to characterize a "bad" politics of selection. Some anthologies may present themselves as a *Blütenlese*, a florilegium, and yet they smell like a scavenging, "the exploitation of a virginal stock."[32] Borchardt's anthology, however, like translation and criticism, manages to add a certain quality that goes beyond the individual writings. Anthology, translation, critical commentary: these forms are all similar in nature in that they emerge from and manifest the *Fortleben* of works. Borchardt's anthology, to Benjamin, combines its writings

> zu einer neuen Gestalt, einer Größe . . . , die nun nicht im abstrakten Sinne ›historisch,‹ sondern unmittelbares, wenn auch bedachteres, wehrhafteres

Fortblühn des Alten ist. Was hier gewirkt wird, ist Wirkung des ursprünglichen Schrifttums selber, gehört in den Lebenskreis seiner Großen genau so hinein, wie Übersetzungen und Kommentare ihrer Schriften. (GS III: 91–2)

into a new gestalt, a greatness . . . that is not in an abstract sense "historical," but immediate, albeit more deliberate, more watchful continued blossoming of the old. What is effected here is the effect of the original literature itself, it belongs to the life circles of its greats just the same as translations and commentaries of their writings. (My translation.)

The Borchardt-review hints at an intellectual constellation that became crucial to Benjamin around the beginning of the 1930. Most explicitly, Benjamin resumed this idea in 1931, in an essay with the programmatic title "Literary History and the Study of Literature."[33] This essay belongs to a number of texts that Benjamin wrote between 1930 and 1931, which he wanted to turn into a book about literary criticism.[34] The book never saw the light of day, but the surviving drafts and notes outline at least what the book was supposed to look like. There is a draft for an introduction, entitled "The Task of the Critic," and tellingly, while the book was supposed to include Benjamin's critiques on Keller, Hebel, Hessel, Kraus, Walser, Green, Proust, and Gide, it was also supposed to include two of his essays, namely the one on surrealism and "The Task of the Translator." All this speaks to the kinship between criticism and translation, and their relation with (literary) history. Benjamin even argues that criticism must not only be part of literary history; it must be its *Grundwissenschaft*, its "fundamental discipline" (SW 2: 415), as the title of a brief fragment from 1930 or 1931 insinuates. Eventually, at the end of "Literary History and the Study of Literature," Benjamin summarizes:

Deren [literarische Werke, B.H.] gesamter Lebens- und Wirkungskreis hat gleichberechtigt, ja vorwiegend neben ihre Entstehungsgeschichte zu treten; ihr Schicksal, ihre Aufnahme durch die Zeitgenossen, ihre Übersetzungen, ihr Ruhm. Damit gestaltet sich das Werk im Inneren zu einem Mikrokosmos oder viel mehr: zu einem Mikroaeon. Denn es handelt sich ja nicht darum, die Werke des Schrifttums im Zusammenhang ihrer Zeit darzustellen, sondern in der Zeit, da sie entstanden, die Zeit, die sie erkennt—das ist die unsere—zur Darstellung zu bringen. (GS III: 290)

The entire circle of their lives and effects must become equal, indeed predominant alongside their histories of origins; their fate, their reception by contemporaries, their translations, their fame. With this, the work on the inside takes the shape of a microcosm, or indeed: a microaeon. What is at stake is not to portray literary works in the context of their age, but to represent the age that perceives them—our age—in the age during which they arose.[35]

Some of the threads that this text has followed up on intersect in this quotation. Translation is where the *Fortleben* of literary works manifests. Thus it is not primary in nature, it is not naïve. Instead, it transforms and adds something. It does not simply give shape to the continued lives of literary works, but makes them fuller, more complete. In that, translation shares a kinship with criticism and anthology. And all of these need to be taken into consideration in order for the literary work to become a microaeon in which we can find—through criticism—the time that recognizes it: ours.

4

Umschmelzungsprozesse, and a Late Return to Translation

The beginning of the 1930s was a difficult time for Benjamin. He experienced bouts of heavy depression and suicidal ideation, which led him to plan his death and write farewell letters. The external circumstances, while not exclusively to "blame," says Scholem (in Jennings and Eiland 2014: 377), cannot be ignored either: the NSDAP had gained ground in recent elections, which paved the path for Hitler's rise to power. The two magazines that had regularly published Benjamin's articles and reviews, *Die literarische Welt* and *Frankfurter Zeitung*, stopped publishing his works and almost entirely closed off their lines of communication. In January of 1933, Hitler was officially made chancellor, and in March of 1933, Benjamin left Germany for good. In his writings, he continued to reflect on the role of the author and the practice of the critic, and he increasingly addressed his own position in the class struggle. The many inner and outer contradictions had to be relentlessly uncovered and addressed; he thus reflected on the role of the bourgeois intellectual who may have been "proletarianized," but remained a member of the bourgeoisie—a contradiction that seemed insurmountable. But at least in his intellectual endeavors, Benjamin did not stop when things appeared insurmountable. His writings do not convey a resigning or fatalistic quality, not even his later texts, in which Benjamin, unlike the later Adorno/Horkheimer, often focused on a possibly emancipatory potential of new media.

While Benjamin's approaches and terminologies shift over time, it is notable that he continuously circles back to earlier ideas. One pertinent example of this lies right at the beginning of his time in exile: in 1933, Benjamin conceptualized what he thought of as "a new theory of language" (1994: 402),[1] and it took the form of two short texts entitled "Doctrine of the Similar" and "On the Mimetic Faculty,"[2] with the latter being a more concise version of the former. To write these, he felt that he needed one of his earlier texts for reference, namely the

Language-Essay from 1916. When Benjamin had written this early text, he had sent a copy to his friend Scholem; and now, twelve years later, he asked Scholem to send a copy back to him. He asked for it to be sent to Ibiza, which was Benjamin's second stop in exile, after only a few weeks in Paris. With the Language-Essay at hand, he reworked "Doctrine of the Similar" into the four handwritten pages of "On the Mimetic Faculty." All three, the Language-Essay and the latter two texts, point to Benjamin's conception of language philosophy; the latter two, however, may be considered as transformative translations into a different terminological and conceptual area (Menninghaus 1995: 60).

Notably, in the later texts, Benjamin avoids any recourse to the book of Genesis. He takes an ontogenetic and phylogenetic turn: instead of looking for the "essence of language" by reference to the Bible, he now thinks about the human mimetic faculty and the nature of similarity by reference to childhood development and "the dawn of humanity" (SW 2: 697).[3] Benjamin begins his argument by saying that nature creates correspondences, which stimulate, or awaken, the human mimetic faculty. This faculty finds its original expression in the desire to imitate, to *become* similar. The natural correspondences, in their imitability, contain "instructions for mastering an already present similarity" (SW 2: 695).[4] But the way in which this assignment is carried out has shifted, from *becoming* similar—to *seeing* similarity (GS II: 210; SW 2: 697).

Benjamin describes this with reference to constellations of stars in the sky. First, there is the desire to become the constellation, for example, in dance; then there is "reading" the constellation, like seers do. It is a particular kind of reading, though, it is "reading per se" (SW 2: 697),[5] which, in the later text, is described in the words of Hugo von Hofmannsthal: "reading what has never been written" (SW 2: 722).[6] In this "reading per se," *seeing* and *becoming* are close: "reading per se" is immediate. In the mind of the seer, things meet in an immediate manner. What we commonly understand as reading, however, means that things meet in our minds in a mediated way, in "their essences, in their most transient and delicate substances" (SW 2: 697).[7] They meet in language. The human mimetic faculty continually changes, as natural correspondences change as well. And as the mimetic faculty has changed, the quality of *becoming* has gradually seeped into language. These processes of transformation, as well as their results, are subsumed in a new term that Benjamin coins: *unsinnliche Ähnlichkeit*, "nonsensuous similarity" (SW 2: 697).

While this new term is coined, translation is nowhere to be found. The latter concept, however, seems to linger behind the new term, nonsensuous similarity. There are a number of more or less subtle references to the Language- and to the Translator-Essay: just like the translational act of naming, the magical kind of reading, "reading per se," is immediate, and it combines a twofold process of reception and creation. In a receptive realm, the seer "reads the constellation from the stars in the sky"; and in a creative realm, they read "the future or fate from it" (SW 2: 697).[8] And just like certain writings contain a demand for translation in their translatability, natural correspondences contain a demand for their "handling" in their imitability. What is more, Benjamin illuminates something in this text that remains obscure in the Translator-Essay, namely the relation between the semiotic, meaning-conveying, and the non-instrumental realm of language, the realm of *Reine Sprache* and nonsensuous similarity. And this is also the only point in this text when Benjamin uses metaphoric language:

> Alles Mimetische der Sprache kann vielmehr, der Flamme ähnlich, nur an einer Art von Träger in Erscheinung treten. (GS II: 213)

> Rather, the mimetic element in language can, like a flame, manifest itself only through a kind of bearer. This bearer is the semiotic element. (SW 2: 722)

The mimetic, which stimulates nonsensuous similarity, is not independent of the meaning-conveying function of language; the semiotic realm is its *Träger*, its bearer, which provides the material basis for it to ignite. It manifests, *blitzhaft*, like a flash, on the semiotic side of language. In addition, Benjamin looks beyond the bounds of languages to further illuminate the nature of nonsensuous similarity:

> Ordnet man nämlich Wörter der verschiedenen Sprachen, die ein Gleiches bedeuten, um jenes Bedeutete als ihren Mittelpunkt, so wäre zu erforschen, wie sie alle—die miteinander oft nicht die geringste Ähnlichkeit besitzen mögen—ähnlich jenem Bedeuteten in ihrer Mitte sind. (GS II: 212)

> For if words meaning the same thing in different languages are arranged about that signified as their center, we have to inquire how they all—while often possessing not the slightest similarity to one another—are similar to the signified at their center. (SW 2: 721)

It may thus be argued that nonsensuous similarity can only be grasped from beyond the limits of one particular language, arguably in an act of translation that aims precisely at making this nonsensuous similarity perceptible.

Yet Benjamin does not use the term "*Übersetzung*" to describe this process. It leaves a terminological gap that vividly demonstrates how, in Benjamin's texts, concepts often pass through complex *Umschmelzungsprozeße*, another Benjaminian term he uses in "The Author as Producer" (1934)[9] to describe powerful, quasi-tectonic processes of melting and re-casting. And "The

Author as Producer" is also one of the few texts in which there is still at least a terminological trace of *Übersetzung*. It was not published during Benjamin's lifetime, but it may have been given as a lecture at the Institute for the Study of Fascism in Paris. In this text, Benjamin's ideas regarding literary history and criticism meet the materialist concept of history. Benjamin thinks about the relation of politics and aesthetics in art and, in doing so, he thinks about how literary forms of expression must be considered in relation to their *technische Gegebenheiten*, "technical factors," conditions, or prerequisites. He qualifies:

> Nicht immer hat es in der Vergangenheit Romane gegeben, nicht immer wird es welche geben müssen; nicht immer Tragödien; nicht immer das große Epos. Nicht immer sind die Formen des Kommentars, der Übersetzung, ja selbst der sogenannten Fälschung Spielformen am Rande der Literatur gewesen, und nicht nur im philosophischen, sondern auch im dichterischen Schrifttum Arabiens oder Chinas haben sie ihre Stelle gehabt. (GS II: 687)

> There were not always novels in the past, and there will not always have to be; there have not always been tragedies or great epics. Not always were the forms of commentary, translation, indeed even so-called plagiarism playthings in the margins of literature; they had a place not only in the philosophical but also in the literary writings of Arabia and China. (SW 2: 771)

This passage establishes the historicity of literary forms, of how they emerge, develop, and fade, in complex interaction with their corresponding relations of production, and technical developments—which, in turn, demand and bring forth different ways of perception. This is the enormous, substantially transformative change Benjamin refers to as an *Umschmelzungsprozeß*, and it is also the idea that ultimately lies at the center of the Artwork-Essay. What is more, "The Author as Producer" is peppered with Marxist terminology, and it is similarly as "dry" in imagery and metaphor as is "On the Mimetic Faculty." Intriguingly, though, like the igniting flame there, the strongest image from this text is also one that exudes heat: describing the abovementioned *Umschmelzungsprozeß*, Benjamin talks about a *glühendflüssige Masse*, a glowing-liquid mass from which new forms are cast, and the respective temperature required for this *Schmelzvorgang*, or "melting-down process" (SW 2: 776), is determined by the current state of the *Klassenkampf*.

What is more, in the previous paragraph, Benjamin again groups commentary and translation; but this time, he adds *Fälschung*, plagiarism. I do not untangle this intricate knot of relations between translation, commentary,[10] and plagiarism and their kinship in criticism, but instead confine myself to pointing out that Benjamin had brought together *Fälschung* and translation before, namely in a brief fragment about Hofmannsthal's writing from 1930 or 1931. In this text, he claims that Hofmannsthal plagiarized, or forged, without knowing it. Unwittingly, Benjamin says, the great writings from the past had filled Hofmannsthal with the impulse that "drives the forger" (SW 2: 421).[11] This is not his way of discrediting Hofmannsthal: he tries to figure out how to grasp the nature of Hofmannsthal's writings. He is looking for terms to describe this process, in which Hofmannsthal became "inspired by the works that blossomed anew within him" (SW 2: 421).[12] The way Benjamin describes it, it clearly relates to translation: translation is posited as a literary form that manifests the *Fortleben*, the continued life, survival, or afterlife of writings—and apparently, this is a dynamic that translation shares with *Fälschung*. The English version of this fragment may speak of the old writings "blossoming anew" in Hofmannsthal, yet the German one explicitly stays with the figure of life: the old writings become alive again within him. And, indeed, Benjamin explicitly introduces *Übersetzung* in the following sentence; however, he states that translation is *not* the right term to describe what Hofmannsthal made of Sophocles' *Ödipus* and other texts.

Looking at bibliographies of Hofmannsthal's writings, he is indeed credited with having translated Ödipus, for instance. But other titles mentioned by Benjamin—*Elektra, Das gerettete Venedig, Jedermann*—are either referred to as adaptations, or simply as works by Hofmannsthal. This may illustrate the issue Benjamin attempted to grasp: What is the nature of Hofmannsthal's own, and his relation with past writings? *Übersetzung*, Benjamin feels safe to say, is not the right term. Instead, he chooses forgery: "the great forger . . . cites the originary image [*Urbild*]" (SW 2: 422).[13] Hofmannsthal does not cite single lines, or passages, but entire works, by transforming them and making them his own, having them come alive anew within him. Consequently, says Benjamin,

> sie sind in jedem Falle die nahezu das Unerträgliche streifende Verdichtung der eigensten Charakterzüge jener Werke. So goethisch ist keine Novelle wie die Frau ohne Schatten, so calderonsch kein calderonsches Drama wie der Turm. (GS VI: 145)

> they amount to an almost unbearable condensation of the most personal features of those works. No novella is as Goethean as *Die Frau ohne Schatten*; no play of Calderón's is as Calderonic as *Der Turm*. (SW 2: 421)

Fälschung thus points toward a tendency in Hofmannsthal's works: utter absorption and thoughtful, transforming creation. The inward direction of this movement leads to almost unbearable condensation; yet, at the same time, something is invariably added: new life. Apart from this generative terminology, the imagery of *Einverleibung* (*Leib* = body), in a literal sense as incorporation, is prevalent in this text: great works of the past begin to permeate the forger/translator's body. He describes how some of the great works carry in them a quality that leads to assimilation, and yet the results, that is, Hofmannsthal's texts, do no longer hold this quality of *Assimilierbarkeit*, assimilability, as he calls it: these are "nourishing, but not really edible. To call them edible would mean they were digestible [*einzuverleiben*], and very little of what Hofmannsthal wrote is digestible" (SW 2: 421).[14] In the context of translation, Benjamin may use other terms and images, but the process is similar: while the *urtext* may be *einverleibt* through translation, the royal robe certainly cannot; a translation is no longer susceptible to translation. It is also notable that Benjamin uses a similar imagery of incorporation when talking about his experience translating Proust, yet while it became poisonous to Benjamin, it is life-giving and productive in Hofmannsthal's text production.

Around the mid-1930s, Benjamin was still a transient. For a while, he stayed with his ex-wife in San Remo, Italy (they had divorced in 1930), where he could live cheaply. Then he spent some time in Monaco, and after that, he went back to Paris, where he met Friedrich Pollock, the acting administrative director of the *Institut für Sozialforschung*. Benjamin had received a monthly stipend from the institute for his regular contributions, and Pollock announced that he would increase the stipend for Benjamin to stay in Paris. At the same time, Pollock urged him to produce an exposé for the big project that Benjamin had announced, the one about the Parisian arcades. Following this meeting, Benjamin plunged into productive work, as he felt that the right time had finally come: he claimed to have written the exposé, that is, an essay entitled "Paris, Capital of the Nineteenth Century,"[15] within a few days. Newly motivated, Benjamin spent much of his time researching this project.

Out of the orbit around this immense project, new topics emerged, and Benjamin produced several shorter writings, some of which have come to be among the most widely read texts Benjamin has written. There is "The Work of Art in the Age of Its Technological Reproducibility,"[16] which may be considered as a kind of small-scale application of the historical philosophy, theory, and method developed in the course of his *Passagenarbeit*. And, of course, "On the Concept of History,"[17] in which Benjamin synthesized his life-long preoccupation with history and temporality, as well as his recent attempts at approaching an *Urgeschichte* of the nineteenth century through the Parisian arcades, into nine concise theses. In these writings from the late 1930s, *Übersetzung* is never much more than a trace; nowhere is it attributed terminological or conceptual space and weight.

Nowhere, but in one brief fragment. It is written in a dialogical form, and it bears the telling title "Translation—For and Against."[18] It represents a last, substantial return to translation, but, like so much of Benjamin's work, it was never completed. In 1971, though, at least its context of production was illuminated: Günther Stern-Anders wrote a letter to Gretel Adorno, in which he inquired whether she had, among Benjamin's writings, found a "dialogue about philosophical problems of translation,"[19] which, Anders said, was based on a discussion the two had in Paris in 1935 or 1936. In response to his inquiry, Rolf Tiedemann sent "Translation—For and Against" to Anders, who replied that this was indeed the fragment he had been looking for. He also clarified, however, that he could not tell which of the statements were his and which were Benjamin's, because their perspectives were so similar at the time. He also added that it was supposed to be broadcast as a radio-dialog in Paris, which was why, Anders said, the title was originally in French.

This fragment stands out to me for various reasons. For one, it is explicitly about translation—at a time when neither term nor concept were attributed much time and space in Benjamin's writings. What is more, it seems much more approachable than other texts about language and translation. This may be due to the fact that it was written for dissemination via the mass-medium radio, which required an explicitly dialogical structure. Yet while it seems more approachable, it still contains the occasional convoluted but quotable nuggets of visual beauty and punch. What must be kept in mind, however, is the question of authorship: we do not know much about Anders' role; whether the dialog partners were supposed to be Anders and Benjamin; whether the turns in conversation mark their respective viewpoints; or whether Benjamin split his own position into a dialogue when he was writing it down.

In the German *Gesammelte Schriften*, this dialogical fragment is printed together with another set of notes, which—due to the similar content, type of ink and paper, and style of writing—was determined to have been written around the same time; the second fragment is entitled "What Can Be Said in Favor of Translation?"[20] Both fragments address interlingual translation, and they do so in a way that is, at first glance, difficult to reconcile with Benjamin's early writings. The first fragment discusses the nature of interlingual translation in general, and the problems of translating philosophical texts in particular. The second fragment represents a collection of notes for future, more detailed consideration; the notes are bundled into paragraphs, each representing a separate thought.

I begin with "Translation—For and Against." Its opening is stunning: in the first sentence, Benjamin uses the Germanized version of a French loanword, in order to conjure up an image with such a strong local-cultural connotation that there is no corresponding word in the German language. It is an image particular not only to France but to Paris: *die Bouquinisten*, the bouquinistes,[21] *les bouquinistes*; the antiquarian booksellers alongside the Seine. The speaker tells us that he was walking alongside the bouquinistes, when he came across the French translation of a German book he was well acquainted with—Nietzsche, as he later qualifies. He was looking for the passages that he knew so well, the ones he had frequently and diligently thought about, but "the passages were not there" (SW 3: 249).[22] Dialogue partner "B,"[23] slightly baffled, asks why he could not find them. The speaker replies that he *did*, but "when I looked them in the face, I had the awkward feeling that they no more recognize me than I do them" (SW 3: 249).[24] This image is intriguing. For one, it has an uncanny connotation: he describes the textual sites, *Stellen*, in a double-state of being there and not being there at the same time; the sites that he was *vertraut*, familiar with, now suddenly *befremdet*, alienated[25] him. What he does not recognize about them is their physiognomy, their faces. And this non-recognition is mutual. The textual sites themselves are ascribed the ability to recognize. This draws back to, but also moves beyond Benjamin's Language-Essay: while we know from the early essay that all things and events of animate and inanimate nature have their own language, they now also share in the capacity to recognize. At the same time, this is indicative of his late, materialist "definition" of the "aura," which—in its various versions—is built around an exchange of glances. In "On Some Motifs in Baudelaire,"[26] which he wrote in 1939, Benjamin states: "to experience the aura of a phenomenon we look at means to invest it with the ability to look back at us" (SW 4: 338).[27]

This awkward situation of mutual non-recognition, however, is not due to "bad" translation. The speaker points out that the French translation of Nietzsche is highly estimated, and reasonably so. Responsible for the uncanny turn from familiar to alienating is not a deficiency, lack or incompleteness of translation. Instead, what had happened may be seen as an excess of translation: "the horizon and the world around the translated text had itself been substituted, and become French" (SW 3: 249).[28] Dialogue partner "B" objects. The world around philosophical texts, he argues, is beyond all national characteristics, a universal world of ideas. The speaker negates this by making a strong point:

> Es gibt keine Gedankenwelt, die nicht eine Sprachwelt wäre, und man sieht nur das an Welt, was durch die Sprache vorausgese(t)zt ist. (GS VI: 158)
>
> There is no world of thought which is not a world of language, and one sees of the world only what is provided for by language. (SW 3: 249)

As a response to the universalist idea of a world of thought beyond national characteristics, this reads like a concise, programmatic statement of linguistic relativity. And this pairing of *Gedankenwelt*, world of thought, and *Sprachwelt*, world of language, is reminiscent of the Language-Essay, where Benjamin draws a distinction between the mental, spiritual, or immaterial *geistiges Wesen* and the linguistic *sprachliches Wesen*, both appertaining to all events or things of animate or inanimate nature. There is no mental being, or world of thought, which does not correspond to a linguistic being, or world of language, as the only thing that can be communicated of a mental being is its linguistic being.

Dialogue partner "B" likening this understanding to Humboldt's conception of language,[29] then, closes the first section of this fragment. What follows is a caesura, marked by a page break, that shifts the topic of discussion. Part two of the dialogical fragment is about terminology, and the role of new terms. It begins with a reference to the pervasive use of neologisms in Nietzsche's language. The first speaker poses the question whether Nietzsche's language is of actual intellectual significance. The dialogue partner answers in the affirmative, because he considers them to be of *historical* significance. Nietzsche's neologisms may be *Missbrauch*, misuse, or abuse of the German language; but in mis-/abusing it, Nietzsche reveals that what may be called a stable German *Sprachtradition*, a linguistic tradition, never actually came to be. This, the dialogue partner says, represents a staunch "critique of the unformed state of the German person" (SW 3: 250).[30] Benjamin thus challenges a tendency inherent in any instrumentalization of linguistic relativity to proclaim a national linguistic character, which may lead to a kind of nationalism founded in the idea of *Kulturnation*, in which language, culture, and nation are considered to be a stable unity. Within this framework, then, it is easy to posit one's own language and nation as more developed (cf. Fichte [1808] 2013). Benjamin, however, chooses to stress the incompleteness of (German) language: a stable German language tradition has never come to be, "the German person" remains unformed.

Next, they address the role of translation within this framework, discussing how a particular *Sprachsituation*, a linguistic situation such as the German one outlined earlier, may be translated. The speaker claims that the answer depends on the way in which translation is used, and clarifies, as Benjamin does in the

Peters-letter, that translation is not art: it is science in the service of art. It is *Technik*, and as such, it can and must be combined with others, as for instance with the *Technik* of commentary. It must "acknowledge its own role by means of commentary" (SW 3: 250),[31] and may not veil the different linguistic situations, but instead must make these differences one of its themes. However, translations that meet these criteria have gone lost in modern times; as an example from the seventeenth century, he mentions the bilingual editions of classic works with detailed commentary. These translations became *wirksam*, effective, precisely because the distinctiveness of different language situations was acknowledged. The last sentence of the fragment, then, reiterates that the entire dialogue was about a particular kind of translation, namely the translation of (philosophical) prose, whereas "to apply this technique to poetic texts seems to me highly problematic" (SW 3: 250).[32] This opens up a whole new set of questions, which remain unanswered.

The second fragment, "What can be said in favor of translation?", appears to be a rough outline of arguments for a longer piece of writing. In a brief reading of these notes, I limit myself to only some of the clues it holds, and I begin with the first bullet point, which says: "progress in science on an international scale" (SW 3: 250).[33] In brackets, Benjamin adds two more, uncommented hints: "Latin, Leibniz' universal language" (SW 3: 250).[34] The first part would suggest that translation is necessary to foster international exchange and advances in science, in order to avoid national scientific isolation. Yet the bracketed hints at *linguae francae*, like Latin or today's English, would seem to *prevent* translation in a scientific context, as people no longer write in their mother tongues. At the same time, Benjamin has elsewhere harshly criticized the idea of artificial "universal languages" like Esperanto. This first bullet point thus indicates the way in which the dialectic of "For and Against" permeates each of these propositions.

Later on, Benjamin explicitly addresses the question of the limitations of translation: "The limit: music needs no translation" (SW 3: 250).[35] At this point, the editors hint at an important, hidden reference to Benjamin's second dissertation, where he says that spoken and written language are thesis and synthesis, while music is the antithesis in-between, and, he continues, it is "the last remaining universal language since the tower of Babel" (1977: 214).[36] It is also notable that Benjamin uses a peculiar term here: he talks about music's *Unbedürftigkeit* of translation, that is, there is no substantial need for translation intrinsic to music; he does not, however, talk about its *Unübersetzbarkeit*, untranslatability. And he continues: "lyric poetry: closest to music—and posing the greatest difficulties for translation" (SW 3: 250).[37] Again, Benjamin hints at the difficulties of translating poetry but does not offer additional insights. Through the relation with music, however, Benjamin seems to suggest that the difficulties do not arise from a fundamental untranslatability, but from the fact that there is no intrinsic need for translation in music (and, to a lesser degree, in poetry).

The next point, then, addresses the "the limit of translation in prose" (SW 3: 250),[38] and Benjamin adds: "The value of bad translations: productive misunderstandings" (SW 3: 250).[39] These misunderstandings, he says, begin with the simple fact of which books are being translated at all, as it is usually the ones that could have been written in one's own language and literature. Two names, then, seem to indicate two different paths: *Jean Christophe* is the title of a popular novel in ten volumes written in French by Romain Rolland about a German musician who tries to make it in Paris, and it was widely read and well received in Germany (Rogister 1991: 349). The counter-story, then, is told in keywords, and by reference to Karl Christian Friedrich Krause, a German philosopher and author around the late eighteenth to early nineteenth century:

Krause in Spanien.
Mißachtung der Nuancen
Eine gewisse Brutalität im Geistesbild
Höchste Gewissenhaftigkeit mit größter Brutalität verbinden (GS VI: 159)

Krause in Spain.
Neglect of nuances.
A certain brutality in the mental image.
Combine extreme conscientiousness with utmost brutality. (SW 3: 251)

In Germany, Krause's work was not widely received, but it had an enormous impact in Spain. An influential Spanish philosopher, lawyer, and pedagogue, Julian Sanz del Rio, translated Krause into Spanish around the middle of the nineteenth century—in a very loose, commented translation, which was adapted to what he thought the didactic necessities were in Spain at the time. This led to the rise of *Krausism* in the Spanish-speaking world (Chmielorz 2010). The disregard of nuances combined with a brutality in vision led to the *Wirksamkeit*, the effectiveness or impact, of this translation—thus Benjamin concludes that what makes translations effective is the combination of extreme diligence and utmost brutality. In a final note, then, Benjamin closes the circle back to his conception of fidelity toward the foreign and freedom toward one's own language. He refers to a dictum by a Mr. Stresemann, which he claims was intended as a comical or farcical *bon mot*, and he quotes it as "French is spoken in every language" (SW 3: 251).⁴⁰ Benjamin argues that it has to be taken more seriously than Stresemann intended it to be. He ends in a very quotable statement, arguing that "the purpose [*Sinn*] of translation is to represent the foreign language in one's own" (SW 3: 251).⁴¹

These fragmentary notes constitute a last extensive and explicit conceptual engagement with *Übersetzung* in Benjamin's writing. Yet there is one more thing I want to look at, and that is a cooperation that took place at the beginning of 1936, which may have contributed to this renewed interest in translation that led Benjamin to write these two notes in the first place: the cooperation with his French translator, Pierre Klossowski, who translated Benjamin's Artwork-Essay. It is illuminating to look at the process of Benjamin's own texts being translated into a language that he had previously translated from himself. Unsurprisingly, Benjamin could not refrain from intervening, to which several exchanges of letters not only between Benjamin and his confidents but also between representatives of the *Institut für Sozialforschung* testify. Regarding the process of translating and editing the Artwork-Essay, for instance, secretary Hans Klaus Brill reports to Horkheimer that it was a *Schwerstgeburt*, the most difficult birth. This was, to a large degree, due to time constraints. Brill assumes that when Klossowski agreed to the deadline, he must have been unaware of the difficult nature of the text. Yet he also hints at "difficulties that resulted from the cooperation with Dr. B[enjamin]."⁴² Due to the significant delay that resulted from the prolonged translation process, Brill eventually had to make cuts to the final, French version, without the approval of Benjamin, in order to meet the deadline. Benjamin felt angry and betrayed when he found out. His complaints led to internal struggles regarding the allocation of competencies within the Paris branch of the *Institut für Sozialforschung*, which resulted in further delays and difficulties. However, the dispute was settled eventually, and the essay was printed.

Benjamin's letters provide another side to the story. At first, he reiterates in several letters that the translation of his Artwork-Essay was in good hands with Klossowski, who "does not only meet all the linguistic, but also important scientific requirements."⁴³ It soon became clear, however, that the process was more difficult than expected, and Benjamin began intervening. Even after the translation was done, he writes in a letter to Horkheimer that he is not sure whether their cooperation was successful. He cannot be the judge of that, he says, "the reception by the French readers will decide."⁴⁴ But at least, Benjamin claims, the translation is characterized by *Genauigkeit*, precision, and by the fact that "throughout, it correctly renders the sense of the prototype."⁴⁵ At the same time, Benjamin also reflects on his own intervention in the translation process.

He was warned, he says, that it would be clearly visible in the translated text, and that it would have a negative bearing on it. Nonetheless, he still thought it was indispensable, due to significant *Mißverständnisse* and *Entstellungen*, misunderstandings and disfigurements, which he came across when he went through the first few translated passages. Benjamin puts the blame solely on the limited time-frame; he says, like Brill did before, that Klossowski must have misjudged the extent of this translation, and must have thought it may be finished "within the time-frame of an ordinary translation."[46] But this was no ordinary translation, says Benjamin, and once Klossowski grasped its difficulties, he was very understanding. Eventually, Benjamin claims, the cooperation was "not only fruitful, but also pleasant,"[47] yet he does agree that "the traces of the translation practice"[48] were negatively perceivable in the French text. The only remedy would be more time, so that the text could pass through another cleansing *Umschmelzungsprozeß* to get rid of these traces. But they simply did not have the time to do that.

In a letter to Adorno, Benjamin then goes into more detail as to what he considered fruitful about the joint translation process. For one, the cooperative translation work allowed, he says, for a "distance from the German text that I usually only gain from longer respites."[49] This distance proved to be highly productive, as it made him recognize something in his text that he had not previously perceived: "the cannibalistic urbanity, a cautiousness and circumspection in destruction."[50] This image, the juxtaposition of cannibalistic urbanity and destruction, with cautiousness and circumspection, is reminiscent of the fragment "What can be said in favor of translation?", even though he does not talk about translation, but about the Artwork-Essay here. Still, in both contexts, he discovers a combination of diligence and brutality, circumspection and destruction. The idea of productive distance, which sounds almost like an antidote to the previously perceived intestinal poisoning, is reminiscent of another note from the abovementioned fragment, where he calls it the "liberation from the prejudices of one's own language" by "jumping over our own language" (SW 3: 250).[51] This productive process of estrangement was, in the end, made possible due to initial *Missverständnisse*, misunderstandings, that came up in Klossowski's translation. Keeping these cross-references in mind, it may very well be that the abovementioned fragments, and with them this renewed interest in translation, were influenced by this experience of working with Klossowski on a translation of his own text.

There is yet another side of the story, namely Klossowski's, of the translator translating a translator. In 1952, Adrienne Monnier wrote a letter to Klossowski, asking whether he was involved in the translation of Benjamin's Storyteller-Essay and whether he could write a contribution to the publication of this essay in French, which Monnier was preparing. In response, Klossowski details his encounters with Benjamin, as well as their cooperation on the translation of the Artwork-Essay. Klossowski seems to share Benjamin's conclusion that the translation would have needed more time; "it should be entirely reworked" (2014: 20), Klossowski says. As for the reasons why Benjamin got involved in the process in the first place, he states that Benjamin considered the first drafts "too loose" (2014: 20). But as soon as Benjamin began tampering with the translation, it turned into a perfectly unreadable text, as it "copied exactly certain poor German expressions for which Benjamin accepted no transposition. French syntax often literally gave cramps to this unwavering logician" (2014: 20).

Klossowski then goes on to reminisce about Benjamin. Together with Georges Bataille, the three of them represented a productive clash of opposites. Even though their positions had nothing in common, he estimated Benjamin highly, because "there was in this Marxist-leaning, or rather, extreme criticist, a visionary whose imagery was as rich as Isaiah's" (2014: 20). And he closes his letter with a statement that seems so out of place from today's perspective, and yet it still rings true: "I remain persuaded," says Klossowski, "that Benjamin is one of the greatest unrecognized thinkers of our time whom horrible circumstances have contributed to assimilating in the minds of many to the category of 'Marxist theorist'—a category from which he clearly distinguished himself by a powerful originality" (2014: 21). The era of an unrecognized Benjamin is long gone. Yet it is still hard to grapple with his powerful and contradictory originality, which finds expression in writings that stubbornly resist categorization. His writing questions boundaries and integrates the different influences that he encounters throughout his life in such a way that nothing seems to be replaced by anything else. Everything is present at the same time, in crystallized images of utmost concretion.

Part II

... Meets Cultural Translation

5

Benjamin's Arcade

Die wahre Übersetzung ist durchscheinend, sie verdeckt nicht das Original, steht ihm nicht im Licht, sondern läßt die "Reine Sprache," wie verstärkt durch ihr eigenes Medium, nur umso voller aufs Original fallen. Das vermag vor allem Wörtlichkeit in der Übertragung der Syntax und gerade sie erweist das Wort, nicht den Satz als das Urelement des Übersetzers. Denn der Satz ist die Mauer vor der Sprache des Originals, Wörtlichkeit die Arkade.

(GS IV: 18; my emphasis)

This quotation is taken from "Die Aufgabe des Übersetzers," that is, the preface that Benjamin wrote in 1921 for his own translation of Charles Baudelaire's *Tableaux Parisiens*. Adorno included this preface as an independent essay in his first collection of Benjamin's writings in 1955. It has since been translated into at least nineteen languages[1]—and it has been extraordinarily widely received. "You are nobody unless you have said something about this text" (1985: 11), said Paul de Man. In the following chapter, I trace some of the translation movements that this particular quotation has gone through—between German and English, between different historical constellations, disciplines, and scholars.

To begin with, "Die Aufgabe des Übersetzers" has entered English-language discourse, first and foremost, through Harry Zohn's 1968's translation, "The Task of the Translator," which was included in the first English-language collection of Benjamin's writings, Hannah Arendt's *Illuminations* (1968). Here is Zohn's rendition of the previous paragraph:

> A real translation is transparent; it does not cover the original, does not block its light, but allows the pure language, as though reinforced by its own medium, to shine upon the original all the more fully. This may be achieved, above all, by the literal rendering of the syntax which proves words rather than sentences to

be the primary element of the translator. For if the sentence is the wall before the language of the original, literalness is the arcade. (SW 1: 260)

In the following, I focus mainly on its last half sentence: "literalness is the arcade." As I illustrate, the image of the arcade has become inextricably linked with Benjamin, but it also represents a point of conflict in the translation of Benjamin's German texts into English. I render visible this disturbance, and trace the possibilities it opens up for new theory building in the context of cultural translation, as well as the creation of "new Benjamins" in the process. These "new Benjamins" are then questioned about their role in the discursive formation of said theories of cultural translation, as well as for their potential of decentering the "old" one by illuminating new subtexts in, connections among, and implications for Benjamin's German writings.

The *Arcades Project*

Indeed, the arcade has become emblematic of Benjamin. To no small degree, this is due to the mythos of a "black briefcase" (Fittko 1982: 1187) that Benjamin supposedly carried with him on his run from the Nazis, before he committed suicide in a Spanish border town in 1940. We owe the image of this black briefcase to the autobiography of Lisa Fittko, Benjamin's guide through the Pyrenees. He told her that the briefcase contained a new manuscript: "It is the manuscript that must be saved. It is more important than I am," he supposedly said (1982: 1187). The briefcase has come to signify a search for closure, a life cut short, and a life's work unfinished. It is a search for something that would help us make sense of Benjamin and his writings, where all the loose threads would come together. We hope to find it in his last work, the "theater of all [his] conflicts and all [his] ideas" (1994: 359):[2] The *Arcades Project*. Its final version, it is speculated, may have been in the briefcase.

Even though the briefcase was lost, the story of how we know what we do about the *Arcades Project* is enticing, too: there was another manuscript, recovered after the war in the venerable Bibliothèque Nationale in Paris by Benjamin's friend, Georges Bataille. Benjamin had confided his manuscript to Bataille, who gave it to two friends, librarians of the Bibliothèque Nationale, for safekeeping during the war. Bataille then sent the manuscript to Adorno, the estate trustee, and in 1982, its more than 1,350 pages were made available to German readers as volume five of Benjamin's collected writings, upon which today's English version is based as well. But this is not where the story ends, either: combing through Bataille's literary legacy at the Bibliothèque Nationale, Giorgio Agamben found writings by Benjamin that Bataille had, for whatever reason, not sent to Adorno. In 1982, the very year that volume five of the collected writings was published, Agamben announced in an article the recovery of these additional manuscripts (Agamben 1982); these manuscripts, however, are not yet part of the German, and thus also not part of the English versions of the *Arcades Project*.[3]

It is thus apparent that the (hi)story of the *Arcades Project* is complex and still unfinished. And so is the text itself. The English editors call it an "*Urgeschichte*, signifying the 'primal history' of the nineteenth century" (1999a: IX), which crystallizes in the arcade as its quintessential emblem (Figure 1).

The *Arcades Project* was an immense project, and the sheer sum of collected fragments illustrates that Benjamin put an inordinate amount of work into it. "Nobody will be able to assert that I made things easy for myself," he says in a letter to Scholem in 1928 (1994: 333).[4] Yet it has never been a coherent text. Instead, it is a massive collection of materials, an array of fragments, notes, pictures, and quotations, categorized into what Benjamin called *Konvolute*, bundles of material, each given a letter and a few catchphrases as descriptions. There are also different versions of an exposé, as well as essays that Benjamin wrote about and in the course of the project. And there is the so-called Baudelaire complex that developed from a single convolute into a separate book, which, as Benjamin explains in a letter to Horkheimer in 1938, became a *Miniaturmodell*, a "miniature" (1994: 556) of the whole *Arcades Project*. Most of these materials were published in German by Tiedemann in 1982. However, some of the materials relevant to the *Arcades Project*, particularly the ones recovered by Giorgio Agamben, have not been published in German, or in English, in their entirety.[5] As porous as the surviving materials are, they have become a breeding ground for speculation about what Benjamin *may have* wanted the *Arcades Project* to look like. Some say, like Adorno, that the final version may have been close to the montage of materials suggested in the manuscript found in the Bibliothèque Nationale; some think, like Tiedemann, that it would have looked entirely different. But we do not know. The only thing that seems clear is that Benjamin was devoted to the project. He wanted to write every last word of it in Paris,[6] so he defied all his friends' advice who told him that he had to get out of there as soon as possible to flee the Nazis. He stayed.

At least since 1927 and until his death in 1940, Benjamin dedicated much of his time and attention to his study about the arcades. And he mentions one incentive in particular that triggered this intensive engagement: Louis Aragon's

Figure 1 Passage de l'Opéra, galerie de l'Horloge, Paris Marville, C. ([1866] 2015), "Passage de l'Opéra, galerie de l'Horloge. Paris IXe. Vers 1866," digitally restored by Laurent Gloaguen, Vergue, June 15. Available online: http://vergue.com/post/595/Galerie-Horloge (accessed April 29, 2023). Public Domain.

book, *Le Paysan de Paris* (1926), a surrealist, topographical portrait of Paris, part of which takes place in the Parisian arcades. This book had affected Benjamin intensely;[7] he claimed that he could not read more than two or three pages at night, because his "heart began to pound so hard that [he] had to put the book down" (1994: 588).[8] What had captured his attention in particular was the historical rise and fall of the arcade. In the 1790s, its predecessors had been gradually introduced into the urban environment, spreading from Paris throughout Europe. It developed, architecturally, from a covered walkway;

an alley between two buildings to which a roof was attached. Not any roof, though: a glass and iron roof. Benjamin mentions the beginnings of glass and iron construction as a precondition for the emergence of the arcades. Making use of this material innovation, the glass-roofed passageways represented a response to several problems evoked by the old architecture of European cities: due to poor sanitation and an intimidating incidence of crime in the dark and narrow alleys, bourgeois customers called for "clean, safe places to shop, refined oases separate from the crowded messy chaos of big-city streets" (Fabijancic 2001: 18). These customer needs were met in the enclosed spaces of the shop-lined arcades, which constituted some of the first public spaces solely accessible to pedestrians. As *the* commercial and recreational innovation of the modern metropolis, arcades thus became the centerpiece of the city between the 1830s and 1860s. But the second half of the nineteenth century saw the rest of the city catching up, and it saw the emergence of department stores. Thus the popularity of the arcade began to decline. Eventually, by the early twentieth century, the arcades had become moribund, "home only to ailing small businesses and shopkeepers trading in the goods of a bygone era" (D. Smith 2004: 18).

Its importance began to shift, from being an integral part of urban geography to becoming an emblematic and ambiguous literary setting, as Aragon's *Paysan* demonstrates. And through Benjamin's writings, the rise and fall of the arcade made its way into the theoretical discourse of the twentieth century. In his exposé from 1935, "Paris, the Capital of the Nineteenth Century,"[9] Benjamin calls the arcade of the nineteenth century "a world in miniature" (1999a: 3)[10] that had, by the beginning of the twentieth century, turned into "a past become space" (1999a: 871).[11] It represents a space of consumption and for consumers, between inside and outside, enclosed but transparent due to the new materiality of glass and iron. A space in which the dialectic between individual and masses, observer and observed, plays out—with its quintessential inhabitant, the *flâneur*. The arcade is a transitory space, which is signified not only by the *flâneurs*, the scurrying pedestrians and consumers but also by the transitoriness of the consumer goods it houses, as well as its own historical rise and demise. Thus, to Benjamin, the arcade, as past become space, turns into a bottleneck of historical experience and knowledge.

Unforeseen Constellations: Arkade *and* Passage

Returning to the abovementioned quotation from the Translator-Essay, it would seem that the emblematic image of the arcade did not just come to Benjamin during his work on the *Arcades Project*, but had already been on his mind in the early 1920s: "For if the sentence is the wall before the language of the original," he writes in 1921, "literalness is the arcade" (SW 1: 260). It is not unusual that there would be a sense of continuity running through Benjamin's thinking; significant *Denkbilder*, thought-images, or *Denkfiguren*, figures of thought, often develop in his early works, only to find new expressions in later ones. To trace these developments—of terms, images, and concepts—is often enticing and rewarding. Yet it is also difficult. Attempts at tracking continuities often crash into discontinuities, misunderstandings, and disturbances. But these in particular can be very revealing. One such disturbance is caused precisely by the arcade from the Translator-Essay—because it is *not* the same arcade as in the *Arcades Project*.

To illustrate what I mean, I return to the Translator-Essay, and to the part where the image of the arcade first appears. There, Benjamin outlines his concept of *Wörtlichkeit*, which he positions as an ideal accomplice to break with the paradigm of reproducing *Sinn*, sense, in translation. He contrasts *Wörtlichkeit* with retaining sense on a syntactical level, which results in a translation that does not want to read like a translation, thus standing like a wall in front of the original so that the source language is out of sight. When putting the word, in its wordness, at the center of attention, however, even when rendering the syntax, the target language becomes porous: you can look through it, as if through an arcade, at the source language and the interplay of differences between source and target language. There is no disappearing of one for the sake of the other; both are recognizable and come into play with each other precisely *within the relations* between the words, "no longer governed by sentence grammar" (Weber 2008: 92; cf. De Man 1985: 29–30). In this sense, *Wörtlichkeit* means fidelity to the word.

To flesh out this understanding of *Wörtlichkeit*, it is interesting to take a look at a couple of texts Benjamin wrote at the same time as the Translator-Essay. For instance, Benjamin wrote—upon the publisher's request, and with chagrin—a brief announcement for the publication of his book, in which he indicates that he managed to fulfill his own call for *Wörtlichkeit* in his *Baudelaire* translations. He chose to emphasize three things about his publication: that some of the poems were being published for the first time in German; that the edition was bilingual, and the French version was the first philologically correct one in Germany;[12] and, eventually, he points out that in his translation,

> einerseits das Gebot der Treue, welches der Übersetzer in seiner Vorrede unwiderleglich begründet, gewissenhaft erfüllt, andrerseits aber das Poetische überzeugend erfaßt wird. (GB II: 358)

the demand for fidelity, which the translator established beyond dispute in his preface, is met in the most conscientious fashion. And second, that the poetic element in Baudelaire's work is comprehended in a convincing way. (Jennings and Eiland 2014: 187)

This announcement indicates that Benjamin had followed his own call for fidelity, that is, toward the word—and that he had also convincingly rendered *das Poetische*, the poetic, which he juxtaposes with his understanding of fidelity. A letter to Hofmannsthal illustrates, however, that Benjamin may not have been as sure about the second aspect as the announcement would suggest. Here, Benjamin states that his translations were inadequate, with regard to the simple but important fact that

> die Übersetzung metrisch naiv ist. Damit meine ich nicht sowohl die metrische Haltung der Übertragungen als die Tatsache, daß sie mir nicht im selben Sinne zum Problem geworden war, wie die Vorrede dies von der Wörtlichkeit ausspricht. ... Ich bin der Überzeugung, daß zuletzt nur die metrische Besonnenheit einer Übersetzung der Fleurs du mal intensiver als die meinigen des Baudelaireschen Stils teilhaft macht ... (GB II: 410f)
>
> the translation is metrically naïve—not in the metrics of the translation itself, but in the fact that I had not given it the same kind of thought that the preface expresses regarding *Wörtlichkeit* ... I am convinced that, in the end, Baudelaire's style can only be rendered accessible by way of a metrical thoughtfulness in the translation of *Fleurs du Mal* that is more intensive than mine ... (My translation.)[13]

He concludes that only metrical thoughtfulness could improve his translations, as his first attempt was "naïve" when it comes to meter. Naïveté, in the preface, is a feature of poetry that does not correspond with the thoughtful nature of translation as a form. And regarding metrics—and with it, maybe, "the poetic"— it seems that Benjamin did not think that he had managed to comply. With regard to *Wörtlichkeit*, however, he did: he thought that he stayed true to the thoughtful nature of translation, while, at the same time, staying true to the word in the rendition of syntax. That is what Benjamin's strategy of *Wörtlichkeit* accounts for, with the goal of illuminating an interplay of differences from which we can glance the languages' longing for linguistic completion. In this sense, *Wörtlichkeit* is not a wall that conceals, but an arcade that reveals.

But here is the thing: in this context, Benjamin does *not* talk about the glass-roofed, iron-framed, nineteenth-century arcades from the *Arcades Project*. In the Translator-Essay, he uses the German word "*Arkade*," which refers to an entirely different architectural structure: a series of arches, a vertical structure traditionally built from stone, with a function similar to that of a wall, namely, to support—while letting light flow through. *Wörtlichkeit*, thus, is an *Arkade*, says Benjamin (GS IV: 18)—a series of arches. In his later *Arcades Project*, Benjamin talks about a different structure, as I have outlined earlier, and he uses a different German word, too: he refers to the glass-roofed, iron-framed Parisian passageways of his later texts as *Passagen*; and what remains of his unfinished magnum opus, the *Arcades Project*, is thus known in German as *Passagen-Werk*.

Incidentally, though, both German terms *Arkade* and *Passage* translate as "arcade." For the English-language readers, this shift remarkably leads to the disappearance of the image of the archway: due to the theoretical and biographical importance of the Parisian passageways for Benjamin and his readers, it is almost exclusively the *Passage* from Benjamin's later works that is read into the English word *arcade*, while the image of the archway, the *Arkade*, is lost. This slight shift has often gone unnoticed in the English-language reception. So, in the following section, I trace the "lost" image of the *Arkade* in Benjamin's writings, in an attempt to reinscribe it into the English-language reception.

The *Arkade* in Benjamin's Writings

Architecturally, the *Arkade* is formed from an arch that multiplies into a series. The term denotes this series of arches and the space it creates—which is a very peculiar, in-between space, in which the inside and the outside overlap. Usually located in front of buildings, the *Arkade* belongs to both, the building and the public outdoor space. Indoor functions may be extended into the *Arkade*, so that they attain public character. It is a seam of space, a porous border that may be crossed or walked along. The crossing experiences may differ, depending on varying architectural characteristics: the *Arkade* may be bright and wide, but it may also be dark and compact, creating the impression of stepping into a cave (Figures 2–4).

Walking along the *Arkade*, its sheltered space and rhythmic, continuous series of arches facilitate contemplative strolling. Glancing along the inside, the in-between space may appear as an indoor space, and the series of arches as a wall. Zooming in on this wall, however, it becomes porous, and the columns and arches create a sharp contrast of lights and shadows in a magical interplay (Janson and Tigges 2013: 19–20). With regard to their function in modern urban space,

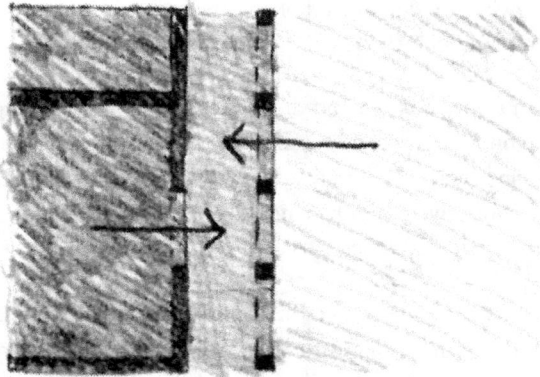

Figure 2 Drawing of the spatial structure of an arcade. Janson, A. and F. Tigges (2013), *Grundbegriffe der Architektur. Das Vokabular räumlicher Situationen*, Basel: Birkhäuser, p. 21. Courtesy Alban Janson.

Figure 3 and 4 Drawings of a cave-like arcade, as well as a light and airy arcade. Janson, A. and F. Tigges (2013), *Grundbegriffe der Architektur. Das Vokabular räumlicher Situationen*, Basel: Birkhäuser, p. 22. Courtesy Alban Janson.

Arkaden are often described as performing a return to an unspecified past: they are, at times, consciously implanted in order to re-instate an air of the ancient, of an indeterminate historicity, as their archaic appearance is counted on to "heal the wounds" of modernity in urban environments (Confurius 1987: 97–8).

In Benjamin's writings, the *Arkade* comes up in early travelogues and thought-images, in his Baudelaire translations, and in his *Arcades Project*. For instance, in his early autobiographical notes about a trip to Italy in 1912:

> Wir treten ein und haben die Stille der großen aufsteigenden Arena vor uns. Nur an einer Stelle wird die Linie des Horizonts durch große Trümmerpfeiler unterbrochen, Reste eines Arkadenumbaus, der zu Goethes Zeiten noch stand.

Treppen sind zwischen den meterhohen Absätzen geschlagen. Wir steigen hinauf bis zum Rand. (GS VI: 272)

We enter, and in front of us, we find the silence of a large ascending arena. The line of the horizon is interrupted in only one place by large debris of columns, the remains of an outer circle of arcades, which was still standing in Goethe's times. Stairwells are driven into the landings that stand meters high. We climb up to the edge. (My translation.)

The *Arkaden*, in this case, are located in front of a very particular building: an amphitheater that is reminiscent of the Roman coliseum due to its double arcade structure. And, as it is often the case in Benjamin's writings, the *Arkaden* appear right next to another in-between space, a space of passage between above and below: the stairs.

Years later, the *Arkaden* re-surface in Benjamin's translation of Baudelaire—not only in the famous preface, of course, but also in one of the poems, namely in "Rêve parisien." It is the second to last poem in Baudelaire's *Tableaux Parisiens*, and it begins in a betwixt state between sleep and awakening. This threshold position is indicative of a special relation between the poem and the entire *Tableaux:* while the *Tableaux* sketch the course of Paris by day and night, the poem, "Rêve parisien," precisely marks the point of passage between nocturnal and diurnal Paris. Also, the term *parisien* in both titles seems to deliberately veil the exact nature of the relation between dream or visual presentation and Paris, which hints at a fundamental ambiguity and difficulty of expressing the subjective, ecstatic experience of an imagined object. In 1929, Benjamin picks up on this ambiguity in his essay on "Surrealism," where he describes Paris as the object that is "the most dreamed-of" (1978: 182), yet the German phrase *Geträumteste* designates Paris not (only) as the most dreamed-of, but as the most imagined of objects. Only a few lines later, then, Benjamin mentions a predecessor of surrealism, Giorgio de Chirico, who has become inextricably linked with his depiction of *Arkaden*. In his "pittura metafisica," *Arkaden* create a sharp and magical contrast of lights and shadows, and they serve as a frame scenery for enigmatic, hidden events. De Chirico describes the secret of the *Arkade* as follows:

Nichts ist wie das Geheimnis der Arkade—von den Römern geschaffen—, das Geheimnis all dessen, was römisch sein kann. (De Chirico 2011: 49)

There is nothing like the secret of the arcade, made by the Romans, the secret of everything that can be Roman. (My translation.)

To de Chirico, the function of the *Arkade* seems similar to that of the *Passage* in Benjamin's later writings: a fragment in which can be found the whole, an enigmatic "world in miniature."

As mentioned before, the poem "Rêve parisien" begins at the very moment between sleep and awakening, when the dream landscape from the previous night returns to the first-person narrator as an image, or *Konterfei*, "distant and dim" (Aggeler 1954: 382), he says:

Ce matin encore l'image, Vague et lointaine, me ravit.... Et, peintre fier de mon génie, Je savourais dans mon tableau L'enivrante monotonie Du métal, du marbre et de l'eau.	Heut morgen noch das Konterfei Entfernt und vage mich berückt.... Und stolz auf meine Bildnerei Genoß, ihr eigener Verfasser Ich ihr berauschend Einerlei Von Marmor und Metall und Wasser.	This morning I am still entranced By the image, distant and dim, ... And, painter proud of his genius, I savored in my picture The delightful monotony Of water, marble, and metal.
(GS IV: 56)	(GS IV: 56)	(Aggeler 1954: 382)

In the next stanza, the "I" sees itself as a painter relishing in the rendering of this image, his *tableau*, *Bildnerei*, or picture. These word choices, *Konterfei* and *Bildnerei*, are interesting to take note of. The latter is a rather outdated word that opens a broad reference frame: it is a synonym of statuary art, but at the same time derives from the German word for image, *Bild*. It thus refers to a visual realm, but does not commit to either process or result, nor to a particular visual medium. Using the term *Konterfei*, however, Benjamin focuses on a very particular facet of meaning contained in the French *l'image*, a particular kind of visual presentation, namely of people and faces. With regard to the medium of artistic expression, *Konterfei* may refer to a painting, but in Benjamin's contemporary use, it is more often used in connection with the medium of photography (DWDS, "Konterfei"). In using these terms to render *tableau* and *image*, Benjamin's translation contrasts a more "traditional" form of artistic expression, that is, painting or statuary art, with a reference to the modern visual medium of photography. This seems fitting. The poem continues to describe an inorganic, shiny, and dazzling urban landscape made "of water, marble and metal" (1954: 382),[14] in which mirror-like ponds are encircled "not with trees, but with colonnades" (1954: 382). And in this shiny mirage, we encounter the image of the archway, the *Arkaden*:

Babel d'escaliers et d'arcades,	Gestuftes Babel von Arkaden	Babel of arcades and stairways,
C'était un palais infini,	Ein unabsehbarer Palast	It was a palace infinite
Plein de bassins	Stand voller Becken	Full of basins
et de cascades	und Kaskaden	and of cascades
Tombant dans	In Gold und Bronze	Falling on dull
l'or mat ou bruni;	Eingefaßt	or burnished gold,
(GS IV: 56)	(GS IV: 56)	(Aggeler 1954: 382)

Compressed into one line, they occur together, once again, with stairs—and with Babel: "Babel of arcades and stairways" (1954: 382). This line conjures one of the most well-known visual presentations of the story of Babel, namely "The Great Tower of Babel" (1563) by Pieter Bruegel. He used the coliseum as a model, but while the arcaded gangways in the coliseum descend, pointing toward the inside arena, they ascend in Bruegel's painting and point, in an impossible construction, toward a not-yet built center at the top. As the art historian and poet Klaus Demus emphasizes, it is not that the tower remains unfinished; it is the visual presentation of something that cannot be built at all (2008: 56)[15]—a counter image, maybe, to the "bottomless depths of language" from the Translator-Essay (Benjamin 1997: 165).[16] Yet in the poem, these arcades are placed within Baudelaire's phantasmagoric urban landscape, taking part in a dialectical *tableau* of myth and urban modernity.

In 1924, then, the image of the *Arkade* returns in Benjamin's writings, namely in a city portrait entitled "Naples."[17] Benjamin describes the city as craggy, as if it had grown into the rock, which was now riddled with small caves and doors. He continues:

> Porös wie dieses Gestein ist die Architektur. Bau und Aktion gehen in Höfen, Arkaden und Treppen ineinander über. In allem wahrt man den Spielraum, der es befähigt, Schauplatz neuer unvorhergesehener Konstellationen zu werden. Man meidet das Definitive, Geprägte. Keine Situation erscheint so, wie sie ist, für immer gedacht, keine Gestalt behauptet ihr "so und nicht anders." (GS IV: 309)
>
> As porous as this stone is the architecture. Building and action interpenetrate in the courtyards, arcades, and stairways. In everything they preserve the scope [*Spielraum*] to become a theater of new, unforeseen constellations. The stamp of the definitive is avoided. No situation appears intended forever, no figure asserts its "thus and not otherwise." (1978: 165–6; my annotation)

Benjamin emphasizes the permeability, the porosity of the rock—an ambiguity, resumed in the juxtaposition of building and action. Again, Benjamin assembles various in-between spaces: to *Arkaden* and stairways he adds courtyards—an outside on the inside. These spaces hold a room-for-play, a *Spielraum*, a potential of becoming sites for new, unforeseen constellations, where that which is not definitive, not defined, not intended, or marked forever manifests. This space of transition and ephemerality is reminiscent of the space of the translation process, revealed by the *Arkade* of *Wörtlichkeit*: "all translation is only a *somewhat provisional way* of coming to terms with the foreignness of languages" (SW 1: 257; my emphasis),[18] Benjamin says in the Translator-Essay.

Biographer Momme Brodersen finds that these characteristics, namely, porosity, permeability, and incompleteness in methodology and composition, convey Benjamin's entire program of an open form of philosophy and perception (1990: 159). He points out that the insistence on these principles expressed in "Naples" marks an opening in Benjamin's thinking that had announced itself in his previous writings. It is an opening toward another way of thinking, in which he increasingly diverges from his metaphysical fundamentals, away from an "Esoteric of the True" (Habermas 1979: 47), toward a methodology and composition based in incompleteness, openness, porosity, and interpenetration.

In this city portrait of Naples, there is yet another hidden in-between space, shaped by similar principles: the glass-roofed passageway, the *Passage*. Benjamin does not yet call it by its name, but he describes its architectural form:

> Glückselige Zerstreutheit im Warenlager! ... Der lange Gang ist bevorzugt. In einem glasbedeckten gibt es einen Spielzeugladen..., der neben Märchengalerien bestehen würde. (GS IV: 313)

> Blissful confusion in the storehouses! ... The long gangway is favored. In a glass-roofed one there is a toyshop ... that would hold its own beside fairy-tale galleries. (1978: 170)

So, in "Naples," *Arkade* meets *Passage*. And at least for a while, the two co-exist, especially in Benjamin's early texts on the Paris arcades, which stem from the time when he wrote the Surrealism-Essay. There is a brief text entitled "*Passagen*," or "Arcades," from as early as 1927, which may have been planned as an essay, and which was probably written together with Franz Hessel; there is a collection of text fragments entitled "Pariser Passagen II," or "The Arcades of Paris," written in 1928–29; and then there is a brief text entitled "Der Saturnring oder Etwas vom Eisenbau," or "The Ring of Saturn," also written in 1928–29. And, in the collection of text fragments entitled "The Arcades of Paris," there is an intriguing note that later made its way into convolute N of the *Passagenarbeit*, in a slightly altered version.

Diese Niederschrift, die von den pariser Passagen handelt, ist unter einem freien Himmel begonnen worden, wolkenloser Bläue, die über Laube sich wölbte und doch von den Millionen Blättern bestaubt war, vor denen die frische Brise des Fleißes, der schwerfällige Atem des Forschens, der Sturm des jungen Eifers und das träge Lüftchen der Neugier (mit) viel-hundertjährigem Staube bedeckt ward. Der gemalte Sommerhimmel, der aus Arkaden in den Arbeitssaal der pariser Nationalbibliothek hinuntersieht, hat seine träumerische, lichtlose Decke über die Erstgeburt ihrer Einsicht geworfen. (GS V: 1059)

These notes devoted to the Paris arcades [*Passagen*] were begun under an open sky of cloudless blue that arched above the foliage and yet was dimmed by the millions of leaves from which the fresh breeze of diligence, the stertorous breath of research, the storm of youthful zeal, and the idle wind of curiosity have raised the dust of centuries. The painted sky of summer that looks down from the arcades [*Arkaden*] in the reading room of the Bibliotheque Nationale in Paris has stretched its dreamy, unlit ceiling over the birth of their insight. (1999a: 884; my annotation)[19]

This image is stunning: Benjamin writes about writing about the Paris arcades, *Passagen*, under a painted sky that looks down from the reading room arcades, *Arkaden*. What plays out here is the complex entanglement of light and shadow, inside and outside—and both structures, *Passagen* and *Arkaden*. Especially in English, but also, to a lesser degree, in German, there is a sense of confusion as to how exactly this visual is supposed to be constructed: while the glass-roofed Paris arcades, together with the cloudless blue and the open sky, invoke a kind of transparency and brightness, this image is immediately juxtaposed with an unlit, painted sky looking down from an archwayed ceiling. How are we supposed to picture this painted sky looking down from the arcades in the reading room? I did go down that rabbit hole and tried to find out in which reading room Benjamin was working in at the Bibliothèque Nationale. And eventually, I found an enlightening picture (see Figure 5), which does not only provide a stunning visual to make sense of the previous quotation but also illustrates Benjamin's awareness of the different structures that are *Arkaden* and *Passagen*. The image illustrates how we may picture a painted sky looking down from reading room arcades. Clearly, this is a series of arches; these are *Arkaden*. Yet at the same time, it appears as if Benjamin consciously plays with the similarities and differences between *Arkaden* and *Passagen*.

Against this background, it is interesting to read the first coherent text fragment from the *Passagenarbeit*, namely, the brief but incredibly dense "Arcades," which was written shortly before the abovementioned note. In this

Figure 5 Salle Labrouste, Bibliothèque Nationale, Paris Freihalter, G. (2017), "Salle Labrouste," July 29. Available online: https://upload.wikimedia.org/wikipedia/commons/0/0f/Paris_2e_Biblioth%C3%A8que_nationale_Salle_Labrouste_713.jpg (accessed April 29, 2023). Wikimedia Commons (CC BY-SA 3.0).

text, too, *Arkaden* and *Passagen* co-exist in the very first sentence. And this is indeed the only English translation I found in which the difference between the two architectural figures is clearly marked:

> In der Avenue des Champs-Elysees zwischen neuen Hotels mit angelsächsischen Namen wurden vor kurzem Arkaden eröffnet und die neueste Pariser Passage tat sich auf. (GS V: 1041)

> On the Avenue des Champs-Élysées, between modern hotels with Anglo-Saxon names, arcades were opened recently, and the newest Parisian passage made its appearance. (1999a: 871)

The text was most likely written in 1927; and indeed, in 1926, the *Arcades des Champs-Élysées* were opened as a new luxury shopping mall in Paris. It seems as if Benjamin plays here with the anachronism of this development: the *Arcades des Champs-Élysées*, in this context, do not denote something ancient, or ahistorical, but rather the newest of the new, the reincarnation of the Parisian Passage as a luxury shopping mall, an *Arcade*.[20]

Overall, Benjamin uses the image of the *Passage* differently than that of the *Arkade*, particularly with regard to their historical embedding and experience:

the Parisian *Passage* is a quintessentially urban, modern, transitory space, constructed from nineteenth-century building materials, mirroring its own rise and fall in the consumer goods it contains; the *Arkade* from the early works, on the other hand, often evokes an archaic, ancient, or biblical context, at times marking a dialectic interference by doing so. The *Arkade* is porous and open in a literal sense, whereas the *Passage* represents an entirely enclosed space, only permeable to light due to its glass and iron roof. Yet there are also conspicuous similarities that Benjamin explores especially in his later texts: for one, the glass-roofed *Passage* belongs to a similar architectural category as the *Arkade*, as they both constitute sheltered in-between spaces that are permeable to light, though in different ways. At the same time, he also plays with the anachronism of their different historical and sociocultural functions, as he hints at the increasing replacement of the *Passagen* by shopping malls, epitomized, paradoxically, by the new *Arcades*, such as the Arcades des Champs-Élysées.

The Arcade and Cultural Translation

The image of the *Arkade* from Benjamin's Translator-Essay has led into a labyrinth of illuminating detours through his works. Now, I return to the beginning. I opened this chapter by quoting from Harry Zohn's translation of "The Task of the Translator." As of today, there are, as far as I am aware, only four English translations, plus one amended version. Two were published simultaneously in 1968: the Zohn translation in *Illuminations* (1968b), and a translation by James Hynd and E. M. Valk, published in the magazine *Delos: A Journal On & Of Translation* (1968c). The latter translation, though, is hardly ever referred to; there is only one reprint I could find, from 2000, in a translation studies reader entitled *Translation—Theory and Practice*, edited by D. Weissbort and A. Eysteinsson. After that, the next one took almost thirty years: in 1997, Steven Rendall published "The Translator's Task" (1997), together with a critical article discussing passages of Benjamin's text that he thought were misconceived in Zohn's translation. Both, the article and the new translation were first published in the journal *TTR: traduction, terminologie, redaction*, and his commentary was eventually incorporated into the *Translation Studies Reader*, edited by Lawrence Venuti in 2000. The most recent translation appeared in 2009, in a new edition entitled *One-Way Street and Other Writings* (2009), with a foreword by the Indian writer and scholar of literary studies Amit Chaudhuri,[21] and with all new translations by J. A. Underwood. Yet in spite of recurring criticism, the translation by Zohn has held its place as the standard translation for almost fifty years, and an amended version of was printed in the *Selected Writings* (1996). Thus we still largely read, criticize, and quote from Zohn's "first" Benjamin, with only relatively minor alterations.

With regard to the one word, the "arcade," there is only one translation that falls out of alignment: Hynd/Valk use the term "colonnade," the others use "arcade," which certainly seems closer to the German *Arkade*. Yet it comes, as I have illustrated, with the challenge of referring to two different architectural forms. Taking this into consideration, the ostensibly deviating choice, "colonnade," appears in a different light. It avoids the ambiguity of the term "arcade," and seems to convey, in spite of all differences, at least a closer relation with the *Arkade* from Benjamin's earlier works: with traditional building materials, an air of the archaic. However, I have not once come across this translation anywhere as a reference. In its translation as "arcade," the image of the *Arkade* thus disappears from Benjamin's works for the sake of the image of the glass-and-iron covered *Passage*. However, this disappearance seems to also have created a space of possibilities, in particular for end of the twentieth-century translation and cultural theory. In the following, I explore this new room-for-play.

Looking at the early reception of the Translator-Essay, with a focus on the *Arkade*-quote, the first thing that confronts the eye is a blank: the image does not appear in the first few English-language readings of Benjamin's Translator-Essay. As far as I am aware, it does not turn up in George Steiner's 1975 *After Babel*, in Carol Jacobs' "The Monstrosity of Translation," or in Paul de Man's 1986 "Conclusions"; in these texts, something else moves to the forefront of concern, namely, the organic metaphors from the Translator-Essay that are connected with life and temporality—like seeds, processes of ripening, and after-ripening, or unfolding. The first of these well-known essays that does include the *Arkade*-quote is Derrida's "Des Tours de Babel." Derrida, too, focuses on the abovementioned metaphors in order to highlight his own conception of translation's *survivre*, but the "stony" arcade also turns up. He briefly outlines Benjamin's earlier theory of name-language and illustrates that Benjamin's reference to *Wörtlichkeit* in the Translator-Essay goes back to the early Language-Essay. Outlining Benjamin's way of privileging the word, Derrida quotes the paragraph about *Wörtlichkeit*, and he adds: "Whereas the wall braces while concealing (it is in front of the original), the arcade supports while letting light pass and the original show (we are not far from the Parisian passages)" (1985a: 187–8). Indeed, Derrida seems to have an *Arkade* in mind, which offers support as a structural, architectural element similar to a wall, but it differs from the wall in that it lets light pass through. At the same time, Derrida sees the architectural proximity between *Arkade* and *Passage*, and thus provides a short, bracketed, but significant reference to Benjamin's later works: *Arkaden*, he says, are "not far from" the Parisian *Passagen*. This formulation signifies proximity as well as distance; Derrida knows that *Arkaden* are not the same as *Passagen*, but they are "not far from" each other.²² This tentative connection opens the floodgates for the subsequent English-language reception, in which Derrida's "not far from" develops into an equation—with interesting consequences.

Over the years, there have been numerous other prominent readings of Benjamin's Translator-Essay. Yet it is the poststructuralist commentaries by Derrida and De Man that have become almost as canonical for the English-language reception as the Translator-Essay itself, such that this constellation of Benjamin–De Man–Derrida has generated its own strand of secondary literature. In 1992, one of the first to turn her attention to this "Translation Trinity" (Ingram 1997: 213) is Tejaswini Niranjana, in her study *Siting Translation: History, Poststructuralism and the Colonial Context*. She calls for the "siting" of translation, its careful contextualization, as well as for translation to become recognized as a crucial site where unequal relations between different languages and cultures play out, where the colonial "Other" is produced, and questions of representation, power, and historicity must be raised.

In this study, translation is "not just" (1992: 8) an interlingual process. Niranjana does take textual, interlingual translation between India and Great Britain into consideration, as she looks at how these translation processes underpin and constitute British colonial power, and how they have contributed to the construction of a colonial "Other" (e.g., 1992: 174f). At the same time, Niranjana goes beyond that. Her main objective is to look at translation as "an entire problematic" (1992: 8), which entails an investigation of how "traditional" translation theories function as tools to cement Western notions of reality and representation, such as representational realism. Within this framework, an "original" is rendered according to the ideal of equivalence—while veiling its own process of construction. This theoretical premise is based on the idea of a "neutral" *tertium comparationis* that is, however, ideologically and conceptually preinscribed with Western universals.²³ Niranjana, then, follows a poststructuralist critique of these "traditional" theoretical premises. In short, she attempts to "reclaim the notion of translation by deconstructing it and reinscribing its potential as a strategy of resistance" (1992: 6).

For this to work, Niranjana needs to establish a backdrop against which this new, subversive strategy of postcolonial translation may be defined; a "traditional" concept of translation she can deconstruct and reinscribe. To do so, she examines translation studies and ethnography, two disciplines involved in the colonial project by translating non-Western texts and "translating... one culture into terms intelligible to another" (1992: 47), and she looks at the way in which these two fields conceptualize translation. The duality suggests a split of translation into literary and cultural translation—the former as an interlingual, textual procedure, and the latter as the translation of cultures into the technical language of ethnographers. And indeed, this is the line of argumentation Niranjana follows.

Translation studies, Niranjana argues, builds its "notion of text, author, and meaning... on an unproblematic, naively representational theory of language" (1992: 48–9). This results in a blindness and unwillingness to question its "humanistic" founding concepts, she says, which eventually leads the field to ignore the complicity of translation in the colonial enterprise,[24] the historicity of translated texts,[25] or unequal power relations in general.[26] With regard to ethnography, on the other hand, these power relations are inscribed in the very conception of their task, as the "birth" of the discipline around the 1920s goes hand in hand with the decentering of Europe through the experience of colonialism. Ethnography thus also functions within a framework of logocentrism, which depends on notions of reality and representation complicit with the conceptual grids of liberal humanism and empiricism. Yet this complicity is more readily acknowledged here than in the field of translation studies, Niranjana argues, and it has increasingly become a topic of discussion, for example, in the *Writing Culture*-debate. Yet within the framework, Niranjana sees a danger of this kind of criticism "troping 'politics' into 'poetics'" and focusing too much on rhetoric, which may lead back into ahistoricism (1992: 86).

Building on her critique of these two fields' understandings of and engagement with translation, Niranjana attempts to arrive at a "post-colonial practice of translation, wary of the rhetoric of humanism, informed by a critique of telos and origin, alert to relations of power and historicity" (1992: 86). Through detailed readings of De Man and Derrida, she develops a poststructuralist critique of the abovementioned "traditional" theoretical premises. However, she argues that the two poststructuralists do not effectively theorize translation in its relation to history, which is why she heavily draws on Benjamin to criticize them for their "refusal... to address the question of history" (1992: 5). In her reading of Benjamin, then, she blends his figure of the translator with that of the materialist historian, as she argues that his "early writings on translation are troped[27] in significant ways into his later essays on the writing of history" (1992: 4–5). In tracing this movement, Niranjana operationalizes the disruptive energies of both figures, the translator and the materialist historian, for her own postcolonial project, challenging the primacy of syntactic meaning and syntagmatic linearity. Thus, it is essential for her argument to find correspondences between Benjamin's writings on translation and his writings on history, for example, the Translator-Essay and the *Arcades Project*. Twice in the course of her argument (1992: 119, 155), she links these two works by means of a term that appears in both texts: the arcade. In the first of these instances, Niranjana comments the respective parts from the Translator-Essay, and adds:

> The arcade was to be the central figure of Benjamin's great unfinished *Passagenarbeit*, also known as the *Arcades Project*. In this massive work, Benjamin planned to write a new kind of history of Paris in the 19th century. The literal translator of "Task" was to become the literal historian of the arcades. (1992: 119)

Niranjana is particularly interested in the notion of *Wörtlichkeit* as a strategy that provides a "critique of representation [which] prepares the way for the critique of historicism in his later writings" (1992: 118). As she outlines how *Wörtlichkeit* challenges the reproduction of sense and "splinters the linearity and symmetry of the sentence" (1992: 119), Niranjana draws subversive energies from this disruptive concept, and then goes on to superimpose this "literal" translator and "the literal historian of the arcades": her word-for-word translator explodes the continuity of a sentence, thus advancing like the materialist historian from the *Passagenarbeit*, who works against historicist historiography by bursting open the continuum of history.

She details this task of the materialist historian later on in her text. Quoting Derrida, she talks about the innate citability of words, which "are citations, already, always" (Derrida 1986: 1), and explains that no word is bound to an "original" context. She then likens this gesture of citation to Benjamin's idea of *Wörtlichkeit*-as-an-arcade: his focus on the word in translation prioritizes the paradigmatic over the syntagmatic level of syntax, which, in the terms of Benjamin's writings on history, parallels the way in which the temporal structure of dialectical images challenges the continuity imposed by historicism. Thus again, Niranjana says, the image of the arcade from the Translator-Essay "brings us close to the great unfinished materialist history of nineteenth-century Paris" (1992: 155), in which Benjamin argues that dialectical images, too, are grounded in a gesture of citation, through which "a past charged with now-time . . . [is] blasted out of the continuum of history" (SW 4: 395).[28] The translational concurrence of *Arkade* and *Passage* in the word *arcade* thus creates a terminological bridge for Niranjana, which allows her to bring together the figure of Benjamin's translator and his materialist historian, and to tap into the disruptive energies of *Wörtlichkeit* to attack both syntactic meaning and syntagmatic linearity in the service of her own postcolonial strategies of subversion. Dissecting De Man and Derrida, she supplements their readings with Benjamin's materialist philosophy of history, in order to construct her subversive concept of postcolonial translation, in which "the post-colonial desire to re-translate is linked to the desire to re-write history" (Niranjana 1992: 172).

Three years after Niranjana's *Siting Translation*, postcolonialism, translation and the "Translation Trinity" again take center stage in Rey Chow's *Primitive Passions: Visuality, Sexuality, Ethnography, and Contemporary Chinese Cinema* (1995). She shares many of Niranjana's approaches and ideas; however, in looking at films, Chow criticizes Niranjana for promoting an expanded understanding of translation, while still singularly applying it to literary texts. Chow counters this approach by moving from writing to visuality, zooming in on processes of translation that occur within and between different media, and between different historical media developments. To begin with, Chow discusses the construction of an intellectual dominance of writing over visuality, and the traditionalist repression of visuality, which had come to be seen as an element of modernity, of a "global movement in media technology" (1995: 17). At the same time, Chow links the increasing dominance of visuality not only to modern media, such as photography and film: she also challenges the genealogy of medialities according to which writing "comes first," by discussing the way in which visuality is inscribed in modernist and pre-modernist writing as well. Looking at the effects of this move toward visuality in a Chinese context, Chow argues that it entails an inevitable confrontation with processes of democratization, as the literary sign is de-centered and dislocated. This dislocation is twofold: the literary sign is increasingly replaced by the visual sign, which leads to a decline of literary language for the sake of visual (mass) media. The literary and literate elites are thus increasingly "disowned" as the sole agents for documenting history, culture, and society.

These profound transformations are structured, according to Chow, by what she calls "primitive passions." This term is never very precisely defined, but Chow provides the readers with several key characteristics (e.g., 22–3) that outline primitive passions as a dynamic that becomes particularly effective in times of cultural crises, as it allows for thinking the unthinkable, for the reconstruction of something after the fact, something that has never been there in the first place, such as, for instance, an "origin." The "passion" for the "primitive" is always phantasmagoric and ex-otic, and is targeted at marginalized or subaltern characters, such as women or natives. While orientalism and the colonial enterprise are prime examples of the primitivization of a colonial "Other," it is essential, says Chow, to understand and analyze the dynamic of primitive passions *within* constructions of the "Other," too, in order to explore the way in which "this dialectic between formal innovation and primitivism characterizes the hierarchical relations of cultural production in the 'third world' as well" (1995: 21).

In her case studies, Chow mines Chinese films from the 1980s and 1990s for this dynamic of "primitive passions," which find their "most appropriate material expression in film" (1995: 23), she argues. Film shares a cross-cultural, exhibiting function with institutions such as museums and art galleries, in that they are visual media often used to exhibit ethnic cultures. Here, Chow identifies significant structural and analytic correspondences between film, colonialism— and, eventually, translation. She posits that the same presumed transparency and immediacy of film and ethnography has often also been presumed of translation. Similarly, where a "conventional" theory of the gaze establishes a dichotomy of looker and the looked-upon, a "conventional" theory of translation establishes a dichotomy of translator and translated. Chow, like Niranjana, draws on the subversive energies of poststructuralist theory in order to re-theorize these "conventional" set-ups, which is particularly notable as she looks at how Zhang Yimou's films tackle "issues in cross-cultural interpretative politics" (1995: 142): in doing so, she addresses the tension between the "Western" and "non-Western" reception of Zhang's films, as well as the autoethnographic way in which the looked-upon look at the on-lookers looking.

Chow points out that criticism of Zhang's films is almost exclusively formulated in terms of surface and depth, thus one of the most often expressed criticisms is that his films are superficial. At times, the lack of depth is given as the reason why the films are beautiful to look at. Indeed, this beauty and lack of depth is thought of as the reason why these films work abroad, and thus is criticized as a conscious attempt to cater to foreign audiences. Chow proposes, with reference to Barthes' *Mythologies*, that Zhang produces his own primitives, he orientalizes his own origins and makes "use of things, characters, and narratives not for themselves but for their collective, hallucinatory signification of 'ethnicity'" (1995: 144). The created "China" he thus displays is mythically codified, but constructed along the parameters and medialities of modernity. It is not some deep, essential meaning that carries a signifying force; rather, the visual surface details "are there to signify 'I am an ethnic detail; I am feudal China'" (1995: 145). Meaning is thus dislocated from where it belongs, according to Western conventions, that is, transposed from the depths to the surface—a surface "which looks, stares, and speaks" (1995: 150).

Zhang's films thus manifest a quality that challenges audiences' obsession with hermeneutic depth, and their search for authenticity and hidden meaning. And it is also a challenge for those who claim that he caters to foreign audiences by serving up a form of orientalism produced by an "oriental," as what Chow calls "The Force of Surfaces"[29] exposes this criticism as a complex form of nativism. The accusation, effectively, is that the films fail to mediate the "true" depth of a Chinese national character, which, in fact, contributes to the idea that there *is* such a thing as an "original," primordial Chinese national character in the first place. Instead, a strong visual aesthetics that immediately presents itself as signification de-centers such Western notions of hermeneutic depth. For those who have been ethnographized, it constitutes a space to look at the practice of ethnographizing their own cultures—as constructed not only verbally, but mainly visually. "To-be-looked-at-ness" thus becomes a "predominant aspect of that culture's self-representation" (1995: 180), and it should become a predominant aspect of critical engagement, too. In such a practice of auto-ethnography, in which "to-be-looked-at-ness" is the primary event, "'us' and 'them' are no longer safely distinguishable" (1995: 180), the binary is complicated. In autoethnographic films, the force of surfaces thus sheds lights not on an "origin" but on the originary cruelty by means of which the original is constructed in the first place, namely through the exhibitionist confrontation with the foreign gaze.

This touches upon what Chow calls the "problem of origins" (1995: 182), which she ultimately links with translation. She outlines how translation is commonly cast as derivative and secondary to the original; the inherent value lies in the original, and translation must not leave any traces, must be as invisible and noninvasive as possible in conveying the "truth" of the original. In her challenge to such ideas of "origin," Chow does not primarily enlist De Man or Derrida; she goes straight to Walter Benjamin. One reason for that is—and this is an important aspect that I have hardly ever found mentioned in the context of cultural translation—Benjamin's own experience of historical change, as he wrote "at the crossroads of cultural transformation" (1995: 185), particularly with respect to the new media of photography and cinema, as we know from his well-known essay about the status of the artwork in an age of mechanical reproduction.

Chow, then, returns to the critique of Zhang Yimou, who is regarded as an unfaithful, bad translator, who failed to mediate the sum total of Chinese culture and history, of a "core meaning that exists prior to film" (1995: 184). She juxtaposes this critique with her own notion of literal translation, and this is precisely where Benjamin's arcade of *Wörtlichkeit* becomes interesting to her. While Niranjana uses the English translation of the word, namely, literalness, Chow introduces the concept by means of the German word, *Wörtlichkeit*. But not only that: she points out the differences between the English and the German words, arguing that Zohn, in his translation, "supplements Benjamin's text in an unprecedented, perhaps fateful, manner" (1995: 186). While literal does mean verbatim, it also holds a connotation of lack, matter-of-fact-ness, without imagination, without metaphor, or depth. To her, this supplementation in translation via Zohn actually shines light on "the precise sense of Benjamin's *Wörtlichkeit*: a real translation is not only that which translates word by word but also that which translates literally, depthlessly, naively" (1995: 186). By looking at it from this perspective, Chow gets more out of *Wörtlichkeit* than many other commentators. It allows her to locate *Wörtlichkeit*-as-superficial-translation as a third concept between literal (in Derrida's and De Man's sense, she says, as that which is proper and not figurative) and the metaphorical: her "literal translation" is neither; instead, it is that which presents itself as signification.

Directly addressing Niranjana, Chow argues that Benjamin's Translator-Essay may indeed be "useful for a theory of cultural translation," but only if his conceptualization of the relation between original and translation is coupled with his pronounced interest in mass culture—it is not, however, useful "in the opposition between 'language' and 'history' as Niranjana argues" (1995: 193). It is intriguing to see that the very same quotation makes the two theorists follow two very different trajectories. Both argue that we must acknowledge the coevalness of cultures, but in her attempt to get there, Chow looks at new media and mass culture as an anchor for said coevalness, instead of a redefined notion of historicity. On this basis, Chow argues, cultural translation needs to embrace and include mass media—radio, film, television, and so on— which may become sites for a weakening of "the (literary, philosophical, and epistemological) foundations of the West" (1995: 197). These processes can "no longer be thought of simply in linguistic terms," and she adds: "Instead, cultural translation needs to be rethought as the co-temporal exchange and contention between different social groups deploying different sign systems that may not be synthesizable to one particular model of language or representation" (1995: 196–7).

The last section of Chow's book is entitled "The Light of the Arcade." Here, she turns, like Niranjana, to a presumed connection between Benjamin's Translator-Essay and the *Arcades Project* in order to relate the transparency of her literal translation with the transparency of mass culture:

> What is forgotten when critics think of translation only in terms of literary and philosophical texts, is that the arcade, especially in the work of Benjamin, is never simply a linguistic passageway; it is also a commercial passageway, a passageway with shop fronts for the display of merchandise. I would therefore emphasize this *mass culture aspect of the arcade* in order to show that the light and transparency allowed by "translation" is also the light and transparency of commodification. (1995: 199)

In the passage preceding this quotation, Chow points out that some critics, such as Derrida and Fletcher, see the arcade *only* as a "mere" passageway. That way, Chow says, "we are back once again in the classical situation in which 'translation' is a mere vehicle, disposable once it completes its task" (1995: 201). They fail to recognize the arcade itself and what it stands for, she says: the space and process of *Wörtlichkeit*. Thus she pleads for paying attention to the arcade itself, and to the process of construction and commodification that takes place in this in-between space. The arcade we are supposed to pay attention to, here, is clearly the one from the *Arcades Project*, not the one from the Translator-Essay. To her argument, however, this fits perfectly. As a nineteenth-century haven for consumers and consumer culture, this arcade's transparency stands for "the transparency of our media and consumer society" (1995: 201).

Chow and Niranjana thus both draw connections between the Translator-Essay and the *Arcades Project* by means of one simple word: the arcade. A space of possibilities opens up, in which Niranjana and Chow inscribe postcolonial potentials that go way beyond Benjamin's texts. To Niranjana, it is important to draw attention to the fact that translation practice and theory has been complicit, with the colonial enterprise, in constructing the colonial "Other" and, in the process, cementing "Western metaphysics" (1992: 91). Through the veiled nature of these processes, these constructions are not only propagated by the colonial power but internalized by the colonized in such a way that, as Niranjana illustrates, the colonized are in a position to have to ask for colonial history books to find out about their past. As a key dynamic of this process, Niranjana thus identifies the perpetuation of enlightenment historicism, by means of which the "Other" is either constructed as standing outside of history, as pre-historic and mythical, or as too far behind on this timeline, always belated. In the case of the latter, the abovementioned internalization may then conveniently be interpreted as the colonized "desire to be colonized." In order to draw attention to and eventually subvert these dynamics, Niranjana focuses on a re-theorization of translation through poststructuralism (and her critique of poststructuralism), which she develops by reference to Benjamin—as he is the only one, in her opinion, to have thought through the relationship of history and translation.

While operating from a similar starting point, Chow harshly criticizes Niranjana's re-theorized concept of translation. It does not leave the realm of interlingual, textual exchange and remains caught in a good vs. bad dichotomy: "good" translation as cultural resistance on the one hand, and "bad" translation as cultural domination on the other. Chow sums up her charges as "idealism and verbalism" (1995: 191), which keep Niranjana from looking at the issue of translating verbal language into other sign systems, and "more important, of the translation of ethnic cultures from their previous literary and philosophical bases into the forms of contemporary mass culture" (1995: 191). Ultimately, Chow argues that

> It would seem that no consideration of cultural translation can afford to ignore these questions, simply because the translation between cultures is never West translating East or East translating West in terms of verbal languages alone but rather a process that encompasses an entire range of activities including the change from tradition to modernity, from literature to visuality, from elite scholastic culture to mass culture, from the native to the foreign and back, and so forth. (1995: 192)

To me, however, it is most notable that Niranjana's and Chow's readings both elucidate significant correspondences between Benjamin's early and his late texts, in particular between his thinking about translation, and his later concerns with historiography and mass culture. For Niranjana and Chow, this conflict in translation thus opens up a space of possibilities, in which they inscribe postcolonial potentials that go way beyond Benjamin's texts. In doing so, both discursively position Benjamin as an anachronistic partner of poststructuralism, who is called upon to remedy poststructuralism's pitfalls for the sake of postcolonial theory building at the crossroads between translation, history, and mass media.

Let me close with another amalgamation of the image of the *Arkade* and the image of the *Passage*—namely my own. During my studies, I once wrote a seminar paper about the significance of the "arcade" in Gail Scott's *My Paris*

(1999b). In *My Paris*, the protagonist has Benjamin's *Arcades Project* on her night stand. As I clearly remembered the "arcade"-quote from the Translator-Essay, it was easy for me, too, to draw connections between the texts. I liberally took the *flâneur*, who strolls through nineteenth-century *Passagen*, and inscribed him into a space of translation, between languages and cultures—in order to analyze the protagonist in *My Paris* as a flâneuse, not only exploring but settling within this space between languages and cultures. Even as a German native, writing in English, it did not occur to me that *Arkade* and *Passage* were two different things; both were "arcades," and that was good enough for me.

The German literary and media theorist, Ludwig Jäger, claims that processes of understanding are translation-shaped, and that such moments of *Störung*, of non-transmissibility, constitute the conditions of possibility for understanding (2013: 4). These moments are frustrating, yet often revealing. They may offer some indication about how reception movements function as two-way streets: these moments of non-transmissibility open up new rooms-for-play, but they also defer traditional perspectives just enough to realize that the "original" is ever-changing, too. This perspective, in turn, seems to me very close to Benjamin's. Inscribed in his texts is what happens to them: Benjamin anticipates the perpetual preliminarity, incompleteness, and openness of any "original," for which the author seems to be hardly more than a midwife. Benjamin's texts contain invitations to interpretation, wrapped in various forms of imagery, and they spawn manifold, more or less productive (mis-)translations. On reading them as such, I have entered "a theater of new, unforeseen constellations. The stamp of the definitive is avoided. No situation appears intended forever, no figure asserts its 'thus and not otherwise'" (1978: 165–6). Benjamin's texts may not offer up clear answers, but they impart a way of reading and thinking in which a striving for completeness fiercely competes with the awareness of its impossibility, a way of reading and thinking that subsists on disturbance, in which conflict is constitutive and no original is ever set in stone.

6

Benjamin's Afterlife

So wie die Äußerungen des Lebens innigst mit dem Lebendigen zusammenhängen, ohne ihm etwas zu bedeuten, geht die Übersetzung aus dem Original hervor. Zwar nicht aus seinem Leben so sehr denn aus seinem "Überleben." Ist doch die Übersetzung später als das Original und bezeichnet sie doch bei den bedeutenden Werken, die da ihre erwählten Übersetzer niemals im Zeitalter ihrer Entstehung finden, das Stadium ihres Fortlebens. In völlig unmetaphorischer Sachlichkeit ist der Gedanke vom Leben und Fortleben der Kunstwerke zu erfassen.

(GS IV: 10–1)

In this chapter, I start from a linguistic image that is more difficult to pin down than that of the "arcade": I zoom in on the "afterlife." It is harder to grasp and simultaneously seems to be of greater conceptual importance to Benjamin. My objective, though, remains the same: I look in detail at the constitution and significance of the German figure of thought that the English "afterlife" is based on, and explore its reception by English-language commentators. In the end, I probe the possibilities that open up in the process and examine if and how these illuminate new subtexts in, connections among, and implications for Benjamin's German writings.

Unlike the *Arkade/Passage*-discrepancy, the choice of the word "afterlife" in the English translation of Benjamin's Translator-Essay has already been problematized. In 2011, Caroline Disler published an article entitled "Walter Benjamin's 'Afterlife': A Productive (?) Mistranslation," in which she harshly criticizes Zohn's choice of the word, "afterlife," in his translation. By means of the wording in her title, Disler calls upon Benjamin's text fragment, "What can be said in favor of translation?", in which he suggests that "the value of bad translations" is to be found in the "productive misunderstandings" they engender (SW 3: 249). Disler, however, deliberately rejects the notion of "productive misunderstandings" in this case. Instead, she *laments* the fact that this translation has been so productive, quantitatively speaking, and calls this development "downright counter-productive" (2011: 214). She does not consider it to be a "bad" translation, but a downright "mistranslation": the English-language commentators she mentions, many of whom are translation theorists themselves, have canonized, she claims, "a mistranslation that can only augment the negative and destructive image of the profession" (2011: 214). I begin with this "mistranslation."

(Fort-)Leben in Benjamin's Writings

Over the course of Harry Zohn's "The Task of the Translator," he decides for the word "afterlife" five times; for the first time, it occurs in his rendition of the paragraph that I have chosen as an epigraph for this chapter:

> Just as the manifestations of life are intimately connected with the phenomenon of life without being of importance to it, a translation issues from the original—not so much from its life as from its afterlife. For a translation comes later than the original, and since the important works of world literature never find their chosen translators at the time of their origin, their translation marks their stage of continued life. The idea of life and afterlife in works of art should be regarded with an entirely unmetaphorical objectivity. (SW 1: 254)

Attempting to back-translate his choice, the "afterlife," bilingual dictionaries would suggest *Leben nach dem Tod*, life after death; *Nachleben*, quite literally afterlife (*nach* = after, *Leben* = life); or *Jenseits*, the beyond. Going back to the German text, "Die Aufgabe des Übersetzers," one would expect to find at least one of these German alternatives. However, none of them actually turn up. Instead, Benjamin uses the term "*Fortleben*." Yet, as Disler also illustrates, bilingual dictionaries do not actually link *Fortleben* with "afterlife." She thus points out how strange it is that "a century of lexicographers has not deemed *Fortleben* and 'afterlife' to be equivalents yet, curiously, translation scholars persist in ignoring their professional colleagues' opinion in discussion of Benjamin's *Fortleben* idea" (2011: 187).

But the situation becomes all the more complex once you take a closer look at Benjamin's German texts. *Leben*-compounds, in various different forms, appear to be of crucial conceptual importance throughout his writings. Even in the Translator-Essay, Benjamin uses different *Leben*-compounds: he talks not only about *Fortleben* but also about '*Überleben*' (in single quotation marks). The word *Überleben* is most commonly used as a verb, which may be rendered as "to survive," though it also occurs in its nominal form: *Das Überleben*, survival. Benjamin, however, seems to use this word in a very peculiar sense, allowing for ambivalence. In the context of his German text, the focus is on the *life*-part, suggesting that it is a particular kind of life, namely *Über*-life, that is, an extension or expansion of life itself. The emphasis is not primarily on (the process or outcome of) survival, but on this particular kind also of more-than-life: "a translation issues from the original—not so much from its life as from its afterlife [*Überleben*]" (SW 1: 254).[1] And yet Zohn renders both, *Über*- and *Fortleben*, as "afterlife."

Indeed, he is the only translator to do so. I have pointed out before that, so far, there have only been four published English translations, plus one amended version, of "Die Aufgabe des Übersetzers": the most often read, criticized, and quoted version by a Harry Zohn (1968b); a contemporaneous one by James Hynd and E. M. Valk (1968c); "The Translator's Task" by Steven Rendall (1997); the most recent one by J. A. Underwood (2009); and the amended version of Zohn's translation that has made its way into the *Selected Writings* (1996; SW 1). Remarkably, the "afterlife," that "infelicitous word" (Disler 2011: 210), only occurs in the Zohn translation(s). In both versions, from 1968 and 1996, "afterlife" is Zohn's primary choice—for "*Überleben*," as well as for most instances of *Fortleben*. There is, however, no terminological consistency: where, in the 1968 version, three *Leben*-compounds are rendered as "afterlife," others are translated as "continued life," "survival," or simply as "life" (in the amended version from 1996, one "continued life" is replaced by another "afterlife"). In short, context is more important to Zohn than terminological consistency. In all other translations, however, it is the other way around. For *Fortleben*, Hynd and Valk (1968c) and Rendall (1997) consistently use "continuing life," while Underwood opts for "continued existence."[2] These renditions of *Fortleben* suggest that the most emphasized notion is that of continuation; only the Zohn translation, that is, the most widely received, introduces the idea of a clearly distinct before and after by using the word "afterlife," the central contemporary meaning of which refers to the caesura of death, in relation to which a before and after are measured. Disler thus argues that Zohn's translation results in a fundamental misrepresentation of Benjamin's concept of *Fortleben*, which, she says, does not at all refer to the death of the works that are translated, but to their continuation in transformation. By casting *Fortleben* into the word "afterlife," these notions are suppressed, and the English reception becomes almost entirely wound up in ideas of death and destruction: "Afterlife," she says, "Connotations of hellfire and eternal damnation. It is a rather dangerous term, in fact. A deathtrap. The metaphorics of damage and destruction, devastation and sacrifice abound in the secondary literature, yet not all [sic] in *Die Aufgabe*" (2011: 209).

Disler then traces the meaning of *Fortleben* in German. However, she states that she could not find the word in a dozen dictionaries published around the time that Benjamin wrote his essay. So, her conclusion is that *Fortleben* "was not at all in common currency at the time that Benjamin wrote the essay" (2011: 186). She wonders why Benjamin chose this unusual word over other, similar ones. If he had wanted to stress "an identical life that continues unchanged, then he could have chosen the much more common and familiar *Weiterleben*. If he had wanted to indicate 'another life after' the (life of) the original, he could have chosen the more transparent *Nachleben*. If he preferred the implication of 'survival,' he could have maintained his use of the very common *Überleben*" (2011: 189). Apart from the fact that this argument is based on the (perceived) frequency of word usage about a hundred years ago,[3] it leaves no room for the ambivalent simultaneous presence of *all* these references. This is precisely what I intend to look at, namely, the relations and ambivalences between the different *Leben*-compounds in Benjamin's writings. I examine the gradations and overlaps of meaning between *Über-*, *Fort-* and *Nachleben*, in order to arrive at a clearer picture of how Benjamin uses and conceptualizes *Fortleben*—in relation with these other terms.

In doing so, I begin with the prefix, *Fort-*. It denotes a distancing movement in space, as well as an ongoing forward movement in time. If this ambivalent, contradictory understanding of *Fort-* is attached to *Leben*, a spatio-temporally polysemous net of meanings opens up—between forward in life and separation in death, between the forward of and the forward from life. This net of meanings does, indeed, seem to get tied up into a single thread, once it is cast into one English word, "afterlife." Intriguingly, it is this intrinsically ambivalent *Leben*-compound, *Fortleben*, which is by far the most frequently used in Benjamin's writings.[4] It turns up in multiple texts and fragments, first in 1919, and last in a note on his *Passagenarbeit* in the late 1930s. In the following, I comment on a number of particularly illuminating contexts. The first fragment exists in two versions: in a letter written in 1919 and in a slightly augmented note from the same year, which seems to have been copied from the letter. In this fragment, Benjamin discusses the critical value of exchanges of letters. They are underestimated, he says, as their relation to the artists' works, and to the person of the artist, is often misjudged. He is of the opinion that letters are akin to testimony or evidence, to *Zeugnis*, as he calls it in German, thus its reference to the author is as "meaningless as the way in which any pragmatic-historical testimonial (inscription) refers to the person of its originator."[5] As testimony, correspondence instead belongs to the "history of a person's *Fortleben*, and what may be studied in the exchange of letters is precisely the way in which this *Fortleben* reaches into *Leben* with its own history."[6] As individual letters turn into correspondence, they change their constitution: they condense and intensify in correspondence, where one letter immediately follows the next, written by a different author. Thus in correspondence, the letters "live in a different rhythm than at the time when the recipients lived, and in other ways as well, they change."[7] Correspondence requires at least two "participants," but the interesting part is not the aspect of communication or information exchange between the two (of course, one would say, with regard to Benjamin's philosophy of language): instead, there is something else, something "new" that develops in correspondence, independently from the letter-writers and their intentions. As Gert Mattenklott indicates, the idea of testimony or evidence, referred to by the German term *Zeugnis*, holds the verb *zeugen*, that is, begetting or procreating, and thus alerts to a productive force that lies in correspondence (2011: 685). The function of individual letters—of providing historical, psychological, social, or cultural information regarding the person of the author—is thus removed by the frame of correspondence, its significance no longer being limited to a source of cultural history. Still, the situational sociocultural circumstances must be untangled and commented on by the editors of published correspondence, not to shift the focus toward the private, but, on the contrary, to neutralize it by objectifying it, so that the function of the correspondence as testimony may take a more distinct shape (Mattenklott 2011: 685). As testimony, correspondence belongs to a person's *Fortleben*, but it also reveals the way in which this *Fortleben* permeates a person's life with its own history. Thus, what stands out in this context is the idea of the exchange of letters, as opposed to the individual ones, as a form that proceeds from the *Fortleben* of letters; as such, it carries a transformative quality and permeates a person's life ex post facto. This idea of permeation is where correspondence differs significantly from literary and artworks, says Benjamin: it may not be studied in the latter, because they function like a *Wasserscheide*, a watershed, and thus do not allow for that kind of permeation.

Only two years after the note on correspondence, in 1921, Benjamin picks up this very image in his famous Translator-Essay, where he states that, in the holy text, meaning ceases to be the watershed between the flow of language and the flow of revelation. What is more, the Translator-Essay also contains extensive deliberations on *Fortleben*, beginning with Benjamin's discussion of translatability as an intrinsic quality of texts. Translatability, he says, guides the *Zusammenhang*, the connection or correlation of a text and its translation. This correlation is "a natural one, or, more specifically, vital one" (SW 1: 254).⁸ In the same way in which *Lebendiges*, that which lives, proceeds from life, a translation proceeds from the original, he says. But it would not be precise enough to say that translation proceeds from the original's life, translation proceeds from its "*Überleben.*" Benjamin thus introduces the argument that leads into the conceptualization of *Fortleben* by means of the term "*Überleben.*" In doing so, he insinuates not only what I have outlined earlier, that is, an extension or expansion of *Leben*, but also a particular quality of translation, namely that of coming later than. From that, he develops the idea that significant works cannot find their designated translators at their own time. If translation is to correspond to its form, translators must express a new, a different, a later rhythm than that of the "original" and its time. Because, like correspondence, translation also marks a later stage within the life of works, namely—and this is where the term *Fortleben* is introduced in the German version—"their stage of continued life" (SW 1: 254),⁹ as Harry Zohn puts it here.

Benjamin also stresses that his understanding of life, in general, is characterized by an "entirely unmetaphorical objectivity" (SW 1: 254):¹⁰ he incorporates artistic works into his overall understanding of life, without simply extending metaphorically onto cultural objects a biologistic conception. Instead, he shifts the perspective from which the concept of life is to be thought:

> nur wenn allem demjenigen, wovon es Geschichte gibt und was nicht allein ihr Schauplatz ist, Leben zuerkannt wird, kommt dessen Begriff zu seinem Recht. (GS IV: 11)
>
> it is only when life is attributed to everything that has a history, and not to that which is only a stage setting for history, that this concept comes into its own. (1997: 153)

From this, Benjamin deduces the task of the philosopher, namely to "understand all natural life on the basis of the more comprehensive life of history" (1997: 154).¹¹ Life, of which there is history, is much easier to trace and analyze when it comes to literary works than to *Geschöpfe*, creatures, he says. Because, with regard to works, life may be traced in three stages: Benjamin mentions their "descent from their sources," their "shaping in the age of the artist," and the stage of their "basically eternal continuing life in later generations" (1997: 154).¹² Translations that remain true to their form proceed from this last stage, from their *Fortleben*; and in it, the life of the text reaches its "constantly renewed, latest and most comprehensive unfolding" (1997: 154).¹³

Like in the fragment from 1919, Benjamin thus addresses a transformative quality of *Fortleben*. He outlines his idea of a kinship between languages, and of translation as the capacity to express this kinship in a unique and special way, namely by realizing it anticipatively, "intensively." In this respect, translation differs significantly from other modes of performance or expression, and it differs from other types of indicating or pointing toward something, such as analogy or signs. Structurally, this intensive mode of realization cannot be based on similarity, and in order to grasp why, one has to follow the same goal as "critical epistemology in demonstrating the impossibility of a reflection theory" (1997: 155),[14] Benjamin says. The process of cognition does not simply produce mirror images of an outside reality; the task of recognizing and knowing does not lie with a recognizing subject that internally mirrors outside objects. In very much the same way, operating along the lines of similarity or sameness does not correspond to the process of translation; instead, translation intensively realizes a relation between languages. This is where *Fortleben* becomes crucial, because with this concept, Benjamin attempts to grasp a transformative quality that counteracts any striving for similarity:

> in seinem Fortleben, das so nicht heißen dürfte, wenn es nicht Wandlung und Erneuerung des Lebendigen wäre, ändert sich das Original. (GS IV: 13)
>
> in its afterlife [*Fortleben*]—which could not be called that if it were not a transformation and a renewal of something living—the original undergoes a change. (SW 1: 256; my annotation)

Benjamin then substantiates a point that he has made before, namely that *Fortleben* finds expression in various different forms. Besides translation, he mentions criticism, as he discusses the insights of the German Romantics. They had, he claims, a greater awareness of the lives of works than others, yet they focused their entire attention on criticism, which constitutes "another, if less important, moment in the continuing life of a work of art" (1968c: 302).[15] In his later writings, around the beginning of the 1930s, Benjamin returns to thinking about this kinship between translation and criticism. At that time, he was planning to write a book about this topic, and to edit a magazine entitled *Krisis und Kritik*, together with Bertolt Brecht. Both projects failed to see the light of day, but there are notes and fragments that provide at least some insight into what the book project was supposed to look like—and the concept of *Fortleben* was to take a crucial part in it.

Before I discuss the way in which Benjamin conceptualizes *Fortleben* in its relation with criticism, however, I go on a brief excursion to look into something that happened in the meanwhile, namely, Benjamin's second dissertation, *The Origin of German Tragic Drama*. It was written only a couple years after the Translator-Essay, between 1923 and 1925. In this book, *Fortleben* also takes on an important role, particularly as Benjamin outlines his concept of allegory. To very briefly, and roughly, summarize, Benjamin brings together allegory and *Trauerspiel* in a twofold way: for one, the German tragic drama is in itself allegorically structured; at the same time, it is an allegorical reading of Greek tragedy (Menke 2011: 215). This discussion hinges on fundamental questions regarding theology and secularization, which is also where *Fortleben* becomes conceptually important. Benjamin claims that *Allegorese*, allegorical interpretation (here: in the context of Judeo-Christian interpretations of ancient religious subject matters) would never have "succeeded," if the church had managed to fully banish the pagan gods from the minds of faithful people. *Allegorese*, he says, does not testify to some triumphant victory but, rather, to the actual preservation and binding of a pre-Christian life. Allegory is thus much

> mehr ... als die wie immer abstrakte Verflüchtigung theologischer Wesenheiten, nämlich deren Fortleben in einer ihnen ungemäßen, ja feindlichen Umwelt. (GS I: 39)

> more than the "vaporization"—however abstract—of theological essences, their survival [*Fortleben*] in an unsuitable, indeed hostile, environment. (1977: 223; my annotation)

Benjamin emphasizes the preservative quality of *Allegorese*, as he states that "the world of the ancient gods would have had to die out, and it is precisely allegory which preserved it" (1977: 223).[16] There is an intriguing double-structure in this movement. For one, allegory interjects a sense of distance between the "now" and the "source," that is, the world of the Greek gods, in an attempt to replace and get rid of it; yet it is due to this process that the "source" is preserved, kept alive.

He concludes that, as the Greek gods reach into worlds foreign to them, they find expression not only in relics but also in words and names:

> in dem Grade wie die Lebenszusammenhänge verloren gehen, aus denen sie stammen, [werden sie] zu Ursprüngen von Begriffen, in denen diese Worte einen neuen, zur allegorischen Darstellung prädisponierten Inhalt gewinnen, wie die Fortuna, Venus (als Frau Welt) und andere dergleichen es sind. (GS I: 399)

> as the living contexts of their birth disappear, so they become the origins of concepts, in which these words acquire a new content, which is predisposed to

allegorical representation; such is the case with Fortuna, Venus (as Dame World) and so on. (1977: 226)

It is the deadness of these figures, the loss of their life-contexts, that is a necessary precondition for "metamorphosis of the Pantheon into a world of magical terminological creatures" (1977: 226).[17] On this deadness, Benjamin says, rests the *Fortleben* of such creatures as the siren or harpy as allegorical figures in Christian hell. This adds another facet: the *Fortleben* of persistent ideas and concepts in allegorical figures is enabled by their prior mortification; based on stillness and distance, *Fortleben* allows for dynamism and persistence. Thus, allegory may be added to the array of different forms and modes that bear a structural correspondence with *Fortleben*, beyond the exchange of letters, translations, and criticism.

With this in mind, I return to Benjamin's writing about literary criticism. In the book he planned on writing at the beginning of the 1930s, Benjamin wanted to include an essay entitled "The Task of the Critic" as well as a reprint of his essay on "The Task of the Translator," which already indicates the close relation between translation and criticism. And even though the book was never written, there are nine fragments about the planned essay on "The Task of the Critic" that have survived, and they collectively reveal the greatest concentration of references to *Fortleben* outside of the Translator-Essay. From these notes and fragments, it emerges that Benjamin intended to dedicate the third part of his essay to a "theory of the survival [*Fortleben*] of works" (SW 2: 416; my annotation).[18] In this section, he planned to develop the thought that "this survival [*Fortleben*] unmasks the terrain of 'art' as semblance" (SW 2: 416; my annotation).[19] Art, he says, is only a *Durchgangsstadium*, "a transitional stage" (SW 2: 547) of great works.

Thus criticism can, like translation, give shape to artworks' *Fortleben*. But just as only certain translations are able to do so, namely, those that are "more than communications" (2009: 31),[20] only a certain kind of criticism is able to manifest a work's *Fortleben*, which is to say, that in which the critic ideally "forgets to pass judgement" (SW 2: 547).[21] In order to arrive at this kind of criticism, Benjamin outlines two distinct critical perspectives: a subjective one, which he locates in a practice of reading as physiognomy, and a second, an "objective truth" that is "the antithesis to this subjective view" (SW 2: 372).[22] These turn into two very different kinds of critical procedure: the subjective one develops into a polemic-strategic approach, and the objective one into an immanent exegetical commenting kind of criticism (Kaulen 1990: 321–2). With regard to the practice of literary history, the strategic-polemic kind of criticism mainly addresses historical contexts, histories of theory, and relationships between different schools of thought; the exegetical commenting kind, however, proceeds from the work itself, and from its material truth moreover, in an exegetical manner. Only where these two conflicting critical postures are amalgamated, should the region of criticism that Benjamin aims at open up; these two postures "merge in a criticism whose only medium is the life, the ongoing life of the works themselves" (SW 2: 372).[23]

In this region of criticism that Benjamin considers the highest, the study of concrete and singular details converges with an insight into historical contents and relations (Kaulen 1990: 325). Thus, in another fragment, Benjamin refers to this highest kind of criticism as the "Fundamental Discipline of Literary History" (SW 2: 415),[24] and toward the end of a review written in 1931, entitled "Literary History and the Study of Literature," he concludes with regard to this historically oriented task of the critic:

> Deren gesamter Lebens- und Wirkungskreis [literarischer Werke, B.H.] hat gleichberechtigt, ja vorwiegend neben ihre Entstehungsgeschichte zu treten; ihr Schicksal, ihre Aufnahme durch die Zeitgenossen, ihre Übersetzungen, ihr Ruhm. Damit gestaltet sich das Werk im Inneren zu einem Mikrokosmos oder viel mehr: zu einem Mikroaeon. Denn es handelt sich ja nicht darum, die Werke des Schrifttums im Zusammen-hang ihrer Zeit darzustellen, sondern in der Zeit, da sie entstanden, die Zeit, die sie erkennt—das ist die unsere—zur Darstellung zu bringen. Damit wird die Literatur ein Organon der Geschichte und sie dazu—nicht das Schrifttum zum Stoffgebiet der Historie zu machen, ist die Aufgabe der Literaturgeschichte. (GS III: 290)
>
> Their [literary works, B.H.] entire life and their effects should have the right to stand alongside the history of their composition. In other words, their fate, their reception by their contemporaries, their translations, their fame. For with this the work is transformed inwardly into a microcosm, or indeed a microeon. What is at stake is not to portray literary works in the context of their age, but to represent the age that perceives them—our age—in the age during which they arose. It is this that makes literature into an organon of history; and to achieve this, and not to reduce literature to the material of history, is the task of the literary historian. (SW 2: 464)

Benjamin's book about literary criticism never saw the light of day. Instead, he turns toward his own practice of precisely those forms that may best manifest his theory of *Fortleben*: he translates, practices literary criticism, and publishes collections of letters, such as *Deutsche Menschen* (1931–2, 1936) and *German Men and Women*. In a draft for what may have been planned as a lecture or a radio piece, entitled "On the Trail of Old Letters," Benjamin argues—in line with his fragment on correspondence from 1919—that the editor's task begins after having discovered the letters, namely, the work of "making them comprehensible in their proper context from every angle" (SW 2: 555).[25]

In this context, a second text is worth taking note of, namely, the essay Benjamin wrote in 1931 about "Christoph Martin Wieland." In this essay, Benjamin attempts to pay equal attention to the author's reception afforded to him by contemporaries, the translation of his works, and his fame—to the exclusion, in large part, of the works themselves (with which Benjamin was arguably not that familiar). Thus, he comments on Wieland's biography, his contemporary reception, the later editorial history of his work, and Wieland's largely non-existent fame. The latter is Benjamin's starting point: "Wieland is no longer being read."[26] Yet his texts had been received favorably by his contemporaries, and particularly so in Goethe's writings. Benjamin concludes that Wieland had something to give at the time, which was absorbed by contemporaries, and, afterwards, his writing lost its fervor. At the end of the essay, Benjamin gets to the heart of the reason why. Goethe, says Benjamin, formulated a *dämonische Allegorie*, a demonic allegory upon Wieland's death: when looking at the fence lining around Wieland's grave, he sees the horseshoes under the hoofs of a future cavalry that will trample over it, thus predicting that Wieland's *Fortleben* will lack manifestation and thus fame. In the last sentences, Benjamin concludes:

> Es gibt Autoren, für deren Fortleben die Möglichkeit, wieder gelesen zu werden, nicht mehr als ein Standbild zu sagen hat. Ihre Fermente sind für immer in den Mutterboden, in ihre Muttersprache eingegangen. Ein solcher Autor ist Christoph Martin Wieland gewesen. (GS II: 405–6)

> For some authors' *Fortleben*, the possibility of being reread has nothing more to say than a statue. Their ferments have forever sunk into the mother soil, into their mother tongue. Christoph Martin Wieland was such an author. (My translation.)

All he had to give had been absorbed; renewed readings add little to Wieland's *Fortleben*, because there is nothing left to work with, to transform. New translations, comments, critique would instead result in statuesque immobilization and canonization, from which there is no *Gehalt*, no more substance to be extracted.

After these last brief glimpses at different forms of *Fortleben*, Benjamin seems to have left behind this figure of thought that had been so crucial to him before. The term gradually loses its outward conceptual importance; at least from 1933 onwards, Benjamin seems only to use it when taking notes. In 1935, for instance, there is an inconspicuous remark that holds a simple instruction for future Benjamin, namely, to take a closer look at Fourier's *Fortleben* in the works of Zola (GS V: 1212). This note, though, recalls a similar one from a year before, 1934, in which Benjamin states that he wants to think about Fourier's *Nachleben* in the works of Zola (GS V: 1222). *Nach-Leben*, literally "afterlife"— that infelicitous word. In this context, Benjamin uses the terms *Fortleben* and *Nachleben* interchangeably. Indeed, this marks a slight terminological shift overall: especially in his later writings, Benjamin uses the term *Nachleben* more frequently than *Fortleben*, particularly when he writes about history and historiography from a decidedly materialist perspective.

Already in 1926, in the *Moscow Diary*, Benjamin points out that the lives of artists, "abstracted from [their] posteriority [*Nachleben*]" (1986: 39),[27] cannot be the object of materialist analysis; only their material *Nachleben* can be. A couple years later, in a fragment from 1927 or 1928, Benjamin refers back to these notes, writing "Against a theory of the 'unrecognized genius.'"[28] This theory of the unrecognized genius, he says, is a modern concept that provides excuses, functioning according to a *Rentnergesinnung*, a pensioner's attitude: "misunderstood geniuses" can rest comfortably within the framework that this concept provides for their lives, because they pay silently into a piggy bank that will, with reasonable certainty, be distributed upon their demise. But this is deceptive, says Benjamin. There is an intrinsic recognizability in certain great works, which finds expression in their effect on others: "A genius may have lived and died unnoticed," Benjamin says, but "seldom is he going to have been misunderstood by his equals among the contemporaries."[29] Consequently, Benjamin confronts the concept of the unrecognized genius with his own theory of fame. Referring to the *Moscow Diary*, he states that a new Russian mentality counters the bourgeois mystery of the unrecognized genius with its own articulation of the "mystery of success," which proclaims as its prime axiom that "a work is not famous because it is great—it is great because it is famous."[30] For the rest of this brief text, Benjamin explores what this position entails:

> Gesetzt, dem sei so, haben die großen Werke innerlich, funktionell den lebendigsten Zusammenhang, den lebendigsten Anteil an den Veränderungen des Kollektivs, sie wandeln sich realiter mit ihm, denn sie leben in ihm. Man kann im entschiedensten Sinne von ihrem Nachleben sprechen. (GS VI: 136-7)
>
> If this is the case, great works have—intrinsically, functionally—the most vivid connection with, the most vivid share in the changes of the collective.

In reality, they transform themselves together with it, because they live in it. In the most definitive sense, this may be referred to as their *Nachleben*. (My translation.)

Thus Benjamin identifies a correlation not only between the lives of a text and its translation but also between a work and the collective. Great works live, or survive, in the collective; they change it and in the process are transformed themselves. This reciprocal transformation, of the work and the collective, takes shape as *Nachleben*, and "[w]here it appears, the latter is called fame" ("The Task of the Translator," 1997: 154).[31] Only where the *Nachleben* of a work manifests in such a way that it transforms both itself and the collective—only where the work is in this sense famous—may it be considered "great."

The early idea of *Fortleben* thus crystallizes in Benjamin's later writings around the term "*Nachleben*." In convolute N of the *Arcades Project*, for instance, where Benjamin collects his thoughts on theories of knowledge and progress, his idea of *Fortleben* is distilled into the context of historical materialism—and it returns as *Nachleben*:

> "Geschichtliches Verstehen" ist grundsätzlich als ein Nachleben des Verstandnen zu fassen und daher ist dasjenige was in der Analyse des "Nachlebens der Werke, " des "Ruhmes" erkannt wurde, als die Grundlage der Geschichte überhaupt zu betrachten. (GS V: 574–5)
>
> Historical "understanding" is to be grasped, in principle, as an afterlife of that which is understood; and what has been recognized in the analysis of the "afterlife of works," in the analysis of "fame," is therefore to be considered as the foundation of history in general. (1999a: 460)

Just like translation, as the historical existence of language (Hamacher 2001: 186–7), is inherent in works as their intrinsic translatability, a fundamental "understandability" is inherent in what is to be understood, and this "understandability" accounts for its *Nachleben* as historical knowledge. Historical understanding does not emanate from a knowing subject that attempts a retroactive approximation of past events. It emanates from the *Nachleben* of what is understood, and thus from its call for understanding.

Over the course of his writings, Benjamin develops a figure of thought that he captures in different terms: *Über-*, *Fort-*, and *Nachleben*. Daniel Weidner describes this as an illustrative example of the way in which Benjamin, in his thinking and writing, goes beyond straightforward conceptions of metaphors, terms, and concepts:

Solche Denkfiguren sind nicht so feste Verbindungen wie Begriffe, Konzepte oder Ideen, sondern haben etwas Vorläufiges und Vorsichtiges—aber gerade darin ist es ihnen möglich, Grenzen zu überschreiten und sie in dieser Überschreitung auch aufzuzeigen. (2011: 178)

Such figures of thought are not fixed compounds like terms, concepts, or ideas. Instead, they carry an air of the provisional and precautious—which is exactly what makes it possible for them to transgress boundaries, and simultaneously to reveal them in this transgression. (My translation.)

Intriguingly, this *Über-/Fort-/Nachleben* does not only denote a central figure of Benjamin's thought, it actually realizes itself in its own development. Within and between texts, there is a constant process of absorption, adaptation, permeation—without replacement or overcoming—that leads from Benjamin's metaphysical thoughts about language into a historical materialist perspective on history. In the end, the reconfigurations, transformations, and translations of this figure of thought into Benjamin's English-language reception may be read in a very similar light. And in many of these reconfigurations, the hegemony of the "afterlife," which Disler has hinted at, is infiltrated.

Fort: From Benjamin to Bhabha

In tracing Benjamin's *Fortleben* into contemporary English-language discourses around cultural translation, two names are of vital importance: Homi Bhabha and Jacques Derrida. In *The Location of Culture* (1994), a widely discussed, and widely criticized, benchmark when it comes to cultural translation, Bhabha works with Benjamin's concept of *Fortleben*, but in doing so, he crucially refers to Derrida. Thus, I begin with "Des Tours de Babel" (1985a), Derrida's poststructuralist reading, deconstruction or translation, as he would say, of Benjamin's Translator-Essay.

For one, this essay is permeated by translation, and the layers of language, text, and translation are so complexly interwoven that the dichotomy of "original" and translation is challenged from the outset. The essay, which was published in English and French in the same publication, is not only *about* translation, but also tries to make translation tangible within its texture. This becomes expressly notable in the readers' stumbling over the linguistic logic of foreignness, especially in the English text. When Derrida talks about the French translation of Benjamin's text by Maurice Gandillac, readers have the English version of

Benjamin's text in front of them—which Joseph Graham has translated from Gandillac's French version. Readers do not read the German Benjamin or the French one; and it is not even the English Benjamin that we are used to, either: it is not Zohn's Benjamin, but it is Graham's, via Gandillac's—via an interpretation of Benjamin (and Gandillac), by Derrida.

What is more, multiple languages are visible in the text. For instance, when it comes to Derrida's engagement with Benjamin's concept of *Fortleben*, it is notable that he retains the crucial German words, that is, *Fortleben* and *Überleben*. He quotes the passage that I have used as the epigraph for this chapter, but in Graham's (via Gandillac's) translation:

> Just as the manifestations of life are intimately connected with the living, without signifying anything for it, a translation proceeds from the original. Indeed not so much from its life as from its survival [*Überleben*]. For a translation comes after the original and, for the important works that never find their predestined translator at the time of their birth, it characterizes the stage of their survival [*Fortleben*, this time, survival as continuation of life rather than as life post mortem]. Now, it is in this simple reality, without any metaphor ["in völlig unmetaphorischer Sachlichkeit"], that it is necessary to conceive the ideas of life and survival [*Fortleben*] for works of art. (1985a: 178; emphasis in the original)

In his reading of this passage, Derrida addresses Benjamin's proclamation of "unmetaphorical objectivity." He expands on the way in which many of Benjamin's terms and metaphors—such as, for instance, *Fortleben*—may appear biologistic, but they hold within themselves their own reversal. Not from the perspective of biological life are we supposed to look at the life of works, but at our own biologistic notion of life from the perspective of the historical life of works. Derrida takes up on this "challenge from within" and molds it into his own concept of *survivre*, in order to question life and death as biological oppositions, and to re-think the relation between finite and infinite life, that is, empirical life-spans and transcendental time, as well as our relation with both (Hodge 2007: 27–8). "There is life at the moment when 'sur-vival' (spirit, history, works) exceeds biological life and death" (2002: 114), Derrida argues in "The Eyes of Language," and immediately goes on to quote the part from Benjamin's Translator-Essay, in which he defines the task of the philosopher as that of comprehending natural by means of historical life.

It is also worth noting that, in the preceding passage, Derrida—via Graham—draws a clear distinction between *Über-* and *Fortleben*. For one, there is a hyphen (sur-vival, survival), as well as an explanatory note in brackets, which, when it comes to *Fortleben,* stresses a sense of continuation and states that there is no death, no post mortem. In the translator's notes, Graham comments on his word choices in this case, explaining that the French *survie*, which Derrida uses throughout the text, may be rendered as "survival," *as well as* "afterlife." Yet he relinquishes the latter term without telling us why. The hyphen, he admits, is a cheat he used in order to convey Derrida's idea of more-life, or more-than-life (1985a: 206). Thus Derrida, via Graham, does clearly highlight the ambivalence of the concept, yet he gathers these different notions, connotations, and layers of meaning and context into a single French word, which he uses throughout: *survivre*.

This loaded word is also the title of an extensive essay that was published years before "Des Tours de Babel," an earlier text that is also permeated by translation. This one was written with a view to its own translation: although Derrida wrote it in French, it was first published in English; the French version did not come out until seven years later. Intriguingly, the English translator, James Hulbert, chose yet another alternative, apart from "survival" or "afterlife," to translate the title of the French essay, *Survivre*: he settled on "Living on,"[32] with the full English title spelling out "Living on/Borderlines." Fittingly, it is also a two-part essay: one part is written above a line, and the other below, typeset like an ongoing footnote. The upper text is demonstratively polysemous, marked by "semantic accumulation and overloading" (1979: 91). The lower text, by contrast, is written in a telegraphic style. The upper one is supposed to be untranslatable, the lower one is supposed to guarantee utmost translatability. "Such will be the proposed contract" (1979: 89) for the translator, says Derrida—knowing full well, of course, that both texts are going to be translated into English.[33]

Thus, Derrida draws a line, a borderline of translatability, which is demonstrated and deconstructed at the same time. Both, translatability and untranslatabiliy are suspended: translatability, because even when it comes to the supposedly fully translatable part, the translator cannot do without explanatory brackets and French parentheses; untranslatability, of course, because both texts are demonstrably translated, even the supposedly untranslatable one. "Living on/Borderlines": the borderline becomes inhabitable and opens up a space in which notions of familiarity and foreignness of language(s), as well as the borderlines between them, are challenged, as is their un/translatability:

> Totally translatable, it disappears as a text, as writing, as a body of language [langue]. Totally untranslatable, even in what is believed to be one language, it dies immediately. Thus triumphant translation is neither the life or the death of

the text, only or already its living on, its life after life, its life after death. (1979: 102–3)

And with that, I move on to Bhabha's *The Location of Culture*. Already in the introduction, it becomes clear that Bhabha's writing is permeated by Derrida's thinking and terminology. This indebtedness reveals itself, for instance, in an undeclared, but distinct reference to the text "Living on/Borderlines." Even the line break finds itself in the right spot, as Bhabha explains in the first paragraph of his book that "our / existence today is marked by a tenebrous sense of survival, living on / the borderlines of the 'present,' for which there seems to be no proper name other than the current and controversial shiftiness of the prefix 'post': postmodernism, postcolonialism, postfeminism" (1994: 1). It seems as if Bhabha takes all of the ambiguity that Derrida has put into his *survivre*, and turns it into his own border condition of the present as *survival*, which he tries to grasp by means of another prefix, namely the omnipresent, but oh-so shifty *post-*. Like Benjamin's figure of *Fortleben*, the *post-* never simply denotes an "after," it never signifies overcoming. With this *post-*, that is, the present as a condition of "survival, living on the borderlines," the border opens up into an inhabitable space, in which any directional movement is disturbed, as it turns into an "exploratory, restless movement caught so well in the French rendition of the words *au-delà*—here and there, on all sides, fort/da . . ." (1994: 1). This, to me, is characteristic of the way in which Bhabha engages with his sources. He adopts elaborate arguments, distilled into strong and memorable images, and uses them in his own writing. More than that, he incorporates these loaded images into his terminological repertoire, using them over and over again, throughout his texts, without re-quoting them. In consciously tracing the provenance of such phrases, a plethora of arguments, and intertextual presences, becomes visible.

The abovementioned phrase "survival, living on borderlines" seems to become part of Bhabha's terminological repertoire; it recurs repeatedly throughout *The Location of Culture*. In the abovementioned context, the phrase denotes one of many spatio-temporal in-between figures that Bhabha operationalizes in his challenge to the concept of culture as a homogenous entity. He calls upon Derrida's notion of an inhabitable borderline in order to insinuate and, simultaneously, re-think and re-configure a dialectic of opening and closure: in order to transgress borders, they first have to be drawn; and in every act of crossing them, they are revealed and acknowledged. With the help of Derrida, Bhabha challenges this image of the border by means of another one, namely that of an inhabitable border-*space* that does not open up between separate entities labeled "cultures," but within the very heart of culture itself. In doing so, Bhabha contrasts the notion of a multicultural co-existence of homogenous entities—as in cultural diversity politics—with the idea of culture as transformational processuality that grows from cultural difference. Culture, thus, is "a signifying or symbolic activity" (Rutherford and Bhabha 1990: 210) that passes through a third space, in which the relations between system and articulation are created and re-created, always anew, always ambivalent, always contradictory. And these relations are realized in cultural translation.

Bhabha illustrates and expands upon this idea in Chapter 11 of *The Location of Culture*, or, more precisely, in the section on "Foreign relations," where we find his reading of *The Satanic Verses*. Here, Bhabha takes the condition of migration as a starting point, which he also thinks of—like the present of the post-—as a translational as well as a transitional condition, in which the struggle for "the 'survival' of migrant life" (1994: 224) takes place between nativism and assimilation. This is the context in which Bhabha explicitly refers to Benjamin's *Fortleben*. In doing so, he indirectly quotes from the standard translation, but Benjamin does not seem to be of prime importance to Bhabha, as he moves right on to Derrida's *survivre*.

> If hybridity is heresy, then to blaspheme is to dream. To dream not of the past of the present, nor the continuous present; it is not the nostalgic dream of tradition, nor the Utopian dream of modern progress; it is the dream of translation as "survival" as Derrida translates the "time" of Benjamin's concept of the afterlife of translation, as *sur-vivre*, the act of living on borderlines. (1994: 226–7)

This incredibly dense passage illustrates, on the one hand, what I have outlined earlier with regard to Bhabha's approach toward his sources; this is the one reference that reveals his references, which then solidifies and turns into the recurring, yet undesignated phrase, "survival, living on the borderlines." With regard to his own line of argumentation, Bhabha makes use of this image borrowed from Derrida in order to grasp the temporality and performativity, as well as the emancipatory potential of cultural translation. In doing so, he also draws on Derrida's iterability: right after the abovementioned quotation, Bhabha continues that "Rushdie translates this [concept of the afterlife of translation, B.H.] into the migrant's dream of survival: . . . an emergence that turns 'return' into reinscription or re-description; an iteration that is not belated, but ironic and insurgent" (1994: 227).

Cultural traditions, symbols, and meanings turn into reformulations that survive what had been there before, which still lives on within but is not, for that matter, overcome. Yet the impossibility of determining meanings once and for all goes hand in hand with the attempt, still, to stabilize them by means of perpetual, iterative repetition—which only perpetuates the production of cultural difference, because even in "repetition," meanings are re-created in new performances, contexts, temporalities, and so on; they change in an eternal, transformative *Fortleben* of meaning. Cultural translation realizes and performs the reluctant relations between difference and "repetition." In this sense, it is potentially subversive, because in the translational (re-)creation of meaning, un/translatability is performed, tradition is disjointed, and hegemonic symbols are unsettled by their ambivalent enunciation. This is what Bhabha's blasphemy refers to, namely the transgressive act of cultural translation which unsettles, alienates, and de-familiarizes cultural traditions: "Rushdie performs the subversion of [the Koran's, B.H.] authenticity through the act of cultural translation—he relocates the Koran's 'intentionality' by repeating and reinscribing it in the locale of the novel of postwar cultural migrations and diasporas" (1994: 226).

Derrida, in his reading of Benjamin's *Fortleben*—which crystallizes during the 1970s and 1980s around the terms *survivre* and "Living on"—does not only challenge the strict binary of life and death but also develops a particular spatio-temporality of the inhabitable borderline. Bhabha, in turn, subsumes all of the term's ambiguity into his own argumentative context, by means of the dense, recurring phrase, "survival, living on the borderlines." This condensed phrase turns up in different texts, where it no longer reveals its genealogy; yet every time Bhabha uses it, he actually builds into his own argument not only the positions of both authors but an entangled web of reception between postcolonialism, poststructuralism—and Benjamin. This is crucial, as Homi Bhabha is often thought to be singularly responsible for the popularization of cultural translation, and his sources are then traced as a genealogical line, a conceptual history of cultural translation: as I have outlined before, this line is often drawn back from Bhabha through the poststructuralists and Benjamin to German Romantic traditions and theories.[34] This genealogy has become so popular that recent studies attempt to stand out by precisely resisting it. In one of the most encompassing studies to date, entitled *What Is Cultural Translation?*, Sarah Maitland tries to detach both from this and the second most prominent genealogical line: her declared objective is "to provide the first definition of cultural translation not limited to Asad and Bhabha" (2017: 18). In the following section of this chapter, I look in more detail at the way in which Maitland means to do so.

What Is Cultural Translation?

In the introduction, I briefly outline how Asad's article on "The Concept of Cultural Translation in British Social Anthropology" has become a second benchmark in the field of cultural translation, firmly anchoring the concept to the field of cultural anthropology. In the sense of a "translation of culture," the concept is principally understood, here, to describe the entire task of ethnography. Yet in his critical article, or rather, in the entire publication—the text appeared in the seminal book *Writing Culture: The Poetics and Politics of Ethnography* (1986)—difficult questions are raised not only regarding the role of ethnographers as authors and translators but also regarding the underlying idea of cultures as objects. The authors of this publication, too, would argue that cultures cannot be thought of as closed-off, segmentizable systems. Due to these and similar objections, not only the idea of cultures as (translatable) entities is harshly criticized but consequently also the idea of cultural translation as a "translation of culture."

In her 2017 book *What Is Cultural Translation?*, Sarah Maitland calls upon the two names, namely, Asad and Bhabha, in order to invoke these two familiar genealogies of cultural translation—and to distinguish her own from them. Intriguingly, in trying to do so, Maitland recruits the one reference *everybody* seems to rely on, namely, Walter Benjamin. More precisely, her theorization is founded, as she argues herself, "in Ricoeur's hermeneutic philosophy and [looks] to Benjamin's complementary notions of survival, afterlife and 'fame'" (2017: 29). Thus, from the very beginning, Benjamin is positioned close to hermeneutic philosophy, and considered—together with Ricoeur—as a theoretical reference that will delimit Maitland's from other understandings of cultural translation. Against this backdrop, it is particularly interesting to observe how Benjamin, here, is incorporated seamlessly into an entirely different philosophical tradition.

According to Maitland, "we exist insofar as we interpret" (2017: 7). We attempt to understand the world around us, and in doing so, we turn toward cultural artifacts, events, actions, and people—which are all thought of as texts, narratives, and stories, and our attempt to understand them is seen as a process of reading and interpreting. This process of stepping outside, of reaching out, always leads back to ourselves, as it is only because of this detour through our interpretation-shaped interaction with the world that we are able to construct and narrate ourselves. Consequentially, concepts like "identity" are configured as story-like. Yet it is important to Maitland to point out that these "stories" are not fixed or finite, but they are continually being written. And, crucially, they include everything "we say and do" (2017: 6), that is, gestures, performances, and actions. They are texts to be expanded by engaging with others in attempts at understanding, and, in turn, they make themselves available to be read by others. What announces itself with this broad understanding of "text" is at least a family resemblance with cultural anthropology's semiotic concept of culture-as-text, according to which all aspects of culture are "webs of significance" to be analyzed not as "an experimental science in search of law but an interpretive one in search of meaning" (Geertz 1973a: 5).

Maitland also engages with the very same debate around cultural translation that I discuss in the Introduction. With her own work, she intends to address two of the most crucial concerns. On the one hand, there is an ethical point of criticism, which states that cultural translation has lost touch with social and political realities, and that it discursively perpetuates and reinforces unequal power relations through its predominantly Western academic discourse (e.g., Pym, Bery, Chesterman, Ha). Maitland's goal is, thus, to lift cultural translation "above the level of fashionable trope to that of a measurable and transferable political discourse" (2017: 24). Secondly, she mentions the struggle for cultural translation's methodological validity, and the uncritical transfer of theories of interlingual translation to the field of cultural translation (e.g., Tymoczko, Pratt, Wagner). In answering to that point, Maitland posits an irreducible connection between the two, and her response is to build a theory of cultural translation on a close reading of interlingual translation—which she considers a "hermeneutic enterprise par excellence" (2017: 9)—from the perspective of hermeneutic philosophy.

This "hermeneutic enterprise par excellence" is her starting point. Translators are, in the first place, readers who attempt to understand something that refuses to be understood: a text written in another language, at another point in time and in another place. This special attempt at understanding thus includes reading and interpreting across distances, the articulation of that understanding at another point in time and in another place, as well as intricate forms of appropriation and expression. Maitland breaks this process down into five dimensions: interpretation, distanciation, incorporation, transformation, and emancipation. Roughly speaking, *interpretation* is posited as a fundamental human impulse to engage with cultural, social, and political stimuli, that is texts, in the hopes of understanding; spatial and temporal *distanciation* is considered the structural and mental prerequisite for that interpretation; while appropriation is seen as a constitutive element of the process itself, which plays out in a field of tension between *incorporation* and *transformation*, and may be operationalized for potentially *emancipatory* ends. To expand the conceptual potential of cultural translation, to flesh out its defining characteristics and give it a distinct shape, Maitland discusses these five dimensions in detail against the backdrop of a hermeneutic-anthropological understanding of (culture-as-)texts. Interlingual and cultural translation are both triggered by a desire to understand; yet while interlingual translation starts from an attempt at understanding a text written in another language, the process of cultural translation can be triggered by any meaningful "cultural, political or social stimulus in the world [that] sets in motion the interpretive work of translation led by a human actor" (2017: 608). And even though it requires a human actor, it does not necessarily have to take place within the realm of language; for meaning may also be expressed by way of gestures, glances, actions.

Now, the entire section on *transformation* is based on readings of Benjamin's Translator- and his Artwork-Essays. Maitland's premise, here, is that a desire to understand, to "solve" the mystery that results from distanciation, goes hand in hand with a "desire to conquer" (2017: 85), and thus with a process of appropriation.[35] Distanciation and appropriation enter into a dynamic that outlines a fundamental cultural struggle to come to terms with estrangement. In the context of interlingual translation, this struggle plays out in the confrontation between the foreignness of the "source" text and the familiarity of the "target" language—whereby the foreign is usually bound by the familiar. A new closeness is produced, which counters distanciation by means of "a cognitive process of familiarization, a conscious embracing of the otherness of the other within the horizon of the own" (2017: 87). As a "text" is appropriated, "devoured," by the reader, the process of interpretation is "both embodied and historical" (2017: 92). This entails an agential shift from authors to readers; and of the readers, this requires the distillation of the infinite potentialities of meaning into one's own. This appropriative act, *An-Eignung*, is performative, in the sense that readers express their own here and now, their own horizons of experience. This performative act "also breathes life into the words of the other text and makes them anew" (2017: 106), in a way that is never neutral or automatic, but transformative. And with that, Maitland arrives at *Fortleben*.

Before I delve into Maitland's reading of Benjamin's *Fortleben*, though, I interject a brief digression in order to take a closer look at her underlying understanding of language, which, I think, becomes strikingly relevant in the context of said reading. Maitland states that words are "simply empty vessels" (2017: 42) filled with meaning by the performative act of interpretation. For this understanding, she actually credits Benjamin's Language-Essay (1916), and the distinction he draws between linguistic and mental being. In this text, Benjamin says:

> Was teilt die Sprache mit? Sie teilt das ihr entsprechende geistige Wesen mit. . . . Das geistige Wesen teilt sich *in* einer Sprache und nicht *durch* eine Sprache mit. (GS II: 142; emphasis in the original)

> What does language communicate? It communicates the mental being corresponding to it . . . Mental being communicates itself in, not through, a language. (SW 1: 63)

Maitland interprets this as follows: "Language has no being. It is we who communicate things using language. Language does not communicate anything except the person behind it, who communicates in language—that is, using language, not 'through' it" (2017: 43). Words, to Maitland, are vessels filled with situational meaning by people; they do not hold anything else but the speakers' position. What is especially notable, here, is Maitland's own interpretation of Benjamin's insistence on the preposition *in*. Benjamin claims that the mental being is communicated *in* language, not *through* language—yet this is paradoxically inverted in Maitland's reading, as she paraphrases Benjamin's "in language" into an instrumental "using" of language. Maitland thus establishes a firm hermeneutic primacy of meaning over materiality—even if it is framed by the perspective of the recipients, not the authors—while Benjamin, throughout his writings, attempts at countering an instrumental understanding of language, or media in general.

Returning to Maitland's reading of *Fortleben*, she stresses that the relation between "original" and translation is by no means one-sided, but rather one of mutual interconnectedness. A translation proceeds from the text and realizes its latest expression; it is "appropriative, to be sure, but in its dependence upon this previous life it also makes its source material shine, for it is the work that gives life to the translation" (2017: 113). This is what Maitland calls the compensatory side of appropriation, "for translation can offer the text a range of survival it would otherwise lack" (2017: 118). Responsible for this dynamic, according to Maitland, is the paradox that translation is both creative and derivative at the same time, and thus that it perpetuates a dynamic of re-enactment. Maitland, then, quotes the paragraph that introduces this chapter, yet she deliberately decides *not* to quote from Zohn's standard translation, but instead chooses Rendall's version:

> It is clear that a translation, no matter how good, cannot have any significance for the original. Nevertheless, it stands in the closest connection with the

original by virtue of the latter's translatability. Indeed, this connection is all the more intimate because it no longer has any significance for the original itself. It can be called a natural connection, and more precisely a vital connection. Just as expressions of life are connected in the most intimate manner with the living being without having any significance for the latter, a translation proceeds from the original. Not indeed so much from its life as from its "afterlife" or "survival" [überleben]. Nonetheless the translation is later than the original, and in the case of the most significant works, which never find their chosen translators in the era in which they are produced, indicates that they have reached the stage of their continuing life [Fortleben]. (Rendall, qtd. in Maitland 2017: 116)

Like Derrida, Maitland thus marks the different levels of meaning and terminology that Benjamin uses in the German text. Starting from a basic differentiation between *Überleben* and *Fortleben*, she reiterates the paradox of mutual interconnectedness: translation survives the text (*Überleben*), but does not replace it, instead giving expression to a new and different life (*Fortleben*).

To Maitland, it is precisely this new and different expression that we should focus on: we must not be overly concerned with what happens to the authority of the "original," but rather look forward to find out what is gained in transformative translation. Translation, in itself, is forward-looking, proceeding from the text while not overwriting it, yet it must still acknowledge its point of departure as the trajectory-defining spot where the journey begins, as "the source continues to live on within and inside the translation" (2017: 117); it is incorporated. It is precisely because of this paradoxical, non-sensical, lingering presence that a translation gains its status as a translation: a translation reveals what it is based on, and simultaneously realizes, within itself, a particular relation with the "original" that may not be thought of as replacement. By conceiving of translation that way—as incorporating the text-to-be-translated in order to transform it, displaying the process of transformation within itself—Maitland is able to convincingly analyze various forms of satire and parody as processes of cultural translation.

At this point, Maitland moves on to Benjamin's Artwork-Essay, and his conception of the aura, in order to make the transformative quality of translation even more tangible. In reproduction as well as in translation, what gets lost is the work's unique presence in time and space. There is something to be gained, however, in exchange: for one, there is a greater sense of independence from the original that comes from the particular medial and apparative dispositions in which the "reproduction" takes place, which allow for new perspectives and perceptions; at the same time, a liberation from the here and now opens the artwork to new and, until then, unattainable situations. Maitland illustrates this point by the example of art-selfies posted on Facebook or Instagram: the click of a camera brings these works closer—"spatially and humanly" (SW 4: 255),[36] as Benjamin says in the Artwork-Essay, thus not only illustrating a spatial closeness with the artwork but also codifying one's own experience of closeness, while simultaneously revealing the text-to-be-translated. In the process of approximation and appropriation, this kind of translation holds the potential of renewal and renovation—precisely by means of the destructive act of disturbing uniqueness and permanence; it is a way of "keeping translation's sources alive" (2017: 123) by translating and transforming them. The translator must not aim at a particular meaning that lies within the confines of the "original's" authority, but rather create an entirely new meaning-event, triggered by the "original." This is an intriguing and fruitful part of Maitland's reading that brings together Benjamin's thinking about translation with what is maybe his most famous insights regarding the question as to what happens to the original artwork in the age of technical reproduction. Yet, as I have insinuated, Maitland's priority of meaning over mediality and materiality stifles her analysis, at this point: she traces the relations and correspondences between Benjamin's thinking about translation and his thinking about new media in an interesting new way, but she does not, in the final analysis, apply them. The specific materialities and media dispositions remain blind spots in her analyses and theorizing: the examples she considers as cultural translations are phenomena and meaning-making processes bound to specific media dispositions (paintings, tweets, YouTube, etc.), yet she analyzes all of them the very same way.

The central aspect of Maitland's argument, however, is that the transformative quality of translation carries a revolutionary potential. Purposeful acts of translation may bring interpreters into the hermeneutic circle, thus possibly affecting change, especially if "ideologically motivated interpretations are interpreted for subversive reasons" (2017: 156). That way, "authors of ideology" may be placed at a distance from their own texts, which they must, in turn, confront. For the cultural translators, ideologically marked interpretations become the source material, which is translated back to the authors in order to place them in a position in which they become interpreters of their own, alienated position—and in that process, translation unpacks one of its most powerful tools, namely, the "reminder of the fallibility of the presumption to knowledge" (2017: 158). In the foreignness of the text/language-to-be-translated lies the power for recipients to change, due to the challenge posed by the perspective of the other. To emphasize this revolutionary potential, Maitland once again refers to Benjamin's Translator-Essay, yet not to his own words (even if she attributes them to him): she quotes a passage that Benjamin quotes from Rudolf Pannwitz, a passage that has become emblematic for a "foreignizing" concept of translation:

> der grundsätzliche irrtum des übertragenden ist dass er den zufälligen stand der eignen sprache festhält anstatt sie durch die fremde sprache gewaltig bewegen zu lassen. (GS IV: 20)

> The fundamental error of the translator is that he holds fast to the state in which his own language happens to be rather than allowing it to be put powerfully in movement by the foreign language. (qtd. in Maitland 2017: 127)

Intriguingly, this passage has come to signify a starting point for precisely the genealogical line of cultural translation that leads from a German Romantic tradition to Bhabha—with Bhabha also quoting that very passage in his *The Location of Culture*.

In his approach to cultural translation, Bhabha looks at culture as a symbolizing practice from the perspective of "cultures of survival," that is, marginalized and primarily migrant cultures "who have suffered the sentence of history—subjugation, domination, diaspora, displacement" (1994: 172). Maitland, too, begins her theorization of cultural translation by referring to the heated debates in Europe around the refugee crisis of 2015. To her, the question at the core of the debates is "how we imagine other people, the extent of their suffering, and our duty to act upon it" (2017: 2). She argues that the way we try to understand people may be influenced by empathetic and emancipatory acts of cultural translation in the above sense. Both authors negotiate extremely complex and loaded topics, from the question of how cultural meaning is generated, to the relation between language(s) and culture(s), how people approach and imagine others, how borders are drawn and crossed, and suffering is triggered, under strikingly unequal relations of power. The acuteness and complexity of these issues is certainly one, if not the main, reason why the debates around cultural translation have become so heated and often emotional. Yet there is also something else: in this already difficult terrain, seemingly irreconcilable theoretical and terminological approaches clash. And still, these different approaches idiosyncratically meet in their recruitment of Walter Benjamin. In the following chapter, I investigate in more detail the peculiar discursive role that Benjamin plays in this context.

7

Benjamin's Untranslatability

> ... *auf den es aber dennoch in einer wunderbar eindringlichen Weise wenigstens hindeutet als auf den vorbestimmten, versagten Versöhnungs- und Erfüllungsbereich der Sprachen. Den erreicht es nicht mit Stumpf und Stiel, aber in ihm steht dasjenige, was an einer Übersetzung mehr ist als Mitteilung. Genauer läßt sich dieser wesenhafte Kern als dasjenige bestimmen, was an ihr selbst nicht wiederum übersetzbar ist.*
>
> (GS IV: 15)

Harry Zohn's 1968 translation of "Die Aufgabe des Übersetzers" has been criticized a lot, but especially and explicitly for its rendering of the preceding passage (e.g., Rendall 1997). Here is Zohn's translation in full:

> Yet, in a singularly impressive manner at least it points the way to this region: the predestined, hitherto inaccessible realm of reconciliation and fulfillment of languages. The transfer can never be total, but what reaches this region is that element in a translation which goes beyond transmittal of subject matter. This nucleus is best defined as the element that does not lend itself to translation. (1968b: 75)

In this chapter, I outline in detail why and how this rendition has been criticized. Suffice it to say, for now, that even the editors of the *Selected Writings* decided in 1996 to adapt this passage for re-publication. Yet by 1994, Homi Bhabha had already provided his very own, immensely influential "re-translation" of this passage: working from Zohn's 1968 version, he turned the "element that does not lend itself to translation" into the "untranslatable element," and consequently into an "element of resistance." Due to the wide dissemination of Bhabha's understanding of cultural translation, his own reading of Benjamin in the light of the "untranslatable" has spread as well.

In the following, I take a step back and look at the construction of the above passage in the German text, tracing how it relates to Benjamin's other writings, in order then to look at how Zohn's 1968 translation affects Bhabha's reading of Benjamin. In the end, this conflict that occurs in translation allows me to touch upon the contemporary debate about the viability of the concept of cultural translation: as I illustrate, it is especially where the intellectual diligence of cultural translation theorists is challenged that Walter Benjamin once more serves as a go-to reference point.

Translating "the Element That Does Not Lend Itself to Tanslation"

Within the context of the Translator-Essay, the above quotation is located right after the section in which Benjamin outlines his idea of *Fortleben,* and the kindship of languages. Translation, says Benjamin, manifests the *Fortleben* of works, and, in doing so, it advances a *heiliges Wachstum,* a "sacred growth of languages" (1997: 157). In this process, translation takes on a key function: by "intensively" realizing the kinship of languages over and over again, at different points in time, it has a testing function that Benjamin outlines with reference to the idea of revelation:

> wie weit ihr [der Sprachen, B.H.] Verborgenes von der Offenbarung entfernt sei, wie gegenwärtig es im Wissen um diese Entfernung werden mag. (GS IV: 14)
>
> to determine how distant what is hidden within them [languages, B.H.] is from revelation, how close it might become with knowledge of this distance. (1997: 157)[1]

Translation can never claim permanence, as it "tests" the distance from revelation over and over again, through time. But the direction of its growth reveals a trajectory toward a "final, ultimate, and decisive stage of all linguistic development" (1997: 157).[2] Benjamin thus recalls an idea from the Language-Essay, namely, the notion of a flow of language through all of nature toward a moment of unity.

Throughout the following passage, then, which includes the epigraph of this chapter, Benjamin creates an encompassing linguistic image, namely, that of a growing tree that bears fruit. I do *not* use Zohn's translation, here, in order to better mark the *shift* in imagery that occurs in his rendition, as compared to the other versions. The image begins with the hidden or veiled seed of a higher language that lies in our own. In translation, then, the "original" grows into a "a linguistic sphere that is both higher and purer" (1997: 157).[3] It may not live there permanently, but by the trajectory of its growth alone, it at least points toward "the realm, predestined and denied, where language is reconciled and fulfilled" (1968c: 302).⁴ This realm, however, can never be reached by the "original" "root and branch" (1968c: 302),⁵ with *Stumpf und Stiel*. This is where the epigraph in this chapter finds its place, as Benjamin outlines which aspects of the "original" may reach said higher sphere: only what is more than *Mitteilung*, "more than communication" (1968c: 302).⁶

To specify in more detail this *wesenshaften Kern*, this "essential kernel" (1997: 158)⁷ that is more than communication, Benjamin then continues with the image of a fruit. In an "original," *Gehalt* and *Sprache*, content⁸ and language, relate to each other like *Frucht* and *Schale*, "a fruit and its skin" (1997: 158). In a translation, however, language envelops its "content" like "a royal mantle," (1997: 158)⁹ a *Königsmantel*. The language in a translation has been enhanced—and, it seems, artificialized—which results in the fact that there is no longer a "naturally fitting" relation with its "content." In this enhanced state, the language of translation is *gewaltig* and *fremd*, "inappropriate, violent, and alien" (1997: 158)¹⁰. This is, Benjamin continues, precisely the reason why a translation may not, or need not be, *translated any further*: "This nucleus is best defined," says the 1996 version of Zohn's translation, as the "element in the translation which does not lend itself to a *further* translation" (SW 1: 258; my emphasis). The 1968 version, however, entirely deletes the question that Benjamin raises regarding "further translation."

In the German version, the purpose of outlining the different relations between language and "content" in an original vs. its translation is to clarify why that which is more than communication can and need not further be translated. The question of *further* translation, then, is where the translational dialectic between permanence and ephemerality plays out. Having realized a relation between the original and its translation at a certain moment in time, translation has done what it was supposed to. It has grown some aspects of the original into this higher sphere of language, and they are saturated now. Going forward, translation may only elevate *other* aspects, by realizing a different relation between this original and its translation, at another moment in time and space. This is ironic, says Benjamin, because in a way, even though translation is always preliminary, it *verpflanzt*, transplants or shifts (in German, this verb is specifically used for plants), parts of the "original" into a more final realm, from where they can and need no longer be relocated. Furthermore, it is crucial to note that the "element" that is more than communication is only *created* in translation; it turns into the nucleus, into that which needs no further translation, *because* the translators have fulfilled their task: "One can extract from a translation as much communicable content as one wishes, and this much can be translated; but the element toward which the genuine translator's efforts [had been] directed remains out of reach" (1997: 158; my annotation).[11] In Zohn's 1968 version, however, the nucleus is an element of the original "that does not lend itself to translation" in the first place, and it is this element which translators are supposed to aim at *in order to* fulfill their task.

Homi Bhabha, though, read Zohn's 1968 translation. For him, it is a small argumentative step to turn "the element that does not lend itself to translation" into an untranslatable "element of resistance" that is at the core of any process of translation. This corresponds with a tendency throughout plenty of secondary literature about the Translator-Essay to read it in the light of untranslatability. Yet in Benjamin's writings, while the notion of translatability is fundamental, its seeming opposite, untranslatability, is notably absent.

Un/Translatability in Benjamin's Writings

There are two more passages in the Translator-Essay in which Benjamin talks about translatability. The first one is located right on page one, and it begins with a seemingly simple sentence that has become very well known: "Translation is a form/mode."[12] To be able to grasp it as such, Benjamin deems it necessary to go back to the original, because it "contains, in its translatability, the law that governs the translation" (1968c: 298).[13] This "issue," however, is not only about whether a work allows for translation, but whether it demands it, as this demand is a crucial part of its peculiar form. Translatability is enabling and demanding, it is a structural quality that lies in the original and holds the law and trajectory of its translation.

What is more, Benjamin detaches translatability from the necessity of human actors. Common understandings of translatability may, first and foremost, raise questions about (the availability and capacity of) adequate translators, says Benjamin. But in his understanding, translatability is one of a number of *Relationsbegriffe*, "relational concepts" (1997: 152), that should not be thought of as limited to the realm of human actors. In this respect, Benjamin compares translatability to unforgettability: certain moments or lives hold an intrinsic unforgettability—a quality, a call, a demand not to be forgotten. Yet even if we, humans, are not able to fulfill this demand, even if we forget this moment that holds unforgettability, it is still unforgettable to the extent that it *points toward* the "realm in which it could be satisfied: the memory of God" (1968c: 299).[14]

Translatability may be similarly thought of as not immediately dependent on human actors, and some texts may indeed be *unübersetzbar*, untranslatable, to mankind:

> Entsprechend bliebe die Übersetzbarkeit sprachlicher Gebilde auch dann zu erwägen, wenn diese für die Menschen unübersetzbar wären. (GS IV: 10)

> Analogously, the translatability of linguistic creations ought to be considered even if men should prove unable to translate them. (SW 1: 254)

Zohn decides once more for a rather liberal translation: Hynd/Valk, more literally, render the latter part of this sentence as: "even if they were untranslatable for man" (1968c: 299). While Zohn's translation emphasizes that translation may reach beyond the realm of human *ability*, the German and Hynd/Valk's versions center the paradox of texts being translatable and untranslatable at the same time: they can be both, untranslatable for humans and translatable within the larger framework of translatability that Benjamin outlines.

The second crucial passage about translatability is located toward the end of the Translator-Essay, where Benjamin returns to the idea of translation as a form/mode. It is notable that, once again, he detaches the discussion of translatability from the ability of translators. He claims that the quality of translatability is what dictates the degree to which a translation may stay true to, or be in keeping with, translation as a form. "The higher the work's constitution" (1994: 164), the *höher geartet* a work is, the more distinct is its translatability. The language of such works of a higher level is marked by a particular *Wert* and *Würde*, a "value and dignity" (1994: 164), not by its communicative or informational value. On the contrary, the more a work is written for its informational value, the less may be gained from it in translation. At this point, however, Benjamin reiterates that the differentiation he has just outlined is only true for texts that are *not* themselves translations:

> Übersetzungen dagegen erweisen sich unübersetzbar nicht wegen der Schwere, sondern wegen der allzu großen Flüchtigkeit, mit welcher der Sinn an ihnen haftet. (GS IV: 20)

> Translations, on the contrary, prove to be untranslatable not because meaning weighs on them heavily, but rather because it attaches to them all too fleetingly. (1997: 164)[15]

Benjamin describes the relation of translation and *Sinn*, sense, by degrees of *Schwere* and *Flüchtigkeit*, heavi- and fleetingness. "Low-grade" translatability in works of largely communicative value results in an overweight of sense, which makes translation strain from its "true" form. "High-grade" translatability in works of great language allows for translation to only fleetingly relate to sense, which provides the space for translation to follow its "true" form. These gradations of heavi- and fleetingness are brought to a conclusion in the insight that translatability is not an inherent quality of *translated* texts, because a "form-ful," *formvoll*, process of translation has, basically, absorbed what little sense there was. Thus there is nothing left to nourish further translation. Another paradox: what stands in the way of "form-ful" translation is an overweight of sense or communicative intent in a source text; yet what stands in the way of translating a translation is not a heaviness of sense, but its utmost fleetingness (like the way in which the folds of the king's robe swirl fleetingly around what lies beneath). Benjamin gets to the heart of his argument by means of Hölderlin's Sophocles translations: "In them the harmony of languages is so deep that meaning is touched by language only in the way an Aeolian harp is touched by the wind" (1997: 164).[16] While the relation between sense and language in Hölderlin's translations has become utterly fleeting—too ephemeral for further translation—the harmonic relation of languages has been realized in such a profound and overwhelming way that further translation would be impossible and unnecessary.

Toward the very end of the essay, Benjamin returns to the gradations of translatability. In Hölderlin's translation, sense, in its fleetingness, is instable: it falls from abyss to abyss and gets lost in the depths of an expanded, boundless, bottomless language. There is only one text in which there is a halt to this plunging of sense, namely, the holy text. In the holy text, sense—this unstable, ephemeral linkage—dissolves entirely: it has ceased

> die Wasserscheide für die strömende Sprache und die strömende Offenbarung zu sein. Wo der Text unmittelbar, ohne vermittelnden Sinn, in seiner Wörtlichkeit der wahren Sprache, der Wahrheit oder der Lehre angehört, ist er übersetzbar schlechthin. (GS IV: 21)

> to be the watershed dividing the flow of language from the flow of revelation. Where the text belongs immediately to truth or doctrine, without the mediation of meaning, in its literalness [*Wörtlichkeit*] of true language, it is unconditionally translatable. (1997: 165; my annotation)

Translations may no longer (need to) be translated due to the utter fleetingness with which their language relates to sense; the holy text, however, is unconditionally translatable, because there no longer *is* any intent to communicate. The same way in which there no longer is a boundary between language and revelation in the holy text, its translation must unite *Wörtlichkeit* and *Freiheit*, "literalness and freedom" (1997: 165)—and this confluence takes shape in an interlinear version of the holy text, which Benjamin thus describes as the *Urbild*, or ideal, of translation. But, in the end, all great texts are translatable, as they hold this *Urbild* as a virtual translation between the lines.

While translatability, in the Translator-Essay, is clearly one of its most fundamental concepts, it is also difficult to grasp, which is why it would make sense to look for clarification outside of this text. However, Benjamin rarely speaks of translatability in his other writings; the only other text in which he discusses translatability in detail is, unsurprisingly, the Language-Essay from 1916. Within the framework of this obscure text, language is principle and it is expression, all things and events partake in the principle of language, and they all have their own ways of expression *in* language. There are no languages as enclosed, discrete systems, but there are different *orders* of language, such as the language of things, or the language of humans. And they relate with each other in a very particular way, namely through their translatability:

> jede höhere Sprache [kann] als Übersetzung aller anderen betrachtet werden ... Mit dem ... Verhältnis der Sprachen als dem von Medien verschiedener Dichte ist die Übersetzbarkeit der Sprachen ineinander gegeben. Die Übersetzung ist die Überführung der einen Sprache in die andere durch ein Kontinuum von Verwandlungen. Kontinua der Verwandlung, nicht abstrakte Gleichheits- und Ähnlichkeitsbezirke durchmißt die Übersetzung. (GS II: 151)

> every evolved language ... can be considered a translation of all the others. By the fact that ... languages relate to one another as do media of varying densities, the translatability of languages into one another is established. Translation is removal from [*of?*] one language into another through a continuum of transformations. Translation passes through continua of transformation, not abstract areas of identity and similarity. (SW 1: 70; my annotation)

Benjamin conceptualizes the biblical act of naming as an act of translation, namely of the language of things into human language, in which a receptive and creative force come together. This act of translation is only possible because there is a fundamental translatability that lies in the gradual relationship between languages: different languages, like media of different densities, represent various gradations of incompleteness; the more incomplete language can enter into a less incomplete language only through transformative translation—or, as Benjamin calls it, through "continua of transformation," which stresses both continuity as well as change. Here, too, the concept of translatability is intrinsically connected to the idea of a kinship of languages. Mankind would not be able to solve the task of naming, Benjamin stresses, "were not the name-language of man and the nameless language of things related in God and released from the same creative word" (SW 1: 70). There may be different languages, but they relate to each other like media of different densities, because they share a common vanishing point, a kindship in God—which accounts for their fundamental translatability.

An entirely different perspective on translatability, however, may be extracted from a peculiar text published in 1929 in the *Frankfurter Zeitung*. The short essay is entitled "Wat hier jelacht wird, det lache ick,"[17] and in it, Benjamin muses about local, urban dialects, particularly that of Berlin. In a brief analysis of dialect literature, Benjamin traces a supposed inferiority complex back to an ambiguous position of the Berlin dialect between High and Low German. Yet the *Sprachgewissen*, the language-conscience is strong in Berliners, Benjamin says, and it leads to various strategies of compensation—resulting, for instance, in the "interpenetration of the most delicate with the crude," or in insults being presented in a mode of "steely objectivity while beating around the rose bush."[18] The careful, roundabout element of the dialect extends toward the temporal realm: particularly when Berliners rant, ridicule, or threaten, they celebrate taking their time. Yet this peculiar sense of celebrating duration does not survive its own preservation: to collect dialect phrases in a written form does them a disservice, because dialect lives in a particular temporality, in particular situations and in improvisation. And on other aspects of dialect, a purely lexical collection necessarily misses out as well, such as grammar, or, most importantly, "facial expressions and physiognomics, . . . the untranslatable gestures."[19] The area of the gesture, he says, is a *Grenzbezirk*, a border district,

> weil das Unbestimmte, Mystifizierende, das jedem Dialekte hin und wieder eignet, hier leicht die Oberhand bekommt und dann am Ende den Ausdruck nicht nur unübersetzbar, sondern undeutbar macht. (GS IV: 540)
>
> because the indeterminate or the mystifying, which is sometimes immanent in each dialect, easily prevails here, and in the end, it renders the expression not only untranslatable, but also uninterpretable. (My translation.)

As an example, Benjamin describes how a Berliner says *von wejen*, "as if," while giving an expressive glance—a combination that lies "beyond articulated language."[20] This *Ausdruck*—a combination of physiognomy, facial expression, and dialect articulation—turns untranslatable, even uninterpretable, because that which is undetermined, mystifying becomes too overwhelming. Interestingly, Benjamin describes a similar physicality in an entirely different fragment, namely, a note for his *Passagenarbeit*: very briefly and without further comment, he describes "the untranslatable literature of flanerie 'Paris rue par rue maison par maison.'"[21] Like the border district of gesture, the literature of walking is bodily as well as literary; a portrait of Paris that must be walked, street by street, house by house. As such, it also deserves this label: *unübersetzbar*, untranslatable (to human actors).

In a later fragment, then, Benjamin raises the question of the *limits* of translation. In "What can be said in favor of translation?", he states: "The limit: music needs no translation" (SW 3: 249). In the German version, there is no sentence after the colon, there is only one word: *Übersetzungsunbedürftigkeit*— an awkward literal rendering of which may be "translation-un-neediness," which expresses the absence of a need, or call, or demand for translation. As such, this "translation-un-neediness" may be seen as the opposite of the enabling and demanding structural quality of translatability. It is still not, however, a concept of untranslatability.

Bhabha's Untranslatable Element of Resistance

Yet, still, it is the idea of untranslatability that moves to the forefront of concern in many readings of Benjamin, as it does in Bhabha's. In "How Newness Enters the World," chapter 11 of his seminal publication, *The Location of Culture*, Bhabha further develops and complicates earlier notions of cultural translation. As Robert J. C. Young points out, the titular phrase of chapter 11 is a citation from an essay that Rushdie wrote in response to the controversy around *The Satanic Verses*. In the essay, Rushdie states that the novel "celebrates hybridity, impurity, intermingling, the transformation that comes of new and unexpected combinations"—which is, to him, "how newness enters the world" (qtd. in Young 2017: 193). Indeed, Bhabha uses the term "cultural translation" for the first time in 1989, when he comments on the fatwah that was issued in response to Rushdie's *The Satanic Verses* in a magazine article entitled "Beyond Fundamentalism and Liberalism." He later fleshes out the concept theoretically in several essays and interviews, and especially in chapter 11, "How Newness Enters the World"—once again, in a reading of Rushdie's famous novel.[22]

The chapter begins with an epigraph: a Benjamin quote from the Language-Essay (the one about translation passing through continua of transformation[23]). What follows is a critique of Frederic Jameson's Marxist framework in *Postmodernism, or, The Cultural Logic of Late Capitalism*. Bhabha primarily questions the primacy of the category of "class," as it clashes with the "subject" of postmodern negotiations of the local and the global. When it comes to the difficulty of cognitively mapping the latter from the perspective of the former in terms of class, Jameson acknowledges, according to Bhabha, that difficulties arise from the fact that postmodern subjects are spatially de-centered by demographic plurality, as they are fundamentally shaped by forces of global exchange and migration, particularly in postmodern cityscapes. Yet, to Bhabha, in order to "revise the problem of global space from the postcolonial perspective [we need] to move the location of cultural difference away from the space of demographic *plurality* to the borderline negotiations of cultural translation" (1994: 223). Concepts such as demographic plurality, cultural diversity, and multiculturalism need to be deconstructed, and Bhabha suggests we do so by turning to the borderline condition, the spatio-temporal moment of cultural translation. What follows is a discussion of the postmodern migrant condition in Western metropoles, by means of their literary construction in *The Satanic Verses*.

To begin with, Bhabha describes the irresolvable liminality of the migrant condition as a conflictual relation between nativist atavism and assimilation. Right then and there, Bhabha argues that, living in this interstitial condition, "the subject of cultural difference becomes a problem that Walter Benjamin has described as the irresolution, or liminality, of 'translation,' the *element of resistance* in the process of transformation, 'that element in a translation which does not lend itself to translation'" (1994: 224). This is the exact passage that exists only in Zohn's 1968 version of the Translator-Essay. Working with this early translation, Bhabha does not consider the additional wrinkle that Benjamin had folded into the German text, that is, the fact that Benjamin talks about that which, *in a translation*, is not translatable any further. In Zohn's first translation, and thus to Bhabha, the element of resistance is crucial because it occurs in *any* process of translation; more than that, it is a precondition that establishes the *liminality* of translation—an irresolution between translatability and untranslatability. This liminal space triggers a confrontation with ambivalence and hybridity, and thus, on a fundamental level, goes against "the assimilationist's dream, or the racist's nightmare, of a 'full transmissal of subject-matter'" (1994: 224).[24]

It is the irresolution of this liminal condition that is so crucial to Bhabha, and to him, it is also what accounts for the charge of blasphemy brought against *The Satanic Verses*, which is much less about misinterpretation than about an unresolved ambivalence. Minority positions articulate "problems of identification and [their] diasporic aesthetic in an uncanny, disjunctive temporality that is, at once, the *time* of cultural displacement, and the *space* of the 'untranslatable'" (1994: 225). In short, the transgressive moment of cultural translation does not have its roots in the misinterpretation of content. Reinscribing cultural traditions in a different time and space, Rushdie performs an iterative act that displaces what is considered to be authoritative, singular, original. This process alienates the familiar in such a way as to disjoint and dislocate authoritative and universalist claims, exposing them to historical and cultural particularity. Bhabha sums up this argument by stating that blasphemy derives from "a moment when the subject-matter or the content of a cultural tradition is being overwhelmed, or alienated, in the act of translation" (1994: 225)—a Bhabharian forshadowing of his future argument, by means of an (unacknowledged) nod to Benjamin, namely, to the image of the overpowering, alien royal robe.

In order to outline the disjunctive temporality and performativity of cultural translation, Bhabha calls upon Benjamin's *Fortleben* and Derrida's *survivre*, as I discuss in the previous chapter. He argues that the complex temporality of cultural translation grows out of necessity, out of survival. The particularity of this temporal structure, too, lies in its irresolution, its liminality, its refusal of both, and back and forth between, tradition and the Utopia of progress. It is this *act* of survival, of back and forth, of "living on the borderlines," that marks the way in which newness sneaks into the world, experimentally, creating links through unstable elements—in a "dangerous tryst with the 'untranslatable'" (1994: 227). This newness that enters the world through the act of living on the borderlines, Bhabha says, "is akin to what Walter Benjamin describes as the 'foreignness of languages'—that problem of representation native to representation itself" (1994: 227). This phrase, "the foreignness of languages," is also part of Bhabha's repertoire of shortcuts: he uses it repeatedly to invoke the problem of an inherent non-identity of language that necessitates representation. In Benjamin's Translator-Essay, though, the "foreignness of languages" is mentioned only once and in passing: it is that which the tentative, ever-incomplete process of translation tries to come to terms with. Bhabha, though, reads Benjamin's "foreignness of language" as coming closest to "describing the performativity of translation as the staging of cultural difference" (1994: 227). Developing this argument, Bhabha juxtaposes his own understanding of "foreignness of languages" with an earlier part of the Translator-Essay, in which Benjamin refers to the complementarity of language. Bhabha argues that Benjamin's example of *Brot* and *pain* illustrates the way in which complementarity relates to contestation: while *Brot* and *pain* may share a common vanishing point with regard to their intentions,[25] their modes of signification[26] are in conflict, they even "strive to exclude each other" (1968b:

74). It is only through ongoing contestation that complementarity emerges, says Bhabha. And this process is "the seed of the 'untranslatable'—the foreign element in the midst of the performance of cultural translation" (1994: 227).

In this passage, Bhabha attempts to re-configure the seed of the untranslatable as a process, a dialectic at work, unresolved, between complementarity and contestation. This strangely processual seed, Bhabha says—and here, he picks up on the thread he laid out before—"turns into the famous, overworked analogy in the Benjamin essay: unlike the original where fruit and skin form a certain unity, in the act of translation the content or subject matter is made disjunct, overwhelmed and alienated by the form of signification, like a royal robe with ample folds" (1994: 227). To Bhabha, the process he describes as "the seed of the untranslatable" is alienating; it leads *beyond* content or subject matter[27] due to the fact that, in its iterative performance, it creates space—the space beneath the royal robe. "The seed of the untranslatable" is contention and complementation, negation, and negotiation, a "splitting of skin and fruit through the *agency* of foreignness" (1994: 228), which sets meaning in motion, destabilizes the idea of stable or ahistorical meaning. It is worth noting, at this point, that in Benjamin's German text, too, the nucleus dissolves, where it refers to the relation between language and "content," and as this relation becomes fleeting in translation, it is also given ample and artificially created space under the royal robe (see p. 130f). To Bhabha, the strangely processual nucleus refers to the inherent foreignness of language, the problem of non-identity that necessitates representation. The image of the royal robe, then, illustrates the way in which the performance of translation overpowers signification. Difference, Bhabha argues, is articulated in performance, much more so than in slippages on the level of content (which are usually celebrated as an articulation of difference).

This understanding of cultural difference is fleshed out in another chapter, "Dissemination: Time, Narrative and the Margins of the Modern Nation"—where Bhabha also prominently discusses the idea of a "Foreignness of Language":

> It is only by engaging with what [Benjamin] calls the "purer linguistic air"—the sign as anterior to any *site* of meaning—that the reality-effect of content can be overpowered which then makes all cultural languages "foreign" to themselves. And it is from this foreign per-spective that it becomes possible to inscribe the specific locality of cultural systems—their incommensurable differences— and through that apprehension of difference, to perform the act of cultural translation. In the act of translation the "given" content becomes alien and estranged; and that, in its turn, leaves the language of translation *Aufgabe*, always confronted by its double, the untranslatable—alien and foreign. (1994: 164)

In Benjamin's German text, the "purer linguistic air" may be read as a reference toward the metaphysical concept of language and translation in the Language-Essay, a call-back to the imagery of a stream flowing from lower-grade to higher-grade languages, enabled by translation. In the Translator-Essay, it is a starting point for Benjamin to discuss whether it is possible, or necessary, to translate a translation; which, Benjamin says, it is not. This argument also holds a dialectic of permanence and ephemerality, as Benjamin argues that even though it is always necessarily ephemeral, tentative, provisional, and momentary, a translation that lives up to its form may *generate* that which—in a translation and through translation—is more than communication, that which reaches a higher and more permanent realm from which it may no longer be removed. To Bhabha, however, this paragraph of Benjamin's text is not so much about a dialectic of permanence and ephemerality, and even less about the translation of a translation, but about a dialectic of translation and the untranslatable. To Bhabha, Benjamin's "purer linguistic air" turns into the sign that precedes any attempt at situating meaning, a kind of reference point that seems to help shift the focus away from the primacy and verisimilitude of content, in order to destabilize and alienate. Only from this vanishing point of self-alienation, the specificity, the particular context and historicity of cultural systems, their incommensurabilities, may be performed in cultural translation. The language of translation, that is, one's own language enriched by another, is left in an irresolvable state, always confronted by its supplement,[28] the untranslatable.

In the last section of chapter 11, then, Bhabha returns to his critique of Jameson. He poses the question of how collective agency and solidarity may be formed outside of the discourse of "class." Bhabha thus urges his readers to consider community as a performative discourse (not as a category). In this performative discourse of community, minority discourse takes on a crucial role as a foreignizing agent, a positionality that enables the emergence of a new kind of solidarity. Quoting Abdul Janmohamed and David Lloyd, Bhabha stresses that building community as a performative discourse does not require *being* minor, but *becoming* minor; it is "not a question of essence . . . but a question of subject position" (qtd. in Bhabha 1994: 328). Bhabha then maps what he had outlined before with regard to the process of negation-and-negotiation, which he locates in the spatio-temporal realm opened up by the foreign element, onto the global-local divide: "Community is the antagonist supplement of modernity: in the metropolitan space it is the territory of the minority, threatening the claims of civility; in the trans-national world it becomes the border-problem of the diasporic, the migrant, the refugee" (1994: 231). He argues for a conception of community as performative discourse, in which minority positions carry the crucial potential of alienating and unsettling the majority in such a way as to create the conditions for a new sense of community that could be built upon affiliative solidarity. It is precisely on the borderline, through this process of cultural translation, that such new forms of affiliative solidarity may arise.

Bad Philosophy?

Bhabha's concept of cultural translation, and with it the discourse of the untranslatable, has become equally prevalent and infamous in discussions *about* the concept of cultural translation. In the following, I look at two texts in particular: a sort-of-response to the *Translation Studies Forum* debate about cultural translation by Anthony Pym, entitled "On Empiricism and Bad Philosophy in Translation Studies" (2009), and Birgit Wagner's "Cultural Translation. Explorations on a Travelling Concept" (2009).[29] I chose these two texts, because in both, Bhabha's concept is harshly criticized—mainly for its philosophical and philological carelessness toward Benjamin.

I begin with Birgit Wagner's text. Engaging with cultural translation as a traveling concept, Wagner raises crucial questions about the development and status of theory in the contemporary study of culture, as she argues that "certain terms follow a career path that may be described by the stages of emergence, hegemonial presence and a subsequent inflationary devaluation" (2009: 1).[30] This is, it becomes clear, precisely the path that the concept of cultural translation is currently on. For the concept to step onto this path, it required a process of metaphorization; in this case, of "translation" into "cultural translation"—of "translation in a verbatim sense" (2009: 1),[31] and its metaphorical extension into a cultural realm. Wagner's allocation of the corresponding disciplinary grounds seems equally clear-cut: the former understanding of translation is curated by translation studies, *Übersetzungswissenschaften*, the latter may be covered by all disciplines, and thus has no discipline. Its objects are unspecific and varied, as the concept covers the transfer of the "contents of imagination, values, patterns of thought, patterns of behavior, and practices from one cultural context into another" (2009: 1).[32] On the "verbatim" side, then, stands translation as a process of "molding a text from one natural language into another" (2009: 1).[33]

It was Bhabha, Wagner says, who catapulted this "metaphorized" concept of cultural translation into its hegemonial stage, from where, since the 1990s, it has moved into its current stage of inflation and devaluation. In Bhabha's formulation, cultural translation was fully detached from its "literal" realm. Very briefly summarizing Wagner's main argument, she claims that it is precisely in his interpretation of Benjamin's text that Bhabha repeatedly crosses the threshold between a "verbatim" and a metaphorized concept of translation. She reiterates that Benjamin's Translator-Essay must be read within the context of his earlier Language-Essay and thus his philosophy of language. Philosophy of *language*; adding, not of culture. Bhabha does not once provide his readers with this contextually relevant information, she says, but instead simply takes Benjamin's verbatim understanding of translation, and jumps into the metaphorical realm. To substantiate her point, Wagner provides her own reading of the passage that I chose as a epigraph for this chapter, where Benjamin talks about the "aspect of language which eludes translation, or rather, according to Benjamin's premise, the aspect that will only be translatable from a messianic perspective" (2009: 5).[34] Wagner does *not*, in fact, criticize Bhabha's *reading* of Benjamin in the light of untranslatability at this point—instead, she largely seems to share it: he may rightly, in a way, use Benjamin's Translator-Essay to theorize an untranslatable aspect of culture, but he fails to provide the context, that is, that Benjamin is talking about language, within a particular framework that she refers to as messianic. However, neither Bhabha nor Wagner provide the context needed to signal the fact that Benjamin discusses the impossibility, or needlessness, of *further* translating a translation.

Wagner's main point of contention is thus with an unreflective metaphorization of translation, and with a kind of decontextualization that allows Bhabha to carelessly jump the line between what she describes as verbatim and metaphorized understandings of translation. Benjamin's theses, or at least her readings of them, are "metaphorically turned," which results, says Wagner, in "a struggle between one verbatim and two metaphorical ways of using the term" (2009: 5).[35] I assume that Benjamin's usage represents the verbatim understanding of translation; the two metaphorizings in question here seem to lie within Bhabha's proposition that the migrant experience is *übersetzend*, actively translating, while migrant culture is, at the same time, supposed to (passively) demonstrate culture's fundamental untranslatability to the majority population (2009: 5). The two metaphorical realms may thus refer, on the one hand, to an understanding of culture as translated *by* migrants, and, on the other hand, to migrants themselves becoming "un/translated" elements.

Indeed, Bhabha avoids ever deciding on a clear distribution of activity or passivity. He speaks of a condition, or an experience, rather than of particular groups or individuals; yet he characterizes this condition or experience as *translational*—nowhere does he refer to it as actively translating, *übersetzend*. The only time Bhabha refers to agency, in this context, is when he describes the agency of foreignness that cracks open illusions of unity, splitting fruit from skin. Wagner comments on this argument of Bhabha's as well, and she considers it to be very persuasive, as it leads him to think of translation as a performative practice in Butler's sense, alienating and transformative. Yes, Bhabha once again transposes a "literal" understanding of translation into a cultural realm, and he again refuses to acknowledge its "original," language philosophical context. But, in doing so, he arrives at the "most fruitful designation of what cultural translation may be" (2009: 5),[36] namely, "the staging of cultural difference" (1994: 227).

To me, Wagner's argument, straightforward and conclusive as it may be, is difficult to align with the framework of Bhabha's theory and intertextual practice. The dynamics that define his concept of cultural translation are rooted in a fundamentally linguistic and discursive conception of the world which is, I would argue, shaped not only by poststructuralist thought but also by Benjamin's encompassing understanding of language. Wagner's argument is based on assigning a "verbatim" understanding of translation to Benjamin, and a "metaphorized" one to Bhabha, yet especially in the context of the Language-Essay, Benjamin's truly fundamental concept of translation may by no means be reduced to a transfer between natural languages. On the contrary, it works *against* precisely the idea of "natural languages" as discrete and enclosed systems. Bhabha picks up on this notion in order to even more decidedly deconstruct systems of categorization that would promote understandings of what is "original" and what is "derived." In the end, Wagner's argument is based on an un-transferability of theories about "verbatim" translation into a "metaphorized" realm, and Benjamin's thinking of translation is clearly framed as belonging to the former: while languages, "as Benjamin stated, may fundamentally not be translated without any residue" (2009: 6),[37] this untranslatable residue of language is not necessarily analogous to the untranslatable residue of culture, says Wagner. Once more, this illustrates that her critique remains under the auspices of untranslatability, and it is not directed at a perceived misinterpretation, but at the undue transfer of theory, the metaphorization and decontextualization of Benjamin's thought.

At the beginning of her text, Wagner raises a suggestive question, namely, whether "the inflationary devaluation of some terms that [Bhabha] uses [can] be attributed to what the French so beautifully refer to as 'le flou théorique,' or [whether it is] actually his audience that should take the blame?" (2009: 2).[38] In the end, she answers this question in a roundabout way, as she indirectly stresses the responsibility of the recipients, for instance when (literary) translations are "foreignizing" to such a degree that the text becomes multilingual, because elements of the source language are retained in translation—then the task of translation lies with its audience. She closes her article with a quotation by Patrick Chamoiseau, whom she indirectly juxtaposes with Bhabha:

> Wir wünschten uns, dass eine Übersetzung vor allem die irreduzible Undurchsichtigkeit jedes literarischen Textes ehren möge, damit in dieser Welt, in der endlich die Möglichkeit besteht, dass sie zu sich selbst findet, der Übersetzer der Hüter der Diversität [le berger de la Diversité]—werde.
>
> Nous étions d'accord pour qu'une traduction ho-nore avant tout l'opacité irréductible de tout texte littéraire, pour que, dans ce monde qui a enfin une chance de s'éveiller à lui-même, le traducteur devienne le berger de la Diversité. ("Pour Sergio" np)
>
> We agreed that a translation was to honor, above all, the irreducible opacity of all literary texts, so that, in this world that finally has the chance of rising to itself, the translator becomes the shepherd of diversity.[39]

Chamoiseau, to Wagner, expresses "a deep sense of respect for difference, based in the appreciation of, and love for, the diverseness of languages. Hybridity, from this perspective, is not a value in itself, but a surplus-value that makes existing values stand out" (2009: 8).[40] I read this final sentence in two ways. To me, it is hard to argue that Bhabha holds anything less than a deep respect for difference, or that he sees hybridity as a simple mixture that obscures diversity, but this sentence clearly does express a potent fear of losing linguistic diversity where one language— English—is considered sufficient for theorizing translation. At the same time, and above all, Wagner demonstrates that we carry the responsibility to work against the canon, and to not reproduce and disseminate only firmly established theories and theorists. Challenging the authority of Bhabha's omnipresent understanding of cultural translation, Wagner clearly aims at following up on this responsibility. In a convoluted turn, though, she does so by reference to the way in which Bhabha recruits Benjamin, one of the most canonized figures throughout the humanities, for his cause. While Wagner does support parts of Bhabha's reading of Benjamin, she criticizes its decontextualization and unacknowledged transferring of theory from the field of "literal" to that of "cultural" translation. To Wagner, this transfer uproots the firm grounding of Benjamin's concept of translation within his philosophy of language. To Bhabha, this process may be considered as a positively blasphemous way of engaging with the canon.

Pym's argument in "On Empiricism and Bad Philosophy in Translation Studies" (2009) is similar to Wagner's, in that Bhabha's way of referring to Benjamin turns into one of the main examples of weaknesses in the theoretical discourse about cultural translation. However, Pym criticizes not only a questionable transfer of theory but also (or, mainly) Bhabha's (mis-)reading of Benjamin. Before addressing Bhabha, though, he challenges other recent approaches to translation, which have developed from a particular brand of translation studies that he does not consider productive. He situates himself within an empirical tradition leading back to Russian formalism, and he argues that the approaches he criticizes—"cases of non-optimal theorization, loosely and probably unfairly labeled as bad philosophy" (2009: 29)—do not meet the requirements of the empirical perspective that he advocates; a large part of these non-optimal theorizations are made up, he says, of "recycle[d] snippets of Benjamin, Derrida, Borges and the like" (2009: 29).

In a section of his article entitled "Translation as Survival," then, Pym addresses Bhabha. Primarily, he dissects Bhabha's practice of citing Benjamin, and he argues that Bhabha pieces two remote parts of Benjamin's text together haphazardly, namely, "untranslatability" and survival. In order to build this argument, Pym goes back to Benjamin's text, diligently mentioning both, the German version and an English version of the Translator-Essay in his bibliography (i.e., Zohn's 1968 translation, as it is re-printed in Venuti's *Translation Studies Reader*). Yet as he quotes from the English version, the quotation is marked as stemming from the German version of the essay. I assumed that this was just a simple mislabeling, but the passage Pym cites does not even occur in the English translation, at least not the way he quotes it: he states that Bhabha's idea of untranslatability is indebted to Benjamin's "passing" claim that "'translations themselves are untranslatable' (Benjamin 1923/1977: 61)" (2009: 31). For one, this is, as I have illustrated earlier, not at all a "passing" claim to Benjamin. And, later in his essay, when Benjamin discusses the fleeting vs. heaviness of sense in translation, Zohn indeed translates Benjamin as stating that "translations, in contrast, prove to be untranslatable" (SW 1: 262). But this is not the way Pym quotes it. And the reference he gives does not help either, because, as I said, it directs the readers to the German text. I may be nitpicking here: the quotes are sufficiently similar. But, after all, it is Pym who faults Bhabha for his lack of philological diligence. Even more substantially, though, the claim that "translations themselves are untranslatable" is precisely *not* what Bhabha bases his reading of Benjamin on; as I have illustrated in detail, Bhabha's reading is based on Zohn's early translation of "the element that does not lend itself to translation," which entirely dismisses the question of "further translation." To Pym, though, Bhabha turns the "apparently untranslatable quality of translations [into] a point of resistance, a negation of complete integration, and a will to survival found in the subjectivity of the immigrant" (2009: 31).

For this argument to work, Pym claims that Bhabha needs to bring together two supposedly disjointed parts of Benjamin's Translator-Essay, namely this argument regarding the "untranslatability" of translations and the part where Benjamin discusses "translations as extending the life of the original" (2009: 31), that is, the part where he talks about *Fortleben*. For one, I would argue that there is a clear conceptual interrelation between these parts of the essay: it is more than relevant to look at the relation between Benjamin's understanding of translations manifesting the *Fortleben* of works and the fact that translations may or need not themselves do so. But even more literally, there is a connection between these two parts of the essay: in the paragraph right before Benjamin discusses "the element that does not lend itself to [further] translation," he outlines how translation "catches fire from the eternal life [*Fortleben*] of the works and the perpetually renewed life [*Aufleben*] of language; for it is translation that keeps putting the hallowed growth of language to the test" (SW 1: 257).[41] This notion of perpetual preliminarity vs. eternal *Fortleben* turns into the starting point for Benjamin's discussion of a dialectic of ephemerality and permanence in translation, part of which is the argument that translations do not lend themselves to further translation. Yet Pym does not see this proximity, because with respect to the discussion of untranslatability, he solely refers to the very *last* part of Benjamin's essay, in which there is indeed no reference to *Fortleben* (Bhabha does, in fact, refer to both passages).

Pym summarizes Benjamin's argument with regard to *Fortleben* as follows: "translations give the original an 'after-life' (*Fortleben*, 'prolonged life')" (2009: 31)—and he also specifies what guarantees this after-life, namely "the 'fleeting' way in which meaning adheres to them (Benjamin 1923/2004: 61)" (2009: 31). Again, this citation has remained puzzling to me. Let me begin by addressing my philological confusion, before I address the argumentative content of this statement. This time around, Pym actually refers to the English version of the Translator-Essay. Yet in the publication he quotes from, the Translator-Essay is printed on pages 15–23; there is no page 61. Again, a mix-up: on page 61 of the *German* version, Benjamin does talk about the fleetingness of sense. Still, and now I move on to the argumentative content of this statement, nowhere does Benjamin argue that this fleetingness of sense is what guarantees an "original"'s *Fortleben*. Pym himself seems to "knit[s] the concept together" (2009: 31) so that it supports his argument. What is more, he avoids a close reading of Benjamin's text, while still proclaiming authority over its interpretation.

Pym's main concern with regard to Bhabha's notion of "survival" is how he gets there. He does not mention that Benjamin himself uses the term *Überleben* in the German Translator-Essay, which is rendered—in the English standard translation—as "survival." Instead, he argues that Bhabha needs a detour through Derrida in order to get there. To Pym, Derrida helps Bhabha to arrive at "survival," because Derrida is the one who argues that Benjamin uses *Überleben* (i.e., survival) and *Fortleben* interchangeably, and thus translates both as *survivre* (2009: 31). If you look up the pages that Pym refers to, you indeed find Derrida commenting on the fact that Benjamin uses both the German terms *Überleben* and *Fortleben* in the Translator-Essay, yet Derrida states: "At times he says 'Überleben,' at times he says 'Fortleben.' These two words do *not* mean the same thing" (1985b: 122, my emphasis)—before outlining where he sees the differences between the two. Eventually, Pym quotes the passage from Bhabha's *The Location of Culture*, in which he states that his reading of Benjamin's "afterlife" includes notions of Derrida's *survivre*. To Pym, this constitutes a "chicane of interlingual interpretations [in which] a few nuances have been shaved off, with alarming certitude" (2009: 32). What follows, then, is Pym's own attempt at *reinstating* these shaved-off nuances, as he provides several juxtapositions between the "original" and Bhabha's reading of it. Most of these juxtapositions follow a familiar line of argumentation: he describes interpretational shifts from texts to people, from multiple languages to one language, and from the "border between an individual's life and death for Derrida" (2009: 32) toward the "cultural border of migration" (2009: 32). All of these may be challenged in themselves; yet I want to zoom in on the juxtaposition that confuses me most: "what for Benjamin was 'fleeting' has become 'resistance,' which is almost an opposite" (2009: 32).

As my own explorations in this chapter illustrate, the way in which Bhabha constructs his untranslatable element of resistance from Benjamin's Translator-Essay is certainly debatable. It is hard, though, for me to reconstruct why the "chicane of interlingual interpretations" turns fleeting relations into elements of resistance. What Benjamin describes as fleeting with remarkable consistency throughout his text is the relation between sense and language—in the original vs. in translation. At first, he argues that just "as a tangent touches a circle fleetingly and at only a single point, . . . a translation touches the original fleetingly and only at the infinitely small point of meaning [*Sinn*]" (1997: 163).[42] And this definite but fleeting relation, in turn, does re-occur in a discussion of translatability, as Benjamin states that the *höher geartet*, "the higher the work's constitution" (1994:

164), the more may be gained from it in translation, "even in the most fleeting brush with its sense" (2009: 43).⁴³ Now, the element of resistance, to Bhabha, draws its subversive energies from (the irresolution of) the untranslatable. In Benjamin's text, the quality of not being translatable any further results from the *wesenhafte Kern*, the nucleus of a translation, yet this nucleus actually refers to a relation, namely the between language and "content": and it is the particular quality of this relation that does not allow for further translation. Arguably, and somewhat paradoxically, this relation is too fleeting: the language of translation may be heavy, *gewaltig*, yet it touches the sense of the original only lightly, in the fleeting way in which the folds of the king's robe touch what lies beneath.

Thus, it may indeed be argued that it is the fleetingness of this relation that causes resistance to further translation—an idea that is restated later in the essay, as Benjamin argues that translations "prove to be untranslatable not because meaning weighs on them heavily, but rather because it attaches to them all too fleetingly" (1997: 164). So, it may indeed be argued that "fleetingness" causes "resistance" to (further!) translation; a reading that did not at all require me to consult Derrida in a "chicane of interlingual interpretations." To Pym, however, the vexatious way in which Bhabha engages with Benjamin via Derrida turns the "actual" Benjamin upside down, which illustrates, to him, how "a trite and ultimately empty conclusion is made to appear substantial through the authority and complexity of past theories" (2009: 32). As a final assignment, or warning, he adds: "If so, it is bad philosophy, and readers should check each of its sources" (2009: 32).

Writing this section has provoked a sense of irritation in me, which I know manifests in my writing. The more I have become aware of this, the more I have come to see this irritation in Pym's argument as well. His text includes expressions of seeping sarcasm and demonstrative self-depreciation, which may be intended to counter the text's overall gesture at a supposedly deeper understanding, a "correct" way to approach things empirically. Pym indeed frames the experience of reading the impulse text for the *Translation Studies* forum in highly emotional terms, to such an extent that it may have provoked his need for writing his own text in the first place: for one, he explicitly states that he felt a "profound frustration" (2009: 35), which went hand in hand with the insight that he "actually agreed with almost everything the authors say about translation" (2009: 35). This general sense of agreement, however, clashed with a profoundly experienced sense of insult: "I can generally agree with where these people want to go, but I feel insulted by the good/bad oppositions that make their text overtly propagandistic" (2009: 36). Whether consciously or not, Pym astoundingly mirrors what he defines as the source of his frustration in his own writing—and he seems to be passing it onward.

Together, Wagner's and Pym's articles cover almost the entire spectrum of criticism directed at the concept of cultural translation, and, to a large degree, I too tend to agree with many of the issues that Pym and Wagner raise. Yet against the background of this study, the most striking aspect, to me, is the way in which their criticism is presented, what it is tied to, and what is apparently at stake: the way they both invoke Benjamin in order to criticize the invokation of Benjamin by authors engaged in theorizing cultural translation—a concept that is, in one way or another, seen as symptomatic, if not jointly responsible, for worrisome tendencies in the field of translation studies, or in the overall study of culture. Their criticism is not *directed* at Benjamin, though, but at Bhabha's reading of Benjamin. Bhabha is charged with instrumentalizing, decontextualizing, and unrestrictedly metaphorizing Benjamin's concepts. Yet in making this argument, it is necessarily a "correct," fully contextualized and literal understanding of Benjamin's texts, or of translation, that is mobilized. No matter in which contexts and debates, Benjamin is summoned not only in support of particular theoretical or philosophical positions but also to criticize entire discursive formations.

Now, Bhabha's is, without a doubt, a wild reading of Benjamin's Translator-Essay in general, and of the epigraph for this chapter in particular. Yet it is not the only one in which untranslatability moves to the forefront of concern; Bhabha may have found support for his own reading in Derrida's. And it is actually Paul de Man who alerts his readers to the fact that Derrida's reading is based on a mistranslation of the German Translator-Essay into *French*. Toward the end of the Translator-Essay, Benjamin states that the sacred text is "unconditionally translatable" (1997:165); yet the French translator, Maurice Gandillac, renders it as *un*translatable: "il est purement et simplement intraduisable" (Gandillac, in De Man 1985: 19). De Man, then, anecdotally recounts that Derrida based part of his reading of Benjamin on this idea of *un*translatability, until he was notified by a student about his mistake. To this, de Man adds: "I'm sure Derrida could explain that it was the same—and I mean that in a positive sense, it is the same, but still, it *is* not the same without some additional information" (1985: 19). In *The Ear of the Other*, Derrida does indeed give additional information. At first, he states, in accordance with Gandillac, that "a sacred text is untranslatable, says Benjamin" (1985b: 103), because in the sacred text, meaning and language are one and cannot be split. Yet Benjamin, then, continues his argument by proclaiming that the "interlinear version of the Scriptures is the archetype or ideal of all translation" (1968c: 307).[44] This is perfect for Derrida to break down the barriers between un/translatability: sacred texts are untranslatable, yet they are translated, and their translation represents the ideal of all translation. Derrida thus reiterates: "don't forget that for Benjamin . . . the sacred text in which the sense and the letter can no longer be dissociated . . . is both the untranslatable and the pure translatable" (1985b: 150). And, if the sacred text is untranslatable, the untranslatable is what makes a text sacred: "every time there is a text that is not totally translatable, in other words, every time there is a proper name, it gets sacralized. . . . Benjamin tells us that sacralization or the sacred is the untranslatable" (1985b: 148). And from this reading by Derrida, it is only a small step, an invitation almost, for Bhabha to turn the sacred untranslatable into blasphemy. Both, it seems, the English and the French Benjamin, pave the way for untranslatability to move to the forefront of concern. So, maybe, there is something to it.

Conclusion
Unforeseen Constellations

Anthropophagy and the Apocryphal

In a letter to Adorno, dated March 18, 1934, Walter Benjamin comments on the fact that their writing had not yet been widely received by suggesting: "But then are we not destined to an apocryphal influence" (1994: 35)?[1] This difficult phrase has stuck with me. Is he insinuating that his and Adorno's writings are destined to become effective only outside of the canon, which is to say that they would have a resistant, or maybe simply a belated influence? If so, how does this relate to Benjamin's contemporary reception? During his lifetime, Benjamin's writings may not have had a broad impact, mainly because he had "gained for his writings the reputation of incomprehensibility," says Gershom Scholem (2003: 147). But since then, Benjamin's writing has, as this study details, indeed become part of the humanities and social sciences canon. He has become an iconic scholar—a status that subsists on ubiquitous reference, and reverence.

From this omnipresence of allusion and invocation, though, certain moments of synchronicity stand out. In 1980, the Brazilian critic, poet, author, and translator Haroldo de Campos wrote an essay entitled "Da razão antropofágica," translated into English as "The Rule of Anthropophagy." In this text, de Campos presents a reading of Brazil's national and literary culture informed by anthropophagy, a cultural metaphor that will go on to develop a life of its own in various subsequent discussions of postcolonial translation and cultural theory.[2] De Campos traces his own reading of anthropophagy back to Oswald de Andrade's "Manifesto Antropofago," the "Cannibalist Manifesto." In this manifest from 1928, anthropophagy gives shape to a counter-cultural stance that formulates and performs a cultural, social, and epistemological critique feeding on the complexity of postcolonial relations between Europe and Brazil, as well as on precolonial cultural traditions. De Campos revives these critiques in his 1980 text, for which he chose the tenth thesis from Walter Benjamin's "Critic's Technique in Thirteen Theses" as an epigraph: "A true polemics takes up a book as lovingly as a cannibal prepares himself a small child" (qtd. in de Campos 1986: 69).[3] This passage is part of Benjamin's book *One-Way Street*, which was published in 1928—the very same year when de Andrade's "Manifesto Antropofago" came out as well.

This synchronicity leads into a complex, transatlantic history of creating, projecting, and metaphorizing anthropophagic figures. Since the early sixteenth century, cannibalism is mainly attributed to the "New World," in repeated acts of colonial imagination. Claudia Hein argues that "it is not a figure that is simply there. Much rather, the cannibal is created at the precise moment when European explorers, or conquerors, encounter indigenous people in the 'New World'" (Hein 2014: 88).[4] Hein outlines a correlation between an act of defining the self by defining the other and concrete historical situations of colonialism,[5] in which the "charge" of cannibalism seems to be ubiquitous: if the "Other" is marked as cannibalistic, then oppression and, in "return," cultural cannibalism as imperialism is "justified" in accordance with the dictum of "eat or be eaten" (Kilgour 1990: 148). Imaginations of cannibalism thus have a central identity-establishing function for early modern Europe. And, intriguingly, this process of self-definition through defining the "Other" by means of the figure of the cannibal also turns into a central instrument *within* Western discourse, to primitivize and attribute cultural inferiority to marginal groups (Guest 2001: 2).

At the same time, though, discourses of anthropophagy in Europe also inform a fundamental critique from within (Guldin 2008: 110). In 1580, for instance, Michel de Montaigne wrote an essay "Of Cannibals," in which the dichotomy of civilization vs. savagery still remains present, yet the relativity of assigning the one or the other is up for debate, as the question is raised whether European methods of torture may even be more savage than the "humane" cannibalism of the Tupinambá.[6] The bitingly satirical criticism of an emerging Western-industrialized capitalism formulated by Jonathan Swift in "A Modest Proposal" (1729) even goes one step further. Swift proposes, as the subtitle suggests, using Irish babies for sustenance: "For Preventing the Children of Poor People from Being a Burthen to Their Parents or Country, and for Making Them Beneficial to the Publick." In this case, it is Western culture that turns cannibalistic through its ruthless exploitation of nature and humanity. The complex entanglements of (post/colonial) constructions of the "Other" within the framework of cannibalism thus reveal fundamental "anxieties that haunt the apparently stable center of western culture" (Guest 2001: 3).

Around the turn of the twentieth century, anthropophagy finds its way into the European avant-garde, as indicated, for instance, by Alfred Jarry's essay on

"Anthropophagie" (1902), Francis Picabia's "Manifeste Cannibale Dada" (1920), or Tristan Tzara's magazine entitled *Cannibale*.[7] The chiffre of anthropophagy is increasingly positively connoted, as the arguably destructive-productive act is seen to connect the shock value of taboo with a longing for a cultural renewal. One would think that de Andrade had placed his 1928 "Manifesto Antropofago" directly within this discourse. And he does, in a way, yet in doing so, he appropriates the ambivalent history of the chiffre's appropriation by European intellectuals, bringing forth its own discourse of Brazilian modernity by doing so. De Andrade affirms anthropophagy,[8] embraces the complexity of references, cracks open genealogies and illusions of "original" meaning, and thus devours not only the labeling, cannibalism, but also the entire cultural and epistemological disposition it stems from. He replaces a bipolar image of unilateral progression, which is only think- and narratable in dependence, as a one-sided recipient relation with Europe, with a more complex image of anthropophagy as perpetual difference and transformation—a perpetual "transfiguration of the Taboo into a totem" (de Andrade 1991: 42), which refrains from fearing the "Other," but instead devours and appropriates it in order to create a new relation with the world.

The efficacy of de Andrade's anthropophagic chiffre, which codifies processes of re-and-re-appropriation, has found new expressions in Brazilian movements since the 1950s (de Campos 1986: 43), and especially in the writings and practices of the *Noigrandes*-group around Augusto and Haroldo de Campos. In his abovementioned essay on "The Rule of Anthropophagy," the eponymous concept comes to stand for a critical devouring of universalized cultural heritage, not from a perspective of the "noble savage," but "from the point of view of the 'bad savage,' devourer of whites—the cannibal" (1986: 44). It is hardly surprising that this concept lands on fertile grounds in the emerging field of postcolonial studies at the time: a universalized Europe is devoured and thus provincialized, while the de-historicizing mythos of the "noble savage" is decidedly denied.

> Any past which is an "other" for us deserves to be negated. We could say that it deserves to be eaten, devoured. With this clarification and specification: the cannibal was a polemicist (from the Greek *polemos*, meaning struggle or combat) but he was also an "anthologist": he devoured only the enemies he considered strong, to take from them marrow and protein to fortify and renew his own natural energies. (De Campos 1986: 44)

On the one hand, de Campos here refers to the epigraph of his essay, that is, Benjamin's dictum that "[a] true polemics takes up a book as lovingly as a cannibal prepares himself a small child." At the same time, he aligns cannibalism with two other literary forms, apart from translation, which Benjamin also mentions in the same breath: combative polemics and anthology.

In 1928, when de Andrade was writing his manifesto in Brazil, Benjamin was in a high phase of translation practice, mainly working on, and despairing of, Proust. At the same time, Benjamin also published numerous literary reviews and was theoretically engaged with literary history and literary criticism. The latter must, Benjamin insists, be dedicated to the entire circle of a work's life and effects, which includes those literary forms that manifest a work's *Fortleben*. And one of these forms is, as I have indicated in the first chapter of this book, anthology. To correspond with its genuine form, it cannot uncritically follow a logic of representation; a poem, for instance, may not simply stand for a poet, who stands for a certain school, who stands for a certain nation (cf. Benjamin's Kalmer-review, Chapter 3, p. 41f). To compile such an ordinary kind of *Blütenlese*, a florilegium, must be prevented; instead, whoever anthologizes texts or poems must let them complement each other in a new constellation, so that they cast up a new quality that goes beyond the individual writings. In this respect, anthology resembles other forms, such as criticism and translation: these forms, if they are taken seriously, manifest the *Fortleben* of writings, which is transformative, enriching, and concentrating, dynamic and expanding, yet never overcoming; *Fort-Leben* in all its ambivalence, leading along, away, maybe astray.

Apart from anthology, criticism, and translation, Benjamin mentions yet another form that may manifest a work's *Fortleben*, namely, *Fälschung*, or forgery. In the brief fragment about Hofmannsthal, which I have referred to in Chapter 4 (p. 36f), he tries to grasp the nature of Hofmannsthal's writings, and he describes it as follows: great writings from the past had filled Hofmannsthal with the impulse that "drives the forger" (SW 2: 421);[9] in other words, he had become "inspired by the works that blossomed anew within him" (SW 2: 421).[10] So, what was the nature of Hofmannsthal's own, and his relation with past writings? Translation, Benjamin feels safe to say, is *not* the right term. Instead, he describes processes of forgery as citation: "the great forger . . . cites the originary image [*Urbild*]" (SW 2: 422).[11] Hofmannsthal does not cite single lines, or passages, but entire works, by transforming them and making them his own, having them come alive anew within him. *Fälschung* thus points toward a tendency in these works: utter absorption and thoughtful, transforming creation. The inward direction of this movement leads to almost unbearable condensation; yet, at the same time, something is invariably added: new life. Apart from this generative terminology, the imagery of *Einverleibung*, in a literal sense as incorporation, is prevalent throughout this text: great works of the past begin to permeate the forger's body. It is also notable that Benjamin uses a similar imagery of incorporation when talking about his experience translating Proust, yet while it became poisonous to Benjamin, it is life-giving and productive in Hofmannsthal's text production.

For Hofmannsthal, the impulse that drives the forger is triggered by particular past constellations, and in a very particular way: he chooses past works following his instinct, says Benjamin, namely "an infallible instinct for the topical relevance that emanates from what is most remote."[12] These are two characteristics that genuine expressions of all these forms—translation, criticism, anthology, forgery—share: they manifest a deep interrelation with history and historicity, and they follow a particular demand that emanates from a work to be engaged with. With regard to the latter, there is a certain magnetism often expressed by Benjamin through his various abilities (Weber 2008), such as the previously discussed translatability, or assimilability. As for the former, Burkhardt Lindner argues, with regard to criticism in particular, that it must take seriously literary history, and thus primarily a new understanding of history, according to which we must—in the time of the "original" work—find an expression of our own time (GS 3: 290; Chapter 6 p. 56f). That way, says Lindner, the past of a literary work and the present of its interpretation enter a "tension of topical relevance," in which collide "a recognition of the past and a self-expression of a recognizing present,"[13] exposing as a sham the commanding character of art, its *Gebietscharakter*.[14]

Now, with regard to criticism, it is only a particular kind that can do so, and one side of it is constituted by a kind of strategic polemics, which "takes up a book as lovingly as a cannibal prepares himself a small child." Polemics finds its fullest form, says Benjamin, in the satirist Karl Kraus, about whom he wrote an expansive essay in 1930–31. Especially in the third part of this text, which is entitled "Unmensch," un-human, brute, or "Monster" (SW 2: 447), the figure of the anthropophagus comes to the fore: "The satirist is the figure in whom the cannibal was received into civilization" (SW 2: 448).[15] Against the background of the outlined transatlantic cultural history of cannibalism, this formulation is as problematic as it is unsurprising, especially in its concise juxtaposition of "cannibal" and "civilization." Yet it also indicates the complexity of these entanglements,[16] especially if it is read in the context of what Benjamin has elsewhere called a "new, positive concept of barbarism" (SW 2: 732).[17] According to Josef Fürnkäs, the Kraus-Essay as a whole may be read as "another version of a dialectic of enlightenment in three acts":[18] part one, "Cosmic Man," stands for enlightenment; part two, "Demon," for mythos; yet this dialectic does not, in the end, turn into critical self-reflection, but into the "real humanism" (SW 2: 456) of the un-human, the monster, the brute. The *Unmensch* may be seen as belonging to the abovementioned positive barbarism; it certainly does not belong to the realm of mythos. These positive barbarians oppose the notion that (cultural) renewal may spring from genial creation, or from hanging on to supposedly continual contexts of tradition. Lindner outlines the loss of experience that is constitutive of this "new barbarism":

> Erfahrungsarmut, das heißt also reinen Tisch machen zu können, den Verheißungen des Humanismus, "des Menschen" und "der Kultur" zu mißtrauen. . . Erfahrungsarmut, das heißt zu allererst: Verzicht auf den kulturgeschichtlichen Reichtum, der in den Händen der Bourgeoisie faulig geworden ist. (1985: 195)

> Poverty of experience: it means to be able to wipe the slate clean, to mistrust the great promises of humanism, "the human" and "the culture" . . . Poverty of experience: it means, first and foremost, to abandon the cultural historical wealth and abundance that has become putrid in the hands of the bourgeoisie. (My translation.)

De Andrade turns the figure of the anthropophagus against colonial rule in a similar way. In a complex, transatlantic entanglement without origins and genealogies, an integral idea of the dialectic of enlightenment is thus rendered productive in a fundamental critique of colonialism. And the figure of the cannibal, as Benjamin outlines it in his Kraus-Essay, functions in a similar way, says Christian Schulte:

> Der Gegner, den der Unmensch in seiner Eigenschaft als kannibalischer Satiriker sich einverleibt, ist jene allmenschliche Ideologie, die sich auf Menschenrechte beruft, welche nie eingelöst worden sind, auf eine Humanität und eine Kultur, die nur noch als Besitz derjenigen figurieren, die sie faktisch mißbrauchen. (2003: 104)

> The enemy, whom the *Unmensch* devours in his capacity as a cannibal satirist, is the cosmic [*allmenschliche*] ideology that acts upon the authority of human rights which have never been redeemed, of a humanity and culture which only function as a property to those who factually mis-/abuse it. (My translation.)

Against the background of this transatlantic history of cannibal imaginations, and in the context of this "new barbarism," Benjamin and de Andrade both, in their criticism, operationalize anthropophagic figures that suspend continuity, genealogy, and genial creativity. If one is read in light of the other, a new constellation of correspondence pops up, which points way beyond individual readings and texts: together, their cannibals unfold intrinsic entanglements between enlightenment and colonialism.

Now, let me briefly return to Hofmannsthal, and the way in which he recognizes the topical relevance that emanates from what is most remote. In an essay about Eduard Fuchs,[19] Benjamin describes, in a similar way, that Fuchs' "interest in [*Blick für*] the scorned and apocryphal constitutes his real strength" (SW 3: 284).[20] And with that, we are back at the beginning. The religious connotation of this complex image leads, of course, back to the biblical Apocrypha, which have, in spite (or precisely because) of their early, resistant influence, *not* become part of a sanctioned biblical canon. It may be argued that the introductory quotation, regarding Benjamin's apocryphal influence, was honored to the effect that his writings, many of which he may have thought were scorned during his lifetime, have not only become influential, but have taken effect—first in a small circle of contemporaries, and then in the increasingly large circle of successive generations. Their resistant quality has allowed them to survive and live on in these circles. They have become effective. They have changed these circles and themselves in the process. Benjamin's writings have not only become famous, but in his own sense "great," because—in their diversified and widespread unfoldings—they point toward a quality of *Wirksamkeit*, an influence and productivity that is intrinsic to such "great" works. Yet in the end, it would seem as if the Apocrypha have indeed become canonized, and ascribed absolute authority.

Benjamin's reception—and especially the English-language one—is thus often measured against the intrinsic authority of his own texts, and charged with instrumentalizing, decontextualizing, and unreservedly metaphorizing Benjamin's concepts. This is particularly notable when it comes to the theorization of cultural translation, which may be studied like a microcosm of more deep-seated issues as encompassing as the direction of translation studies as a discipline, cultural theory, or even the humanities, at large. Indeed, one the most frequently formulated concerns in this context is the idea of "metaphorization," which turns into a knockout argument. The one thing almost everyone seems to agree on is a firm stance against the practice of "merely" metaphorizing translation, in an appeal to a sense of scientificity that is so often called for. Yet the different perspectives diverge when it comes to the question as to where "mere" metaphorization begins or ends, and what, precisely, constitutes that which is not "merely" metaphorical. What makes the premise of this argument even more difficult and perplexing is the fact that the two processes, translation and metaphorization, correspond with each other in so many respects. Yet while much of the discussion around the concept of translation is based on ridding the process of the negative connotation of being "merely" derivative, the opposite may be said for "mere" metaphorization. I would argue that this way of perpetuating the argument produces orthodoxy: in order to claim that something is metaphorized, a "literal," "verbatim," or "true" understanding must be mobilized, which leads to a perpetual (re-)production of doctrine.

To counter this approach, and to bring to light the subcutaneous dogmatism and conservatism that resonates with many findings of loss outlined in this book, I dissect the way in which Benjamin is translated and received, by focusing on what has been added or gained in the process. This book thus follows Benjamin's *Fortleben*, the dynamic, testing, expansive, transformative trajectories of Benjamin's writings that lead *beyond* themselves, in order to counter the tendency of measuring their translation and reception by degrees of loss against a fixed, authoritative meaning perceived as hidden in the "original." Benjamin's enigmatic, substantive, and hardly categorizable way of thinking and writing, as well as the dense interdisciplinarity bound within his texts, unfolds primarily in the subsequent commentaries and translations. And, in tracing these, I have come across two unexpected "partners": anthropophagy and the apocryphal. These figures have come to inform a critical posture motivated by remoteness, friction, and "unforeseen constellations" (1978: 165),[21] de-centralized by a devouring sense of cooperation. There is a contexture of rhizomatic exchange, of cooperation across generations, through which the abovementioned "tension of topical relevance" may emerge as a mutual relation between past and present, a preposterous, transformative, cooperative form of *Fortleben*. It is a critical posture instructed by the *Unmensch*, a "creature sprung from the child and the cannibal" (SW 2: 457), who combines a child-like sense for the magnetism of the apocryphal, for remote, scorned, and disruptive things, with the "creative destruction" of the cannibal.

Benjamin's understanding of language and translation is of an immense scope and range. Especially in his early writings, everything between heaven and earth is translation (Wohlfarth 2001: 92),[22] which is why it is unsurprising, to me, that Benjamin's texts are taken to provide a blueprint for everything, and nothing, to be considered as translation. Yet a crucial part of Benjamin's continued work is his vigorous attempt at pinpointing, as meticulously and concretely as possible, the commonalities as well as the particularities of the abovementioned literary forms. While translation undoubtedly has much to offer—from knowledge to symptoms of poisoning—we may indeed want to inquire more often, as Benjamin did, if it is not "an inadequate term" (SW 2: 421)[23] to describe what we are looking at.

Notes

Introduction

1 I sincerely thank the reviewer of my manuscript for their suggestion to start here, and for all of the other suggestions as well. They made this a better version of my book.
2 Pym (2010: 153f), Bery (2009: 215f and 2007: 15f), Young (2012: 158f), Papastergiadis (2011: 6f), Conway (2012: 21f), Sturge (2009: 68).
3 Implicit or explicit, uncritical or critical, here are some of the examples: Buden and Nowotny (2009: 199ff), Gentzler (1993: 180f), Young (2012: 158f), Conway (2012: 22), Wagner (2009: 23f), and many more.
4 He states that "[we] are embattled in the war between the cultural imperatives of Western liberalism, and the fundamentalist interpretations of Islam, both of which seem to claim an abstract and universal authority" (1989: 112). This antagonism is rehearsed and perpetuated in the media as well as in intellectual debates, Bhabha says, but for many, neither of these perspectives is adequate: "where do we turn, we who see the limits of liberalism and fear the absolutist demands of fundamentalism" (1989: 114)? This is what *The Satanic Verses* is about, Bhabha tells us: it is about "a life lived precariously on the cultural and political margins of modern society," in which "the comforts and continuities of Tradition" are replaced by "the responsibilities of cultural Translation" (114). Bhabha thus contrasts the capitalized Tradition with a capitalized, cultural Translation—and the latter, he says, becomes a responsibility, which always carries "the threat of mistranslation, confusion and fear" (114).
5 Published in 1990 in *The Rushdie File*, edited by Maitland and Appignanesi, which provides a collection of responses and a platform for debate about the issues connected with the publication of *The Satanic Verses*.
6 Bhabha quotes Rudolf Pannwitz, for instance, who advocates against turning "Hindi, Greek, English into German [but] instead to turn German into Hindi, Greek, English" (1994: 228). This sentence has come to stand for the German Romantic translation tradition; Pannwitz, however, is not a German Romantic—he wrote the book from which Bhabha quotes in 1917 (*Die Krisis der europäischen Kultur*). For more on the German Romantic translation tradition, see Snell-Hornby (2006), Pym (2010), Bassnett (2014), and others.

7 Lawrence Venuti (2008) reads the German Romantic, Schleiermacher, as advocating foreignizing, as opposed to domesticating, translation—which, as Juliane House (2009) argues in her article "Moving across Languages and Cultures in Translation as Intercultural Communication" was a misinterpretation, or mistranslation, of Schleiermacher's German expressions "den Ton der Sprache fremd zu halten," that is, to *keep* the tone of the language strange or foreign, as "verfremden," foreignizing, that is, to *make* strange or foreign.
8 This was the title of his 1964 publication: *Toward a Science of Translating*.
9 Nida even argues in his article "A Framework for the Analysis and Evaluation of Theories of Translation," that in 1952, he had already adopted an approach that would anticipate fundamental features of Chomsky's generative-transformation grammar (1976: 71).
10 Regarding the simultaneity of these developments, Toury recalls in 1995: "Interestingly, the first formulations of the *Skopostheorie* by Vermeer (e.g., 1978) almost coincided with the beginnings of my own switch to target-orientedness (Toury 1977)—which sheds interesting light on how changes of scholarly climate occur, especially considering that for quite a while, the two of us were practically unaware of each other's work" (1995: 25).
11 The text was written in German and entitled "Übersetzen als kultureller Transfer."
12 Cf., Snell-Hornby, Pöchhacker and Kaindl (1994).
13 "Anthropology at the time had a virtual monopoly on the concept of culture," says Sewell in his article on "The Concept(s) of Culture" (1999: 36). Throughout this book, I use the designations "ethnography" and "anthropology" to distinguish between an anthropological research method (i.e., ethnography) and the discipline of anthropology (i.e., most often in the context of US-American cultural anthropology).
14 Franz Boas, a German-born anthropologist who immigrated to the United States at the end of the nineteenth century, was a founding father of cultural anthropology. He brought with him a German Romantic hermeneutic heritage, most notably through Johann Gottfried Herder. Conceptually, Boas aimed at separating cultures from the prevailing idea of biologically and physically distinct races. He saw cultures as dynamic and encompassing, including social, symbolic, and material realms (Barth et al. 2005: 262). As complex and relative as they are, they need to be analyzed on their own terms—and in their own languages: Boas was one of the first to strongly advocate for a linguistic training of anthropologists. What is more, he also took a step toward a form of "egalitarian linguistic relativism" in arguing that while languages were distinct and relative, there was no structural hierarchy among them. This general tendency toward complexification and relativization was immensely impactful, particularly in the United States (cf. Barnard and Spencer 1996; Barth et al. 2005).

15 Most influentially, Clifford Geertz developed the idea of culture-as-text in his seminal publications *Interpretation of Cultures* (1973a) and *Thick Description: Towards an Interpretative Theory of Culture* (1973b). To Geertz, the "culture of a people is an ensemble of texts, themselves ensembles, which the anthropologist strains to read over the shoulders of those to whom they properly belong" (1973a: 255).
16 For a more nuanced discussion, including other influential factors, see Sewell (1999), and Brightman (1995).
17 The cultural anthropologist Arjun Appadurai, for instance, proposed in *Modernity at Large. Cultural Dimensions of Globalization* to use the adjectival form instead of the noun, that is, "the cultural" instead of culture, in order to avoid the latter's ontological burden and the "implication that culture is some kind of object, thing or substance, whether physical or metaphysical" (1996: 12), which would risk the concept of culture of being brought back into the vicinity of race. "Resisting ideas of culture that tempt us to think of actual social groups as cultures, I have also resisted the noun form of culture and suggested an adjectival approach to culture, which stresses its contextual, heuristic, and comparative dimensions and orients us towards the idea of culture as difference, especially difference in the realm of group identity" (1996: 13).
18 As well as in Bassnett's article on "The Translation Turn in Cultural Studies" (1998).
19 See Part II of this book, and Chapters 6 and 7 in particular.
20 Sapir may well have been one of the first to conceptually use the term. He does so in the "Language"-entry for the *Encyclopaedia of the Social Sciences,* prepared sometime between 1927 and 1933: "A type of influence which is neither exactly one of vocabulary nor of linguistic form . . . is that of meaning pattern. It is a remarkable fact of modern European culture, for instance, that while the actual terms used for certain ideas may vary enormously from language to language, the range of significance of these equivalent terms tends to be very similar, so that to a large extent the vocabulary of one language tends to be a psychological and cultural translation of the vocabulary of another" (1963: 26). This is interesting especially regarding the famous Sapir-Whorf hypothesis, which, named after him, constitutes a radical theory of linguistic determinism (for additional context and complication, see Silverstein 1973). In this context, he seems to propose that there are similar "meaning patterns" in different languages, which are based on a similar range of significance, but manifest in a different vocabulary through a process of "psychological" and "cultural" translation. Clearly, Sapir's cultural translation would need much more detailed attention, particularly in that it distinguishes between "cultural" and "psychological" translation, and in that this idea is developed with reference to what he calls "European culture."

21 Nida distinguishes between linguistic and cultural translation in a publication coauthored with Charles R. Tarber, entitled *The Theory and Practice of Translation* (1969). Nida argues that Bible translation must be linguistic translation; it "must not be a 'cultural translation'" (1969: 13). The "sin" of cultural translation, to Nida, would be a translator's intervention that results in the adaptation of the historical context of the Scriptures. Nida's glossary defines "cultural translation" as "a translation in which the content of the message is changed to conform to the receptor culture in some way, and/or in which information is introduced which is not linguistically implicit in the original; opposed to Linguistic Translation" (1969: 199). In another section of the book, Nida explains that cultural translation is "the introduction of cultural ideas which are at least absent, if not foreign, to the culture of the text" (1969: 134). This, however, complicates Nida's own idea of functional equivalence: Nida mentions elsewhere that striving for functional equivalence could, for instance, include a change from "Lamb of God" to "Seal of God" for Inuit recipients who do not know what lambs are (however, while this is an often-cited example, Nida later said it was "apocryphal," see Snell-Hornby 2006: 25–6).

22 E.g., in articles like "Action, Morality and Cultural Translation," published in the *Journal of Anthropological Research* in 1987 by the Scandinavian anthropologist Tord Larsen, and "Conventional Metaphors and Anthropological Metaphysics: The Problematic of Cultural Translation" from 1985, published in the same journal, by the US-American anthropologist Roger M. Keesing.

23 Part of the dynamic of turns, Bachmann-Medick argues, is the process of metaphorization that fuels the travel of concepts. This process of metaphorization, however, has to be curbed by the concepts' contextual application-orientedness, in order for them to constitute viable and workable analytical tools throughout various disciplines (2006: 27). It is hard for me to grasp, though, where metaphorization must stop and application-orientedness begin for a concept to turn into what is considered a viable analytical tool. This line seems to constantly shift, depending on who is looking at it. Also, I am generally skeptical of proposing such a rapid progression of turns. For one, as Hartmut Böhme notes in a review aptly titled "From Turn to Vertigo," Bachmann-Medick tends to take self-designations coming from within particular fields to as describing broader inter- and transdisciplinary developments as, for instance, in the case of the interpretive and reflexive turn (which took hold within the field of cultural anthropology). This reflexive turn may have been a critical intra-disciplinary challenge for anthropology, but Böhme points out that similar developments had taken place in other disciplines much earlier, during and even before the linguistic turn—in fact, he argues, such challenges had represented a fundamental condition for scientific production since at least Wittgenstein and Nietzsche. Cultural anthropology was just late in picking up on these developments. Both these points hint at what I find most deceptive and problematic about the movements outlined earlier, which Bachmann-Medick

analyzes as turns: that they are at times constituted so very differently, and at times they refer to developments that seem so tightly interwoven that Bachmann-Medick's reasoning as to why they should be discussed separately is hard to follow.

24 As I was writing my dissertation, I was working with three interdisciplinary academic institutions that advertised a translation-related research focus: The IFK (International Research Center for Cultural Studies) in Vienna has a research focus entitled "Cultures of Translation"; the IKT (Institute of Culture Studies and Theatre History) of the ÖAW, the Austrian Academy of Sciences, have an ongoing project simply entitled "Translation"; and the trans-Atlantic research group IRTG Diversity in Montréal/Saarbrücken held their Spring Lecture Series 2017 under the title "Translating Diversity," and I have attended a summer school on "Cultural Translation," convened in Wolfenbüttel by Doris Bachmann-Medick, in July 2019.

25 My translation. "Sie führen nach und nach diejenigen Dimensionen von Kultur, Lebenswelt, Geschichte und vor allem Handeln wieder ins Feld, die von der Sprachenge des linguistic turns ausgeblendet, ja verdrängt worden sind" (2012b: 36).

26 The critics' different lines of argumentation have been diligently laid out in one of the most recent and most elaborate studies on cultural translation, namely, Sarah Maitland's book-length study on *What Is Cultural Translation?* (2017: 14–27).

27 Of course, there is an array of more recent contributions that do, in one way or another, address numerous concerns outlined in this debate, by looking in more detail at the concept's historical development, its theoretical make-up, and its applications (and applicability) in the form of encyclopedia and handbook entries (e.g., *Routledge Encyclopedia of Translation Studies*, 2009/2019; *Handbook of Translation Studies*, 3rd edition, 2012). Cultural translation has also been included in introductory works on translation studies, for example, *Exploring Translation Theories* (2009), in which it is designated as a distinct, recent paradigm of translation. And there are attempts at structured "maps of meaning" (Conway 2012) which aim at cataloguing and bringing a sense of order to the wide variety of existing contributions. And, above all, there is Sarah Maitland's *What Is Cultural Translation?* (2017): while the overall gesture of most of the abovementioned recent contributions is to *show*—what cultural translation may be and where it may come from—Maitland tries to *define* and theoretically substantiate it, in order to counteract what she perceives as a paradox in light of cultural translation's popularity, namely the fact that it is, as of yet, so ill-defined.

28 These high stakes may explain why the discussion is so heated, so emotional at times, with criticism often directed at the authors instead of their arguments. Some of this *ad hominem* criticism does, on the one hand, make a basic but substantial point: we are dependent on and limited to the texts we have read, the experiences we have made. And there certainly is an intellectual danger that emanates from "not learning the language," literally and figuratively. Still, much of this criticism bothers me. For one, a quick look at the biographies of the chastised authors complicates

the arguments. The criticism Pym directs at Buden/Novotny, for instance, is easy to counter: Buden is from Croatia and "immigrated" to Berlin, at least for his PhD; and while Nowotny was born in Austria, he is now working in London. Pym himself, originally from Australia, "immigrated" to Göttingen in the course of his post-doc work. Pym, Buden, and Nowotny have clearly experienced bi- or multilingual conditions as well as processes of migration—and all of them are white males who have *chosen* to migrate. They may have experienced some, but certainly not all of the realities in question. Should this be a prerequisite? Can, or should, we talk about the German citizenship test only if we have immigrated to Germany at one point in our lives? Are we only allowed to talk about authors if we have read *all* their texts, as Pym insinuates when he provides the "correct" reading of Saussure based on *all* of Saussure's writings? It seems to boil down to the question of whether we can, and should, speak for someone else, or about a reality we have not ourselves experienced. There is a particular irony at play, here, when talking about translation, as Pym himself points out in his book *Exploring Translation Theories* (2010): translation is necessarily a process in which someone, the translator, is forced into a position of having to speak on behalf of someone or something else (155–6).
29 Also, implicit or explicit, uncritical or critical, here are some more examples from "outside" the Forum-debate: Gentzler (1993: 180f), Young (2012: 158f), Conway (2012: 22), Wagner (2009: 23f); and so on.

Chapter 1

1 The best resources to piece together the context of Benjamin's process of writing and publishing "Die Aufgabe des Übersetzers" are Abel (2014), Reuß (2016) and Barck (2012). I have relied on all of these, as well as on Benjamin's letters (esp. GB 2: 118f.), and Scholem's account of their friendship (Scholem 2003).
2 In his appendices 2–8, Reuß reprints the different typographies that were discussed. For Benjamin's discussion with Weißbach, see GB 2 (149–151).
3 Benjamin bought it in May/June of 1921, while visiting Scholem in Munich. The *Angelus Novus* would accompany Benjamin for the rest of his life, and it would find its way into the widely received "Theses on the Philosophy of History."

Chapter 2

1 "Unterricht und Wertung" (GS II: 35–42).
2 *Stilübung* (GS II: 27) in German has a broader and a more narrow meaning; the broader would be an exercise in style, the more narrow one refers to the translation

of modern language texts into Latin or Greek in the course of studies in classical philology. See, for instance, Maurach (2006).
3 "Wertung ... um der Erkenntnis willen" (GS II: 39).
4 "Zwei Gedichte von Friedrich Hölderlin" (GS II: 105–26).
5 See Benjamin (1966: 133); Hellingrath was a member of the George circle; his study about the Pindar-translations was published in George's *Blätter für die Kunst*.
6 My translation: "Interesse für die Philosophie der Sprache" (GS VI: 226).
7 "Über Sprache überhaupt und über die Sprache des Menschen" (GS II: 140–57).
8 "Einheit dessen was ich denke" (GB 1: 436).
9 "Fragen nach dem Wesen von Erkenntnis, Recht, Kunst [hängen] zusammen mit der Frage nach dem Ursprung aller menschlichen Geistesäußerungen aus dem Wesen der Sprache" (GB 1: 436).
10 "in immanenter Beziehung auf das Judentum und mit Beziehung auf die ersten Kapitel der Genesis" (GB 1: 343).
11 "jede Äußerung menschlichen Geisteslebens kann als eine Art der Sprache aufgefaßt werden" (GS II: 140).
12 "eine Sprache der Technik, die nicht die Fachsprache der Techniker ist" (GS II: 140).
13 What I describe as fields, Benjamin refers to as *Gegenstände*, which may refer to both an object (thing, item) and a subject-matter (as in, a topic). In the English translation, the word "subject" is used.
14 *Geistige Inhalte* is variously translated as "mental contents" and "contents of the mind." *Geistig* also holds such connotations as immaterial or spiritual.
15 "Medien, die sich gleichsam nach ihrer Dichte, also graduell, unterscheiden" (GS II: 146).
16 "ununterbrochene Strom ... durch die ganze Natur vom niedersten Existierenden bis zum Menschen und vom Menschen zu Gott" (GS II: 157).
17 "die vollkommen erkennende" (GS II: 154).
18 "als unbenennbar, als namenlos außerhalb der Namensprache" (GS II: 154).
19 "das Wort soll etwas mitteilen (außer sich selbst)" (GS II: 153).
20 "kann nicht anders als etwas dazu tun, nämlich die Erkenntnis" (GS II: 151).
21 "wahre Natur der Romantik" (GB 2: 23).
22 Note that Benjamin uses the same word as in the Language-Essay: *Überführung*. In the translation of the Language-Essay, it was rendered as "removal"; in his dissertation it turned into "transposition."
23 "den ersten Niederschlag meiner sprachtheoretischen Reflexionen" (GS VI: 226).
24 In German, Benjamin states that translation is a *Form*, yet the English translations alternate between "form" and "mode."
25 "... die des Dichters ist naive, erste, anschauliche, die des Übersetzers abgeleitete, letzte, ideenhafte Intention" (GS IV: 16). A note on translation, or, more specifically,

on the translations of "Die Aufgabe des Übersetzers": as I outline in more detail later on in this book, the text has been published in four different English versions (five, if you count one additional, amended version of the first and most well-known translation). Harry Zohn's translation (1968b; amended in SW 1) has become, by far, the most-often cited. Throughout the book, however, I use all the different translations (1968c, 1997, 2009) in order to paint a broader picture of the "translational landscape" with regard to this text. Frequency of use does not correlate with quality: I have used Zohn's translation in cases when I explicitly discuss this particular translation and its reception, of course, and in every other case, I have decided entirely subjectively which translation fits best with what I am trying to say.

26 "ein Letztes, Entscheidendes" (GS IV: 19).
27 "Im Anfang war das Wort" (GS IV: 18).
28 See Chapter 5.
29 For more on that, see Chapter 7.
30 "ganz nah und doch unendlich fern" (GS IV: 19).
31 Aura as "the unique apparition of a distance, however near it may be" (SW 4: 255) "einmalige Erscheinung einer Ferne, so nah sie sein mag" (GS I: 440).
32 "Ankündigung der Zeitschrift: Angelus Novus" (GS II: 241–6).
33 The *heilend*, healing quality has been erased in other translations, which is why I have translated this part myself. English version: "a genre that has always had a beneficial effect on it in its periods of great crisis" (SW 1: 294). German version: "eine Form . . ., welche seit jeher heilsam seine [des deutschen Schrifttums] großen Krisen begleitete" (GS II: 243).
34 My translation, which is very literal, as the translation included in the *Selected Writings* is too liberal for my argument: "Where the latter is at a loss to discover a substance of its own on which it might feed, important works from other, related cultures offer themselves along with the challenge to abandon superannuated linguistic practices, while developing new ones" (SW 1: 294).
35 "als unersetzlicher und strenger Schulgang werdender Sprache selbst" (GS II: 243).
36 "Trauerspiel und Tragödie" (GS II: 133–7); "Die Bedeutung der Sprache in Trauerspiel und Tragödie" (GS II: 137–40).
37 "so eine Art zweites . . . Stadium der frühen Spracharbeit . . ., als Ideenlehre frisiert" (GB III: 14).
38 Referring to the fundamental role of translation in the Language-Essay, Wohlfarth states that there is nothing between heaven and earth that is not translation: "So gesehen gibt es nichts zwischen Himmel und Erde, was nicht Übersetzung wäre" (2001: 92).
39 "Erkenntniskritische Vorrede" (GS I: 207–38).

Chapter 3

1. For more information about the entire debacle, see Jennings and Eiland (2014: 224–6, 232–3).
2. "ein festes Gerüst meiner Arbeit. . . . Als solches kommt natürlich Übersetzen nicht in Frage" (GS VI: 358).
3. "so eingehenden Beschäftigung mit dem großen Meisterwerk wird mir im Laufe der Zeit sehr fühlbar werden" (1966: 405).
4. "Zum Bilde Prousts" (GS II: 310–24).
5. "so etwas wie innere Vergiftungserscheinungen" (Benjamin 1966: 431).
6. My translation: "ungeheuer absorbierenden, auf meine eigenen Schrift[en] intensiv influenzierende Natur" (Benjamin 1966: 480).
7. "unproduktive Beschäftigung mit einem Autor" (Benjamin 1966: 431).
8. "Zudem kann ich mir . . . ein festes Akkreditiv als Übersetzer versprechen, wie es etwa Stefan Zweig hat" (Benjamin 1966: 395).
9. "Hessel und ich mußten es sich gefallen lassen, von D. als Proust-Übersetzer vorgestellt zu werden," (GS IV: 576).
10. "Übersetzungen" (GS III: 40–1).
11. My translation; ". . . sehr weit . . ., um diese Dichtungen ins Deutsche einzubringen" (GS III: 40).
12. My translation; "im allerbeschränktesten Raume die Sicherheit und die Gelassenheit der Geste [bewahren]" (GS III: 40).
13. My translation; "wie die Höllenmaschine einen Palast" (GS III: 40).
14. My translation; "Material—vielmehr: sein Organ—ist neben seiner Muttersprache nicht sowohl der fremde Text als vielmehr dessen Sprache" (GS III: 40).
15. Humboldt includes a similar image in his book, *Über die Verschiedenheit des menschlichen Sprachbaus*, where he says that "language is the formative organ of thought" (My translation, 426). Benjamin knew this text. In a fragment discussed later in this chapter, "What can be said in favor of translation?", he places the reference: "Wilhelm von Humboldt: Verschiedenheit des Sprachbaus" (GS VI: 159).
16. My translation; "ehrfurcht- und liebevoll" (GS III: 40).
17. My translation; "in dem Medium einer seltenen vollkommenen Übersetzung" (GS III: 61). In the *Selected Writings*, it says: "through the medium of an unusually perfect translation" (SW 2: 47).
18. My translation; ". . . in der besten aller deutschen Republiken, dem alten Freistaat ihrer Übersetzungen" (GS III: 182).
19. "Ein grundsätzlicher Briefwechsel über die Kritik übersetzter Werke" (GS III: 119–22).
20. My translation; "Darin kann ich nicht eine loyale Art der Buchbesprechung erblicken" (GS III: 120).

21 My translation; "strengen wissenschaftlichen Gesetzen . . ., um selber außerwissenschaftichen Gebilden zu dienen" (GS III: 121).
22 In a footnote, Benjamin here refers to a particularly harsh review he wrote about a study by Eva Fiesel. In his review, Benjamin attacks Fiesel's work, which he miscategorizes as a dissertation, as a "typische Frauenarbeit" (GS III: 96), a typically female work, and then goes on to list its insufficiencies—one of which, he claims, is the fact that she only cites primary sources, no secondary literature. Apart from the blatant sexism, Jennings/Eiland argue that this uncharacteristically venomous review may have been due to the simple fact that Fiesel did not cite Benjamin's own dissertation, which had a similar orientation; what is more, they point out that the decision to only print the primary sources was the publisher; Jennings and Eiland (2014: 304–5, 702n64).
23 My translation; "geistige Teil einer Wissenschaft" (GS III: 121).
24 My translation; "nicht ihr Nervengeflecht, aber das System ihrer Gefäße" (GS III: 121).
25 My translation; "eine ausgeglichene, unproblematische Arbeit" (GS III: 121).
26 My translation; "als Wagnis, als gefährliches Kunststück" (GS III: 121).
27 "Symeon, der neue Theologe, Licht vom Licht" (GS III: 266).
28 My translation; "Verse . . . sind keine Informationen" (GS III: 65).
29 My translation; "tiefere Quellen des Vertrautseins" (GS III: 65).
30 My translation; "ein linguistischer Don Juan" (GS III: 66).
31 My translation; "ein Gedicht ist . . . vor allem Repräsentant" (GS III: 65).
32 My translation; "unbefugten Ausbeutung eines jungfräulichen Bestands" (GS III: 91).
33 "Literaturgeschichte und Literaturwissenschaft" (GS III: 283–90).
34 At the same time, he also planned to edit another journal, which was supposed to be entitled *Krise und Kritik*. See, "Memorandum zu der Zeitschrift *Krise und Kritik*" (GS VI: 619–21). He drew up the plans together with someone who had become one of his most important personal and intellectual relations at the time: Bertolt Brecht. Their relationship had started to develop in 1929 and it had grown ever since.
35 I re-translated the first part of this passage, because the standard translation does not retain the German text's linguistic imagery: "Their entire life and their effects should have the right to stand alongside the history of their composition. In other words, their fate, their reception by their contemporaries, their translations, their fame. For with this the work is transformed inwardly into a microcosm, or indeed a microeon" (SW 2: 464).

Chapter 4

1 "eine neue . . . Sprachtheorie" (Benjamin 1966: 563).
2 "Lehre vom Ähnlichen" (GS II: 201–10) and "Über das mimetische Vermögen" (GS II: 210–13).

3 "Urzeit der Menschheit" (GS II: 209).
4 "die Anweisung . . ., eine vorhandene Ähnlichkeit zu handhaben" (GS II: 206).
5 "Lesen an sich" (GS II: 209).
6 "Was nie geschrieben wurde lesen" (GS II: 213).
7 "Essenzen, flüchtigsten und feinsten Substanzen" (GS II: 209).
8 "liest den Gestirnstand von den Sternen am Himmel ab," "die Zukunft oder das Geschick heraus" (GS II: 209).
9 "Der Autor als Produzent" (GS II: 683–701).
10 For more on the relation between commentary and translation, see Primavesi.
11 "Impuls des Fälschers" (GS VI: 145).
12 "erfüllt von den Werken, die aufs neue in ihm lebendig wurden" (GS VI: 145).
13 "Der große Fälscher . . . zitiert ihr Urbild" (GS VI: 145).
14 "nahrhaft nur nicht eßbar. Essen nämlich heißt doch: sich einverleiben. Und einzuverleiben ist nur weniges was Hofmannsthal schrieb" (GS VI: 145).
15 "Paris, Hauptstadt des XIX. Jahrhunderts" (GS V: 45–59).
16 "Das Kunstwerk im Zeitalter seiner technischen Reproduzierbarkeit" (GS I: 471–508).
17 "Über den Begriff der Geschichte" (GS I: 691–704).
18 "La Traduction—Le Pour et le Contre" (GS VI: 157–60).
19 My translation: "Zwiegespräch über philosophische Probleme der Übersetzung" (GS VI: 729).
20 "Was spricht für Übersetzen" (GS VI: 159–60). There is no question-mark in German; literally: "What speaks for translating."
21 In the English version, the bouquinistes were replaced by the more "open-air bookstall" (SW 3: 249).
22 "die Stellen waren nicht da" (GS VI: 158).
23 This is my way of identifying this speaker; there are no names given in the text.
24 "als ich ihnen ins Gesicht sah, hatte ich das peinliche Gefühl, sie erkennen mich ebensowenig wie ich sie erkenne" (GS VI: 158).
25 The English translation of *befremdet* in the *Selected Writings* is "disconcerted" (SW 3: 249).
26 "Über einige Motive bei Baudelaire" (GS I: 605–53).
27 "Die Aura einer Erscheinung erfahren, heißt, sie mit dem Vermögen belehnen, den Blick aufzuschlagen" (GS I: 646–7).
28 "Der Horizont und die Welt um den übersetzten Text selbst war ausgewechselt und selbst französisch" (GS VI: 158).
29 ". . . Humboldt was convinced that everyone throughout his life was under the spell of his mother tongue. He thought that it was really [*this!*] language which thinks and sees for us" (SW 2: 249; my annotation); ". . . dass jeder zeit seines Lebens unterm Banne seiner Muttersprache stünde. Sie sei wirklich die Sprache, die für ihn denkt und sieht" [GS VI: 158]). The missing "this" is crucial: it is the mother tongue that thinks and sees for us, not "language as such."

30 "Kritik an der Unfertigkeit des deutschen Menschen" (GS VI: 158).
31 "im Kommentar Rechenschaft von sich selbst ablegt" (GS VI: 159).
32 "die Anwendung dieser Technik auf poetische Texte [erscheint mir] überaus problematisch" (GS VI: 159).
33 "Fortschritte der Wissenschaft im internationalen Maßstab" (GS VI: 159).
34 "Das Lateinische, Leibnizsche Universalsprache" (GS VI: 159).
35 "Grenze: Übersetzungsunbedürftigkeit der Musik" (GS VI: 159).
36 "letzte Sprache aller Menschen nach dem Turmbau" (GS I: 388).
37 "Lyrik: der Musik am nächsten—größte Übersetzungsschwierigkeiten" (GS VI: 159).
38 "Grenze der Übersetzung in der Prosa" (GS VI: 159).
39 "Wert schlechter Übersetzungen: produktive Mißverständnisse" (GS VI: 159).
40 "Man spricht Französisch in allen Sprachen" (GS VI: 160). I did not find any reference to this *bon mot* elsewhere.
41 "der Sinn der Übersetzung ist überhaupt: die fremde Sprache in der eignen zu repräsentieren" (GS VI: 160).
42 My translation; "Schwierigkeiten, die sich aus der Zusammenarbeit mit Dr. B[enjamin] ergaben" (GS I: 989).
43 My translation; "bringt nicht nur alle Bedingungen von der sprachlichen Seite sondern auch wichtige wissenschaftliche Voraussetzungen" (GS I: 986).
44 My translation; "darüber wird die Aufnahme durch französische Leser entscheiden" (GS I: 989).
45 My translation; "den Sinn der Vorlage durchgehend richtig wiedergibt" (GS I: 989).
46 My translation; "im Tempo einer üblichen Übersetzung" (GS I: 989).
47 My translation; "nicht nur fruchtbar sondern auch angenehm" (GS I: 989).
48 My translation; "die Spuren der Übersetzungsarbeit" (Benjamin 1966: 708–9).
49 "dem deutschen Text gegenüber eine Distanz . . ., die ich gewöhnlich nur in längeren Fristen gewinne" (GS I: 990).
50 "die menschenfresserische Urbanität, eine Umsicht und Behutsamkeit in der Destruktion" (GS I: 991).
51 "Befreiung vom Vorurteil der eignen Sprache (Der Sprung über die eigne Sprache)" (GS IV: 159).

Chapter 5

1 Petra Hardt at the Walter Benjamin Archive in Berlin answered to my inquiry that the Translator-Essay has been translated into Chinese, Dutch, English, French, Greek, Icelandic, Italian, Japanese, Catalonian, Korean, Marathi, Norwegian,

Persian, Polish, Portuguese, Russian, Spanish, Turkish, and Ukrainian (in a phone call in 2016).
2 This sentence is part of a letter to Scholem that Benjamin wrote in French: "théâtre de tous mes combats et de toutes mes idées" (1966: 506).
3 The fragments that Agamben found in 1981 made their way into the Frankfurt-Archives in 1997. A selection of excerpts has been published in GS VII, but they have not yet been published in their entirety (Schmider and Werner 2011: 567–9).
4 "Man wird mir nicht nachsagen können, daß ichs mir leicht gemacht hätte" (GB 3: 368).
5 They will, however, probably be part of the new historical-critical collection of *Werke und Nachlass*.
6 "From the first to the last word, I will have to write it in Paris" (My translation.) "Schreiben kann ich sie ... vom ersten bis zum letzten Wort nur in Paris" (GB 5: 99).
7 Benjamin was so taken with Aragon's text that he began translating parts of *Le Paysan* into German.
8 "Herzklopfen dann so stark wurde, dass ich das Buch aus der Hand legen mußte" (GB 5: 87).
9 "Paris, die Hauptstadt des XIX Jahrhunderts" (GS V: 45–59).
10 "eine Welt im kleinen" (GS V: 45).
11 "raumgewordene Vergangenheit" (GS V: 1041).
12 Which, I think, is questionable, as he supposedly chose to replace one of the poems of the second edition with one of the third. He replaced the poem "A une mendiante rousse," which he never seems to have translated, with "La Lune offensée," which was added to the third edition of *Les Fleurs du Mal* in 1868, only after Baudelaire's death, while all the other poems that Benjamin translated were based on the 1861 second edition. This replacement is not marked in the editor's notes (see Reuß 2016: 9n22).
13 I have translated this part very literally, as I consider at least part of the English translation to be misleading (as so often, the German *nicht sowohl/als auch*-construction is mistaken and translated as "not just/but also," instead of "neither/nor"): "By this, I do not mean only the verse form of the translation itself but also that meter had not posed itself as a problem in the same sense as the literalism of the translation did. My introduction attests to this. ... I am convinced that ultimately only by giving more thought to the meter would another translation of the Flowers of Evil approximate Baudelaire's style more closely than mine does" (Jacobson 1994: 229–30).
14 Interestingly, these three words in the three languages are placed in three different arrangements.
15 It expresses "intentional impossibility, ingenious absurdity, inscrutable irony with regard to all rationality" (my translation; in German: "absichtsvolle Unmöglichkeit, ausgeklügelte Absurdität, abgründige Ironie in bezug auf alle Rationalität" [56–7]).

16 "bodenlose Sprachtiefen" (GS IV:21). As Rainer Nägele argues, the "stairwayed" verticality of the *Arkaden*-image from "Rêve Parisien" breaks with the primacy of syntactic linearity, which aims at preserving a linear sense (represented, in the Translator-Essay, by the image of the wall). In doing so, the Babel of arcades hints, according to Nägele, at the idea of *Sinnstufen*, layers (or steps) of sense pursued in allegorical interpretation; walking these steps represents an act of intermittent, momentous suspension, and precarious fixation of sense—an image that may be constellated with the *lack* of suspension expressed in Benjamin's description of Hölderlin's translations, in which sense is thrown from one step to the next, from cliff to cliff, and thus risks plunging into emptiness (Hart-Nibbrig 2001: 31).
17 Published 1925 in the *Frankfurter Zeitung* under both names, Asja Lacis and Walter Benjamin.
18 "alle Übersetzung nur eine irgendwie vorläufige Art ist, sich mit der Fremdheit der Sprachen auseinanderzusetzen" (GS IV: 14).
19 The English translation corrects incoherence in the German text, which Benjamin later corrects himself, when he transfers the fragment to convolute N (GS V: 571).
20 In the rest of the *Passagenarbeit*, there is only one more return to the *Arkade*, namely, in a description of color lithographs, commissioned by the British king and made by Joseph Nash, depicting the crystal palace at the world fair in London, 1851. Once again, the *Arkade* meets the elements that come to define the *Passage*: glass and iron. But, here, the *Arkade* is explicitly linked with capitalist modernity and juxtaposed with the archaic or ancient, to which it previously alluded. The *Arkaden* (pl.) function as a storehouse, while bronze, marble, and fountain create a fairytale-like atmosphere. "The first world exhibition and the first monumental structure in glass and iron! From these watercolors, one sees with amazement how the exhibitors took pains to decorate the colossal interior in an oriental-fairy-tale style, and how—alongside the assortment of goods that filled the arcaded walks—bronze monuments, marble statues, and bubbling fountains populated the giant halls" (Eiland and McLaughlin 1999: 176–7). Apart from that, the *Arkade* only turns up in quotations, in which they are described as a sheltered public space; a space where the most marginal figures of society, like the homeless and prostitutes, find shelter from the weather and city-related inconveniences like carriages, esp. in two quotes from Friedrich Engels, one from *Die Lage der arbeitenden Klasse in England* (1845; Benjamin quotes from the second edition, published in 1848); the other from a brief review of two slanderous pamphlets by two French policemen, which Engels wrote together with Marx under the title *Besprechung von Chenu* (1850; he quotes from the 1886 version in *Die Neue Zeit*); also, in a quotation taken from an 1893 article C. Hugo wrote for *Die Neue Zeit*, "Der Sozialismus in Frankreich während der großen Revolution"; and, eventually, in the quotation from J. Huizinga's 1928 *Herbst des Mittelalters*. Here, an added utopian function of the *Arkade* comes up: Hugo claims that the *Arkaden* described

by the eighteenth-century François Boissel anticipate the later utopian idea of Bellamy's canopies that would come out of buildings at the first sign of rain; and the arcades turn up in the description of the architecture in Ledoux' utopian city Chaux.

21 In its preface, Amit Chaudhuri, Indian author and scholar of literary studies, claims that he always felt a sense of familiarity with Benjamin when looking at pictures of him, because he looked so conversantly Indian.

22 Derrida himself worked with the translation by Maurice de Gandillac.

23 This is something Niranjana shares with Dipesh Chakrabarty, who, in his 2000 study *Provincializing Europe*, outlines the concept of "cross-categorical translation" as a response to this premise (83–6).

24 Niranjana primarily refers the complicity of missionaries and colonialism, and her prime example of a translation theorist that largely remains unreflective with regard to his position in this unequal set of power relations is Eugene Nida (62–3).

25 Here, she mainly criticizes Toury. She claims that by focusing on the life of the translation in the target culture, and neglecting the influence it has on the "original," he refutes the historicity of the "original" (59–60).

26 Niranjana thus paints a dire picture of the discipline, based on a selective sample of translation studies approaches. While translation studies was certainly in its very early stages of development at the time when Niranjana wrote her book, there were many simultaneous movements aiming to reform the discipline from within, as I outlined in the introduction.

27 For her explanation as to why she uses the term "to trope," see Niranjana (1992: 5).

28 "eine mit Jetztzeit geladene Vergangenheit . . . aus dem Kontinuum der Geschichte [herausgesprengt wird]" (GS I: 701).

29 This is the title of Chow's Chapter 2.4.

Chapter 6

1 "Zwar [geht die Übersetzung] nicht aus seinem Leben [des Originals, B.H.] so sehr [hervor] denn aus seinem 'Überleben'" (GS: IV 10).

2 He switches to a gerund construction twice, and "in ihrem *Fortleben*" turns into "in continuing to exist."

3 The *Wortauskunftssystem zur deutschen Sprache in Geschichte und Gegenwart (DWDS)*, that is, a corpora-based platform that provides statistical data regarding word use and the development of meaning within the German language from 1600 to the present, refutes this claim. A search of the abovementioned options illustrates that, at the time when Benjamin wrote his essay (1921), *Fortleben* is actually *more*

frequently used than *Weiterleben* or *Überleben*, especially if the search is limited exclusively to scholarly publications.
4 I found *Fortleben* to occur more than thirty times in the digitized version of Benjamin's *Gesammelte Werke*; *Überleben* turns up only twice (in its nominal form), and *Weiterleben* only once (as *Weiter-Leben*).
5 My translation; "so bedeutungslos, wie die Beziehung irgend eines pragmatisch-historischen Zeugnisses (Inschrift) auf die Person seines Urhebers" (GS VI: 95)
6 My translation; "Geschichte des Fortlebens eines Menschen und eben, wie in das Leben das Fortleben mit seiner eignen Geschichte hereinragt, läßt sich am Briefwechsel studieren" (GS VI: 95).
7 My translation; "Sie leben in einem andern Rhythmus als zur Zeit, da die Empfänger lebten, und auch sonst verändern sie sich" (GS VI: 95).
8 "ein natürlicher . . . genauer ein Zusammenhang des Lebens" (GS IV: 10).
9 "das Stadium ihres *Fortlebens*" (GS IV: 11).
10 "völlig unmetaphorische Sachlichkeit" (GS IV: 11).
11 "alles natürliche Leben aus dem umfassenderen der Geschichte zu verstehen" (GS IV: 11).
12 "Deszendenz aus den Quellen, ihre Gestaltung im Zeitalter des Künstlers und die Periode ihres grundsätzlich ewigen Fortlebens bei den nachfolgenden Generationen" (GS IV: 11).
13 "stets erneute späteste und umfassendste Entfaltung" (GS IV: 11).
14 "die Erkenntniskritik die Unmöglichkeit einer Abbildtheorie zu erweisen hat" (GS IV: 12).
15 "geringeres Moment im Fortleben der Werke" (GS IV: 15).
16 "die antike Götterwelt [hätte] aussterben müssen und gerade die Allegorie hat sie gerettet" (GS I: 397).
17 "die allegorische Verwandlung des Pantheons in eine Welt magischer Begriffskreaturen" (GS I: 399).
18 "Lehre von dem Fortleben der Werke" (GS VI: 174).
19 "dieses Fortleben den Gebietscharakter 'Kunst' als einen Schein entlarvt" (GS VI: 174).
20 "die mehr als Vermittlungen sind" (GS IV: 11).
21 "im Idealfalle vergißt . . . zu urteilen" (GS VI: 172).
22 "objektive Wahrheit als Gegenstück dieser subjektiven Auffassung" (GS VI: 172).
23 "heben als Gegensätze in einer Kritik sich auf, die zum einzigen Medium das Leben, Fortleben der Werke hat," (GS VI: 172).
24 "Grundwissenschaft der Literaturgeschichte" (GS VI: 173–4).
25 "nach allen Seiten und Zusammenhängen greifbar deutlich zu machen" (GS IV: 942).
26 My translation; "Wieland wird nicht mehr gelesen" (GS II: 395).
27 "wenn man von [ihrem] Nachleben abstrahiert" (GS VI: 321).

28 My translation; "Gegen die Theorie des 'verkannten Genies'" (GS VI: 136–7).
29 My translation; "Ein Genius mag unbeachtet gelebt haben und gestorben sein; selten wird er von seinesgleichen unter den Zeitgenossen verkannt worden sein" (GS VI: 136).
30 My translation; "ein Werk ist nicht berühmt, weil es groß ist—es ist groß, weil es berühmt ist" (GS VI: 136).
31 "dieses letzte heißt, wo es zutage tritt, Ruhm" (GS IV: 11).
32 In the essay, Derrida comments on the adverbial "on" of "living on," in which all the ambiguity seems to come together: "Forever unable to saturate a context, what reading will ever master the 'on' of living on? For we have not exhausted its ambiguity: each of the meanings we have listed above can be divided further (e.g., living on can mean a reprieve or an afterlife, 'life after life,' or life after death, more life or more than life, and better; the state of suspension in which it's over—and over again . . .)" (1979: 78).
33 Within the text, Derrida even occasionally wonders how some of his phrases will be translated, for example, "The event—which 'survient' ['takes place,' 'occurs'; lit. 'comes on']—how will they translate this word" (1979: 136)?
34 Bhabha quotes a passage from the Translator-Essay (1994: 326) that Benjamin takes from Rudolf Pannwitz, which has become emblematic for a German Romantic translation preference for foreignizing approaches, even though Pannwitz was a German writer and philosopher contemporary to Benjamin.
35 It is worth noting that Maitland tends to talk about "appropriation" rather than "incorporation" in her theorization, except when it comes to listing the five dimensions of translation.
36 "räumlich und menschlich" (GS I: 479).

Chapter 7

1 Note that in Zohn's version, that which is hidden in languages, their *Verborgenes*, is defined as a hidden *meaning*. This is not the case in the German version, and neither in Rendall's.
2 "verleugnet nicht ihre Richtung auf ein letztes, endgültiges und entscheidendes Stadium aller Sprachfügung" (GS IV: 14).
3 "höheren und reineren Luftkreis der Sprache" (GS IV: 14).
4 "the predestined, hitherto inaccessible realm of reconciliation and fulfillment of languages" (1968b: 75). Zohn's version here includes a "hitherto," which is not there in the German or the other English versions. This realm is simply *versagt*, denied: "den vorbestimmten, versagten Versöhnungs- und Erfüllungsbereich der Sprachen" (GS IV: 15).

5 Zohn: "in its entirety" (1968b: 75).
6 Zohn: "beyond transmittal of subject matter" (1968b: 75).
7 Zohn: "nucleus" (1968b: 75).
8 All translators opt for the word "content" to translate *Gehalt*. With regard to Zohn, however, it is interesting to note that he variously translates *Sinn* as "meaning," "sense," or "content"—within the same paragraph. This makes it particularly difficult to grasp the subtle distinction between *Sinn* and *Gehalt*, for instance, which both happen to be rendered, on different occasions, as "content." Furthermore, *Sinn* is not the only term translated as "meaning"; so is *Bedeutung*. Thus, many of Benjamin's subtle arguments, by means of which he attempts to go beyond simplistic binaries, particularly of form and content, are made in fact to reinforce them in the English version, and at times rather confusingly so. *Bedeutung*, in the context of the Translator-Essay, denotes an intrinsic, structural relevance or significance; the term almost exclusively turns up in relation to translatability. In the beginning, for instance, Benjamin argues that the *demand* for translation is a crucial part of this form's *Bedeutung*, its "significance" (SW 1: 254).
9 Only Harry Zohn and J. A. Underwood use the word that has become so well known in Benjamin's English-language reception: the "royal robe" (1968b: 75).
10 Zohn: "overpowering and alien" (1968b: 75).
11 "Mag man nämlich an Mitteilung aus ihr entnehmen, soviel man kann und dies übersetzen, so bleibt dennoch dasjenige unberührbar zurück, worauf die Arbeit des wahren Übersetzers sich richtete" (GS IV: 15). To stress the point I am making, here, Rendall's translation works best. However, there is a crucial temporal difference between the German and the English versions: Benjamin speaks in the past tense ("sich richtete"), while Rendall remains in the present tense ("are directed"). I have adapted his translation accordingly, in brackets.
12 "Übersetzung ist eine Form" (GS IV: 9). The translators do not agree on this one either. Rendall (1997) and Zohn (1968b) speak of translation as a mode; Hynd/Valk (1968c), Underwood (2009) and Zohn (1996) consider it to be a form.
13 "Denn in ihm [Original, B.H.] liegt deren [Übersetzung, B.H.] Gesetz als in dessen [Original, B.H.] Übersetzbarkeit beschlossen" (GS IV: 9).
14 "Bereich . . ., in dem ihr [der Forderung, B.H.] entsprochen wäre: auf ein Gedenken Gottes" (GS IV: 10).
15 Neither version of Zohn's translation (1968/1996) sticks with the imagery that Benjamin develops in this paragraph. Instead of the "heaviness" of sense, Zohn decides to translate Schwere as "difficulty" (SW 1: 262).
16 "In ihnen ist die Harmonie der Sprachen so tief, daß der Sinn nur noch wie eine Äolsharfe vom Winde von der Sprache berührt wird" (GS IV: 21).
17 The title depicts a slip of the tongue in Berlin dialect. It may be translated into English as "Why are you laughing, I'm laughing!?"—instead of "Why are you

laughing, I'm asking!?" In their rage, the person misspoke. Benjamin had witnessed this *Zufallsbildung*, this coincidental creation, for himself, and describes its context and physicality in detail.

18 "Durchdringung des Zartesten mit dem Rohen," "stahlharte Sachlichkeit durch die Blume" (GS IV: 539). In translating the latter, I have tried to retain the contrast between steel and flowers; "durch die Blume" is a German idiom for "in a roundabout way," or "indirectly," usually in a sugarcoating way.

19 "Mimik und Physiognomik, . . . die unübersetzbaren Gesten" (GS IV: 540).

20 "jenseits der artikulierten Sprache" (GS IV: 540).

21 "Die unübersetzbare Literatur der Flanerie Paris 'rue par rue maison par maison'" (GS V: 1209).

22 According to Young, Bhabha was well aware of the cultural anthropological legacy of the term, cultural translation. He knew of Talal Asad's contributions and even met him at a conference in 1984, where Asad presented an earlier version of his paper on cultural translation. Bhabha, then, decided to revive the concept at a time when it was pronounced dead in cultural anthropology: while Asad argued that cultural translation was an exertion of power by the ethnographer that left nothing of "translated culture's" particularity, Bhabha took up the concept and re-thought it from the perspective of minority discourse (Young 2017: 190, 195n6).

23 This quote also holds a shift in translation, and its provenance is unclear to me. Bhabha does not tell us where he cites it from. In Benjamin's *Selected Writings*, it says: "Translation passes through continua of transformation, not abstract areas of identity and similarity" (SW 1: 70). Bhabha, however, de-spatializes the image, talking not about abstract areas, *Bezirke*, but about "abstract ideas of identity and similarity" (1994: 212).

24 According to Bhabha, the quote about the impossibility of "full" translation is also taken from Benjamin's Translator-Essay. This may be one of the most weirdly mysterious "references" I have encountered. Bhabha's footnote says that the quote is from Zohn's 1968 translation, same page as the previous one. Yet the only thing that reads similar is Zohn's description of "that element in a translation which goes beyond transmittal of subject matter" (1968b: 75). And because only said element moves into this higher realm of language, "the transfer can never be total" (75), says Zohn. Bhabha contracts this translation and switches it around, adding the qualifier "full" here, in order to talk about the dystopia/utopia of full translation. (What is more, I have not found the word "transmissal" in common dictionaries. It seems to me to be an amalgamation of "transmittal" and "transmission.")

25 Bhabha, once again, assumes the premise of Zohn's translation, and argues that the two refer to "the same object" (227); Zohn's translation: "The words *Brot* and *pain* 'intend' the same object, . . . the two words mean the very same thing" (1968b: 74). In the German version, Benjamin shows much less resolve: in *Brot* and *pain*, Benjamin says, *das Gemeinte* is the same; nowhere, however, does he say that *das*

Gemeinte refers to an object. In each language, the *Gemeinte*, he later says, is always in flux, and never stable (GS IV: 14).

26 This is Bhabha's phrase; Zohn: "modes of intention" (1968b: 74), Benjamin: *Arten des Meinens* (GS IV: 14).

27 The Zohn-translation allows Bhabha to equate "subject matter" with "content"; two notions that are not present in the German text: there is only *Vermittlung* and *Gehalt*, which is neither "subject matter," nor "content" (rather, something more in the direction of "mediation" and "substance").

28 Bhabha derives the concept of supplementarity from Derrida: it has a presenting function, cumulative and accumulative; at the same time, it is an adjunct, something "in-the-place-of," marking the absence of something else: "the image is presence and proxy" (1994: 154).

29 This article is based on a lecture Wagner gave at a conference about Bhabha's cultural theory, entitled *Dritte Räume. Homi K. Bhabhas Kulturtheorie. Anwendung Kritik Reflexion*, i.e., *Third Spaces. Homi K. Bhabha's Cultural Theory. Application Criticism Reflection*. The text is written in German and has, as far as I know, not been translated. I have translated the title and the following quotations for myself.

30 My translation; in German: "manche Begriffe einen Karriereweg beschreiten, der sich mit den Stationen Emergenz, hegemoniale Präsenz und anschließender inflationärer Entwertung beschreiben lässt" (2009: 1).

31 My translation; in German "Übersetzung im wortwörtlichen Sinn" (2009: 1).

32 My translation; in German: "Vorstellungsinhalten, Werten, Denkmustern, Verhaltensmustern und Praktiken eines kulturellen Kontexts in einen anderen" (2009: 1).

33 My translation; in German: "einen Text aus einer natürlichen Sprache in eine andere zu gießen" (2009: 1).

34 My translation; in German: "Aspekt der Sprache spricht, der sich der Übersetzung entzieht, bzw., vor Benjamins Prämissen, erst in messianischer Perspektive übersetzbar sein wird" (2009: 5).

35 My translation; in German: "metaphorisch wendet"; "a struggle between one verbatim and two metaphorical ways of using the term" (2009: 5).

36 My translation; in German: "fruchtbarsten Bestimmung dessen, was kulturelle Übersetzung sein kann" (2009: 5).

37 My translation; in German: "wie Benjamin festgehalten, sich prinzipiell nicht restlos übersetzen lassen" (2009: 6).

38 My translation; in German: "ist die inflationäre Entwertung mancher seiner Begriffe dem zuzuschreiben, was man auf Französisch so schön mit 'le flou théorique' bezeichnet, oder ist sie doch vielmehr den Rezipienten anzulasten" (2009: 2)?

39 The German version is the one that Birgit Wagner incorporates in her texts; she has translated it for herself (2009: 7). The French version is the one written by Patrick

Chamoiseau, and I translated the English version from the French and the German one.
40 My translation; in German: "einen tiefen Respekt vor der Differenz, der auf der Anerkennung der und der Liebe zu der Verschiedenheit der Sprachen beruht. Hybridität ist aus dieser Sicht nicht ein Wert an sich, sondern ein Mehr-Wert, der bestehende Werte hervortreten lässt" (2009: 8).
41 "[entzündet sich] am ewigen Fortleben der Werke und am unendlichen Aufleben der Sprachen . . . , immer von neuem die Probe auf jenes heilige Wachstum der Sprachen zu machen" (GS IV: 14).
42 "Wie die Tangente den Kreis flüchtig und nur in einem Punkte berührt, . . . so berührt die Über-setzung flüchtig und nur in dem unendlich kleinen Punkt des Sinnes das Original" (GS IV: 19–20).
43 "in flüchtigster Berührung seines Sinnes" (GS IV: 20).
44 "Die Interlinearversion des heiligen Textes ist das Urbild oder Ideal aller Übersetzung" (GS IV: 21). For Derrida, this turns into the "intra-lingual version" (1985b: 130, 150) for some reason, which he reads as the sacred text containing within itself its virtual translation.

Conclusion

1 "Aber sind wir nicht auf apokryphe Wirksamkeit eingerichtet" (GB 4: 372–3)? Benjamin comments on Adorno relating, in the last letter, a futile attempt at having his own compositions published.
2 E.g., Guest (2001), Kilgour (1990), Barker, Hulme, and Iversen (1998); with an explicit focus on translation: Gentzler (2008), Vieira (1994, 1999), Guldin (2008); Pym (2010).
3 In de Campos' Portuguese version, he quotes Benjamin's German text and then provides his own translation. The passage I quote from the English version is probably María Tai Wolff's translation of Benjamin; the published 1979 translation by Jephcott/Shorter says: "Genuine polemics approach a book as lovingly as a cannibal spices a baby" (2021: 69). German: "Echte Polemik nimmt ein Buch sich so liebevoll vor, wie ein Kannibale sich einen Säugling zurüstet" (GS IV: 108).
4 My translation; German version: "Der Kannibale . . . ist genau betrachtet keine Gestalt, die einfach da ist. Vielmehr entsteht der Kannibale in dem Moment, in dem europäische Entdecker bzw. Eroberer und indigene Bevölkerung der 'Neuen Welt' aufeinandertreffen" (Hein 2014: 88).
5 Hein underscores her argument regarding the tight interlocking of colonialism and "Othering via cannibalism" with reference to an official political-economic decree from the sixteenth century: the Spanish queen Isabel de Castilla banned the

enslavement of "recently discovered" people—except if they were cannibals, "una gente que se dice Canibales" (2014: 89).

6 "I think there is more barbarity in eating a man alive than in eating him dead; and tearing by tortures and the rack a body still full of feeling, in roasting a man bit by bit, in having him bitten and mangled by dogs and swine (as we have not only to read but seen within fresh memory, not among ancient enemies, but among neighbors and fellow citizens, and what is worse, on the pretext of piety and religion), than in roasting and eating him after he is dead" (1958: 155).

7 For more, see Schulze (2015: 68f).

8 He consciously refrains from using the term "cannibalism," though (Hein 2014: 91).

9 "Impuls des Fälschers" (GS VI: 145).

10 "erfüllt von den Werken, die aufs neue in ihm lebendig wurden" (GS VI: 145).

11 "Der große Fälscher . . . zitiert ihr Urbild" (GS VI: 145).

12 My translation; again, I have provided a more literal translation here. In the *Selected Writings*, Rodney Livingston says: "He had an infallible instinct for the topical relevance of even the remotest cultural goods" (SW 2: 422). In German: "Er hatte einen untrüglichen Instinkt für die Aktualitäten, die am Entlegensten auftreten" (GS VI: 146).

13 My translation; "Erkenntnis des Vergangenen und Selbstdarstellung der erkennenden Gegenwart" (1985: 182).

14 *Fortleben* "unmasks the terrain of 'art' as semblance" (SW 2: 416), says Benjamin, or in German: it "[entlarvt] den Gebietscharakter 'Kunst' als einen Schein" (GS VI: 174). In the English translation, however, "terrain" only translates the spatial connotation of a more complex image. While *Gebiet* may be rendered as terrain, area, territory, region, the German version does not contain the word "*Gebiet*," but *Gebietscharakter*, which may be read in the sense of *gebietender Charakter*, that is, "commanding character."

15 "Der Satiriker ist die Figur, unter welcher der Menschenfresser von der Zivilisation rezipiert wurde" (GS II: 355).

16 Benjamin promptly reveals the reference frame into which he places the anthropophagic metaphor: in the following sentence, he refers to Swift's "A Modest Proposal," and thus to the tradition of using anthropophagic figures in satirist critiques of capitalism: "His recollection of his origin is not without filial piety, so that the proposal to eat people has become an essential constituent of his inspiration, from Jonathan Swift's pertinent project concerning the use of the children of the less wealthy classes, to Léon Bloy's suggestion that landlords of insolvent lodgers be conceded a right to the sale of the lodgers' flesh" (SW 2: 448). In German: "Nicht ohne Pietät erinnert er [der Satiriker, Anm. B. H.] sich seines Ursprungs und darum ist der Vorschlag, Menschen zu fressen, in den eisernen Bestand seiner Anregungen übergegangen, von Swifts einschlägigem Projekt

betreffend die Verwendung der Kinder in minderbemittelten Volksklassen bis zu Léon Bloys Vorschlag, Hauswirten insolventen Mietern gegenüber ein Recht auf die Verwertung ihres Fleisches einzuräumen" (GS II: 355).

17 "Experience and Poverty," "Erfahrung und Armut": "neuen, positiven Begriff[s] des Barbarentums" (GS II: 215).
18 My translation; "eine andere Dialektik der Aufklärung in drei Aufzügen" (Fürnkäs 1988: 263).
19 "Eduard Fuchs, der Sammler und der Historiker" (GS II: 465–506).
20 "Blick auf die verachteten, apokryphen Dinge ... seine eigentliche Stärke aus[macht]" (GS II: 505).
21 "unvorhergesehene[r] Konstellationen" (GS IV: 309).
22 Referring to the fundamental role of translation in the Language-Essay, Wohlfarth states that there is nothing between heaven and earth that is not translation: "So gesehen gibt es nichts zwischen Himmel und Erde, was nicht Übersetzung wäre" (2001: 92).
23 "Darum ist Übersetzung ... gar kein adäquater Begriff" (GS VI: 145).

References

Works by Walter Benjamin

Abbreviations (Ger./Eng.):

GS + vol.: page no.: Benjamin, W. (1972–1999), *Gesammelte Schriften*, eds. R. Tiedemann and H. Schweppenhäuser, 7 vols., II supplements, Frankfurt a.M.: Suhrkamp.

GB + vol.: page no.: Benjamin, W. (1995–2000), *Gesammelte Briefe*, eds. C. Gödde and H. Lonitz, 6 vols., Frankfurt a.M.: Suhrkamp.

SW + vol.: page no.: Benjamin, W. (1996–2003), *Selected Writings*, eds. M. Jennings and M. Bullock, 4 vols., Cambridge, MA: Harvard University Press.

Other German editions:

Benjamin, W. (1966), *Briefe*, eds. G. Scholem and T. W. Adorno, Frankfurt a.M.: Suhrkamp.

Other English editions:

Benjamin, W. (1968a), *Illuminations*, ed. H. Arendt, trans. H. Zohn, New York: Harcourt Brace.

Benjamin, W. (1977), *The Origin of the German Tragic Drama*, trans. P. Osborne, London and New York: New Left Books.

Benjamin, W. (1978), *Reflections: Essays, Aphorisms, Autobiographical Writings*, ed. P. Demetz, trans. E. Jephcott, New York: Harcourt Brace.

Benjamin, W. (1979), *One-Way Street and Other Writings*, trans. E. Jephcott and K. Shorter, London and New York: New Left Books.

Benjamin, W., ed. (1986), *Moscow Diary*, ed. G. Smith, trans. R. Sieburth, Cambridge, MA: Harvard University Press.

Benjamin, W. (1994), *The Correspondence of Walter Benjamin, 1910–1940*, ed. T. W. Adorno and G. Scholem, trans. M. R. Jacobson and E. M. Jacobson, Chicago: University of Chicago Press.

Benjamin, W. (1999a), *The Arcades Project*, trans. H. Eiland and K. McLaughlin, Cambridge, MA: Belknap Press of Harvard University Press.

Benjamin, W. and T. W. Adorno (1999b), *The Complete Correspondence 1928–1940*, ed. H. Lonitz, trans. N. Walker, Cambridge: Polity Press.

Benjamin, W. (2011), *Early Writings, 1910–1917*, ed. and trans. H. Eiland, Cambridge, MA: Belknap Press of Harvard University Press.

Five Translations of "Die Aufgabe des Übersetzers":

Benjamin, W. (1968b), "The Task of the Translator," trans. H. Zohn, in H. Arendt (ed.), *Illuminations. Essays and Reflections*, 69–82, New York: Harcourt Brace.

Benjamin, W. (1968c), "The Task of the Translator," trans. J. Hynd and E. M. Valk, *Delos*, 2: 76–99. Reprinted in Weissbort, D. and A. Eysteinsson, eds. (2006), *Translation – Theory and Practice: A Historical Reader*, 298–307, London: Oxford University Press.

Benjamin, W. (1996), "The Task of the Translator," trans. H. Zohn (emendated version of the 1968 translation), in M. Jennings and M. Bullock (eds.), *Selected Writings*, 253–63, Cambridge, MA: Harvard University Press.

Benjamin, W. (1997), "The Translator's Task," trans. S. Rendall, *TTR – Traduction, Terminologie, Rédaction*, 10 (2): 151–65.

Benjamin, W. (2009), "The Task of the Translator," trans. J. A. Underwood, in *One-way Street and Other Writings*, 29–45, London: Penguin Books.

Secondary Literature

Abel, J. (2014), *Walter Benjamins Übersetzungsästhetik: "Die Aufgabe Des Übersetzers" im Kontext von Benjamins Frühwerk und seiner Zeit*, Berlin: Aisthesis-Verlag.

Adorno, T. W. (1955), "Charakteristik Walter Benjamins," in *Prismen. Kulturkritik und Gesellschaft*, 232–47, Frankfurt a.M.: Suhrkamp.

Agamben, G. (1982), "Un importante ritrovamento di manoscritti di Walter Benjamin," *AutAut*, 189/190: 4–6.

Appadurai, A. (1996), *Modernity at Large. Cultural Dimensions of Globalization*, Minneapolis: University of Minnesota Press.

Asad, T. (1986), "The Concept of Cultural Translation in British Social Anthropology," in J. Clifford and G. E. Marcus (eds.), *Writing Culture: The Poetics Politics of Ethnography*, 141–64, Berkeley: University of California Press.

Ashcroft, B., G. Griffiths, and H. Tiffin, eds. (1998), *Key Concepts in Post-Colonial Studies*, London: Routledge.

Bachmann-Medick, D. (2006), *Cultural Turns. Neuorientierungen in den Kulturwissenschaften*, Hamburg: Rowohlt.

Bachmann-Medick, D. (2012a), "Culture as Text: Reading and Interpreting Cultures," in B. Neumann and A. Nünning (eds.), *Travelling Concepts for the Study of Culture*, 99–118, Berlin: De Gruyter.

Bachmann-Medick, D. (2012b), "Translation – A Concept and Model for the Study of Culture," in B. Neumann and A. Nünning (eds.), *Travelling Concepts for the Study of Culture*, 23–44, Berlin: De Gruyter.

Baer, B. J. (2020), "From Cultural Translation to Untranslatability: Theorizing Translation outside Translation Studies," *Alif: Journal of Comparative Poetics*, 40: 139–63.

Barck, K. (2012), "Le baroque de la banalité. Essai sur la retraduction," in J.-F. Vallée, J. Klucinskas and G. Dupuis (eds.), *Transmédiations. Traversées culturelles de la modernité tardive. Mélanges offerts à Walter Moser*, 119–32, Montréal: Les Presses de l'Université de Montréal.

Barker, F., P. Hulme, and M. Iversen, eds. (1998), *Cannibalism and the Colonial World*, Cambridge: Cambridge University Press.

Barnard, A. and J. Spencer, eds. (1996), *Encyclopedia of Social and Cultural Anthropology*, London and New York: Routledge.

Barth, F., et al., eds. (2005), *One Discipline, Four Ways: British, German, French, and American Anthropology*, Chicago: University of Chicago Press.

Bassnett, S. (1998), "The Translation Turn in Cultural Studies," in S. Bassnett and A. Lefevere (eds.), *Constructing Cultures*, 123–39, Bristol: Multilingual Matters.

Bassnett, S. (2014), *Translation Studies*, 4th ed., London: Taylor and Francis.

Baudelaire, C. (1923), *Tableaux Parisiens*, trans. W. Benjamin, Heidelberg: Verlag von Richard Weißbach.

Baudelaire, C. (1954), *The Flowers of Evil*, trans. W. Aggeler, Fresno: Academy Library Guild.

Bery, A. (2007), *Cultural Translation and Postcolonial Poetry*, London: Palgrave Macmillan.

Bery, A. (2009), "Forum: Cultural Translation. Response," *Translation Studies*, 2 (2): 213–16.

Bhabha, H. (1989), "Beyond Fundamentalism and Liberalism," *The New Statesman and Society*, March 2: 34–5. Reprinted in Appignanesi, L. and S. Maitland, eds. (1989), *The Rushdie File*, 112–14, London: Fourth Estate Publishing.

Bhabha, H. (1990), *Nation and Narration*, London and New York: Routledge.

Bhabha, H. (1994), *The Location of Culture*, London and New York: Routledge.

Bhabha, H. (2015), "'The Beginning of Their Real Enunciation': Stuart Hall and the Work of Culture," *Critical Inquiry*, 42 (1): 1–30.

Bhabha, H. and J. Rutherford (1990), "The Third Space. Interview with Homi Bhabha," in J. Rutherford (ed.), *Identity: Community, Culture, Difference*, 207–21, London: Lawrence & Wishart.

Brightman, R. (1995), "Forget Culture: Replacement, Transcendence, Relexification," *Cultural Anthropology*, 10 (4): 509–46.

Brodersen, M. (1990), *Spinne im eigenen Netz. Walter Benjamin. Leben und Werk*, Bühl-Moos: Elster Verlag.
Buden, B. and S. Nowotny (2009), "Forum: Cultural Translation. An Introduction to the Problem," *Translation Studies*, 2 (2): 196–208.
Burke, P. and R. P. Hsia, eds. (2007), *Cultural Translation in Early Modern Europe*, Cambridge: Cambridge University Press.
Carbonell i Cortés, O. (2010), "Forum: Cultural Translation. Response," *Translation Studies*, 3 (1): 99–103.
Chakrabarty, D. (2000), *Provincializing Europe. Postcolonial thought and Historical difference*, Princeton: Princeton University Press.
Chesterman, A. (2010), "Forum: Cultural Translation. Response," *Translation Studies*, 3 (1): 103–6.
Chmielorz, R. (2010), "! Viva el Krausismo !" *Zeit Online*, 7 October. Available online: www.zeit.de/2010/41/Philosoph-Krause (accessed April 29, 2023).
Chow, R. (1995), *Primitive Passions: Visuality, Sexuality, Ethnography, and Contemporary Chinese Cinema*, New York: Columbia University Press.
Clifford, J. (2012), "Feeling Historical," *Cultural Anthropology*, 27 (3): 417–26.
Clifford, J. and G. E. Marcus, eds. (1986), *Writing Culture: The Poetics Politics of Ethnography*, Berkeley: University of California Press.
Confurius, G. (1987), "Die Arkade als täuschendes Bild," in G. Auer, et al. (eds.), *Portici – Arkaden – Lauben*, 97–107, Gütersloh and Berlin: Bertelsmann Fachzeitschriften.
Conway, K. (2012a), "A Conceptual and Empirical Approach to Cultural Translation," *Translation Studies*, 5 (3): 264–79.
Conway, K. (2012b), "Cultural Translation," in Y. Gambier and L. v. Doorslaer (eds.), *Handbook of Translation Studies: Volume 3*, 21–5, Amsterdam: John Benjamins.
Conway, K. (2019), "Cultural Translation," in M. Baker and G. Saldanha (eds.), *Routledge Encyclopedia of Translation Studies*, 3rd ed., London: Routledge.
De Andrade, O. (1991), "Cannibalist Manifesto," trans. L. Bary, *Latin American Literary Review*, 19 (38): 38–47.
De Campos, H. (1986), "The Rule of Anthropophagy: Europe under the Sign of Devoration," trans. M. T. Wolff, *Latin American Literary Review*, 14 (27): 42–60.
De Chirico, G. (2011), *Das Geheimnis Der Arkade: Erinnerungen Und Reflexionen*, trans. M. Schneider, München: Schirmer Mosel.
De Haan, M. (2012), "The Reconstruction of Parenting after Migration: A Perspective from Cultural Translation," *Human Development*, 54 (6): 376–99.
De Man, M. (1985), "'Conclusions': On Walter Benjamin's 'The Task of the Translator,'" *Yale French Studies*, 69: 25–46.
De Montaigne, M. (1958), *The Complete EsCsays of Montaigne*, ed. and trans. D. M. Frame, Stanford: Stanford University Press.
Demus, K. (2008), "Der Turmbau zu Babel," in W. Seipel (ed.), *Pieter Bruegel d. Ä. im Kunsthistorischen Museum Wien*, 56–7, Milano: Skira.

DePue, J., et al. (2010), "Cultural Translation of Interventions: Diabetes Care in American Samoa," *American Journal of Public Health*, 100 (11): 2085–93.
Derrida, J. (1976), *Of Grammatology*, trans. G. C. Spivak, Baltimore: Johns Hopkins University Press.
Derrida, J. (1979), "Living On/Borderlines," trans. J. Hulbert, in H. Bloom et al. (eds.), *Deconstruction and Criticism*, 75–176, New York: Continuum.
Derrida, J. (1982), "Différance," trans. A. Bass, in *Margins of Philosophy*, 3–27, Chicago: University of Chicago Press.
Derrida, J. (1985a), "Des Tours de Babel," trans. J. Graham, in J. Graham (ed.), *Difference in Translation*, 165–207, Ithaca: Cornell University Press.
Derrida, J. (1985b), "Roundtable on Translation," trans. P. Kamuf, in C. V. McDonald (ed.), *The Ear of the Other: Otobiography, Transference, Translation*, 91–161, New York: Schocken Books.
Derrida, J. (1986), *Glas*, trans. J. P. Leavey, Jr. and R. Rand, Lincoln: University of Nebraska Press.
Derrida, J. (1992), "Given Time: The Time of the King," trans. P. Kamuf, *Critical Inquiry*, 18 (2): 161–87.
Derrida, J. (1994), *Specters of Marx, the State of the Debt, the Work of Mourning, & the New International*, trans. P. Kamuf, London and New York: Routledge.
Derrida, J. (1996), *The Gift of Death*, trans. D. Wills, Chicago: University of Chicago Press.
Derrida, J. (1998), *Monolingualism of the Other. Or, The Prosthesis of Origin*, trans. P. Mensah, Stanford: Stanford University Press.
Derrida, J. (2002), "The Eyes of Language," trans. G. Anidjar, in G. Anidjar (ed.), *Acts of Religion*, 189–227, London and New York: Routledge.
D'hulst, L. (2010), "Forum: Cultural Translation. Response," *Translation Studies*, 3 (3): 353–6.
Dingwaney, A. and C. Maier, eds. (1995), *Between Languages and Cultures. Translation and Cross-Cultural Texts*, Pittsburgh: University of Pittsburgh Press.
Disler, C. (2011), "Walter Benjamin's 'Afterlife': A Productive (?) Mistranslation," *TTR – Traduction, Terminologie, Rédaction*, 24 (1): 183–221.
Fabijancic, T. (2001), "The Prison in the Arcade: A Carceral Diagram of Consumer Space," *Mosaic: A Journal for the Interdisciplinary Study of Literature*, 34 (3): 141–58.
Farahzad, F., A. Parviz, and L. Razmjou (2011), "Translation Quality and Awareness of Cultural Translation Theories," *Journal of Language Teaching and Research*, 2 (2): 486–91.
Fichte, J. G. ([1808] 2008), *Reden an die deutsche Nation*, Hamburg: Meiner.
Fittko, L. (1982), "The Story of Old Benjamin," in R. Tiedemann (ed.), *Gesammelte Schriften*, vol. 5, 1184–94, Frankfurt a.M.: Suhrkamp.
Foster, L. A. (2014), "Critical Cultural Translation: A Socio-Legal Framework for Regulatory Orders," *Indiana Journal of Global Legal Studies*, 21 (1): 79–105.

Fürnkäs, J. (1988), *Surrealismus als Erkenntnis. Walter Benjamin – Weimarer Einbahnstraße und Pariser Passagen*, Stuttgart: Metzler.
Gamsa, M. (2011), "Cultural Translation and the Transnational Circulation of Books," *Journal of World History*, 22 (3): 553–75.
Geertz, C. (1973a), "Thick Description. Toward an Interpretive Theory of Culture," in *The Interpretation of Cultures. Selected Essays*, 3–30, New York: Basic Books.
Geertz, C. (1973b), "Deep Play: Notes on the Balinese Cockfight," *The Interpretation of Cultures: Selected Essays*, 412–53, New York: Basic Books.
Gentzler, E. (1993), *Contemporary Translation Theories*, London and New York: Routledge.
Gentzler, E. (2002), "Translation, Poststructuralism, and Power," in M. Tymoczko and E. Gentzler (eds.), *Translation and Power*, 195–218, Amherst: University of Massachusetts Press.
Gentzler, E. (2008), *Translation and Identity in the Americas*, London and New York: Routledge.
Grunig, J. E., et al. (1995), "Models of Public Relations in an International Setting," *Journal of Public Relations Research*, 7 (3): 163–86.
Guest, K. (2001), *Eating Their Words: Cannibalism and the Boundaries of Cultural Identity*, Albany: State University of New York Press.
Guldin, R. (2008), "Devouring the Other: Cannibalism, Translation and the Construction of Cultural Identity," in P. Nikolau and M.-V. Kyritsi (eds.), *Translating Selves: Experience and Identity between Languages and Literatures*, 109–22, London: Continuum.
Ha, N. K. (2010), "Forum: Cultural Translation. Response," *Translation Studies*, 3 (3): 349–53.
Habermas, J. (1979), "Consciousness-Raising or Redemptive Criticism: The Contemporaneity of Walter Benjamin," trans. P. Brewster and C. H. Buchner, *New German Critique*, 17: 30–59.
Hamacher, W. (2001), "Intensive Sprachen," in C. Hart-Nibbrig (ed.), *Übersetzen: Walter Benjamin*, 174–235, Frankfurt a.M.: Suhrkamp.
Hart-Nibbrig, C. (2001), *Übersetzen: Walter Benjamin*, Frankfurt a.M.: Suhrkamp.
Hein, C. (2014), "Der Kannibale," in L. Friedrich, K. Harrasser, et al. (eds.), *Figuren der Gewalt*, 87–92, Zürich: Diaphanes.
Hermans, T., ed. (1985), *The Manipulation of Literature: Studies in Literary Translation*, New York: St. Martin's Press.
Hodge, J. (2007), *Derrida on Time*, London and New York: Routledge.
House, J. (2009), "Moving across Languages and Cultures in Translation as Intercultural Communication," in K. Buhring, J. House, and J. T. Thije (eds.), *Translational Action and Intercultural Communication*, 7–39, London: Taylor and Francis.
Hugo von Hofmannsthal-Gesellschaft (n.d.), "Hofmannsthal Bibliographie Online." Available online: https://hofmannsthal.bibliographie.de/ (accessed April 29, 2023).

Ingram, S. (1997), "The Task of the Translator: Walter Benjamin's Essay in English, a Forschungsbericht," *TTR*, 10 (2): 297–33.

Italiano, F. and M. Rössner, eds. (2012), *Translatio/n. Narration, Media and the Staging of Differences*, Bielefeld: transcript.

Jäger, L. (2013), "Unübertrasgbarkeit. Transkriptionstheoretische Bemerkungen zum Zusammenhang von Verstehen und Übersetzen," *Sprache und Literatur*, 44 (2): 3–19.

Jacobs, C. (1975), "The Monstrosity of Translation," *Comparative Literature: Translation, Theory and Practice*, 90 (6): 755–66.

Jakobson, R. (1959), "On Linguistic Aspects of Translation," in R. A. Brower (ed.), *On Translation*, 232–9. Cambridge, MA: Harvard University Press.

Jameson, F. (1991), *Postmodernism; or, the Cultural Logic of Late Capitalism*, Durham: Duke University Press.

Janson, A. and F. Tigges (2013), *Grundbegriffe der Architektur. Das Vokabular räumlicher Situationen*, Basel: Birkhäuser.

Jennings, M. and H. Eiland (2014), *Walter Benjamin: A Critical Life*, Cambridge, MA: Belknap Press of Harvard University Press.

Kaulen, H. (1990), "'Die Aufgabe des Kritikers.' Walter Benjamins Reflexionen zur Theorie der Literaturkritik 1929–1931," in W. Barner (ed.), *Literaturkritik. Anspruch und Wirklichkeit*, 318–36, Stuttgart: Metzler.

Keesing, R. M. (1985), "Conventional Metaphors and Anthropological Metaphysics: The Problematic of Cultural Translation," *Journal of Anthropological Research*, 41 (2): 201–17.

Kilgour, M. (1990), *From Communion to Cannibalism: An Anatomy of Metaphors of Incorporation*, Princeton: Princeton University Press.

Klossowski, P. (2014), "Letter on Walter Benjamin," *Parrhesia*, 19: 20–1.

Larsen, T. (1987), "Action, Morality and Cultural Translation," *Journal of Anthropological Research*, 43 (1): 1–28.

Lefevere, A. and S. Bassnett (2002), *Translation, History and Culture*, London and New York: Routledge.

Liebsch, A.-C. (2013), "Die deutsch-lateinische Übersetzung im Schulunterricht. Eine bildungshistorische Untersuchung," *Pegasus-Onlinezeitschrift*, XIII (1/2): 153–217. Available online: www.pegasus-onlinezeitschrift.de/2013_1_2/pegasus_2013-1_liebsch_ druck.pdf (accessed April 29, 2023).

Lindner, B. (1985), "Technische Reproduzierbarkeit und Kulturindustrie. Benjamins 'Positives Barbarentum' im Kontext," in B. Lindner (ed.), *Walter Benjamin im Kontext*, 180–223, Königstein: Athenäum Verlag.

Macedo, A. G. and M. E. Pereira, eds. (2006), *Identity and Cultural Translation: Writing across the Borders of Englishness. Women's Writing in English in a European Context*, Bern: Peter Lang.

Maitland, S. (2017), *What is Cultural Translation?* London: Bloomsbury.

Marchart, O. (2007), "Der koloniale Signifikant. Kulturelle 'Hybridität' und das Politische, oder: Homi Bhabha wiedergelesen," in M. Kröncke, K. Mey, and Y.

Spielmann, (eds.), *Kultureller Umbau: Räume, Identitäten und Re/Präsentationen*, 77–98. Bielefeld: transcript Verlag.

Marchart, O. (2008), *Cultural Studies*, Konstanz: UVK Verlagsgesellschaft.

Mattenklott, G. (2011), "Briefe und Briefwechsel," in B. Lindner (ed.), *Benjamin-Handbuch: Leben – Werk – Wirkung*, 680–7. Stuttgart: Metzler.

Maurach, G. (2006), *Lateinische Stilübungen. Ein Lehrbuch zum Selbstunterricht*, Darmstadt: Wissenschaftliche Buchgesellschaft.

Menke, B. (2011), "Ursprung des deutschen Trauerspiels," in B. Lindner (ed.), *Benjamin-Handbuch: Leben – Werk – Wirkung*, 210–28, Stuttgart: Metzler.

Menninghaus, W. (1995), *Walter Benjamins Theorie der Sprachmagie*, 2nd ed., Frankfurt a.M.: Suhrkamp.

Milner, S. and S. Campbell, eds. (2004), *Artistic Exchange and Cultural Translation in the Italian Renaissance City*, Cambridge: Cambridge University Press.

Newmark, P. (1991), *About Translation*, Bristol: Multilingual Matters.

Nida, E. A. (1964), *Toward a Science of Translating*, Leiden: E. J. Brill.

Nida, E. A. (1976), "A Framework for the Analysis and Evaluation of Theories of Translation," in R. W. Brislin (ed.), *Translation. Application and Research*, 47–91, New York: Gardner Press.

Nida, E. A. and C. R. Tarber (1969), *The Theory and Practice of Translation*, Leiden: Brill.

Niranjana, T. (1992), *Siting Translation: History, Poststructuralism and the Colonial Context*, Berkeley: University of California Press.

Opitz, M. and E. Wizisla, eds. (2000), *Benjamins Begriffe*, Frankfurt a.M.: Suhrkamp.

Papastergiadis, N. (2011), "Cultural Translation, Cosmopolitanism and the Void," *Translation Studies*, 4 (1): 1–20.

Phillips, J. and C. Tan (2005), "Langue and Parole," *The Literary Encyclopedia*, 8 February. Available online: www.litencyc.com/php/stopics.php?rec=true&UID=662 (accessed April 29, 2023).

Pratt, M. L. (2010), "Forum: Cultural Translation. Response," *Translation Studies*, 3 (1): 94–7.

Pym, A. (2009), "On Empiricism and Bad Philosophy in Translation Studies," in H. C. Omar, H. Haroon and A. Ghani (eds.), *The Sustainability of the Translation Field*, 28–39, Kuala Lumpur: Persatuan Penterjemah Malaysia.

Pym, A. (2010), *Exploring Translation Theories*, London and New York: Routledge.

Rendall, S. (1997), "Comments on Harry Zohn's Translation of Walter Benjamin's 'Die Aufgabe des Übersetzers'," *TTR*, 10 (2): 191–206.

Reuß, R. (2016), "Nachwort," in R. Reuß (ed.), *Tableaux Parisiens: deutsch und mit einem Vorwort von Walter Benjamin, "Aufgabe des Übersetzers,"* facsimile reproduction, 1–51, Frankfurt a.M./Basel: Stroemfeld.

Rogister, M. (1991), "Romain Rolland: One German View," *The Modern Language Review*, 86 (2): 349–60.

Rushdie, S. (1992), *Imaginary Homelands: Essays and Criticism 1981–1991*, London: Granta Books.

Said, E. (1978), *Orientalism*, London: Penguin Books.
Sapir, E. (1963), *Selected Writings of Edward Sapir in Language, Culture and Personality*, ed. D. G. Mandelbaum, Berkeley: University of California Press.
Schmider, C. and M. Werner (2011), "Das Baudelaire-Buch," in B. Lindner (ed.), *Benjamin-Handbuch: Leben – Werk – Wirkung*, 567–84, Stuttgart: Metzler.
Scholem, G. (2003), *Walter Benjamin: The Story of a Friendship*, trans. H. Zohn, New York: New York Review Books.
Scholem, G. (2007), *Lamentations of Youth: The Diaries of Gershom Scholem, 1913–1919*, Cambridge: Belknap Press.
Schulte, C. (2003), *Ursprung ist das Ziel. Walter Benjamin über Karl Kraus*, Würzburg: Königshausen & Neumann.
Schulze, P. W. (2015), *Strategien "kultureller Kannibalisierung": Postkoloniale Repräsentationen vom brasilianischen Modernismo zum Cinema Novo*, Bielefeld: transcript.
Sewell, W. H. (1999), "The Concept(s) of Culture," in V. E. Bonnell, L. A. Hunt, and R. Biernacki (eds.), *Beyond the Cultural Turn: New Directions in the Study of Society and Culture*, 35–61, Berkeley: University of California Press.
Silverstein, M. J. (1979), "Language Structure and Linguistic Ideology," in R. Cline, W. Hanks, and C. Hofbauer (eds.), *The Elements: A Parasession on Linguistic Units and Levels*, 193–247, Chicago: Chicago Linguistic Society.
Simon, N. (2010), *The Participatory Museum*, Santa Cruz: Museum 2.0.
Smith, D. (2004), "The Arcade as a Haunt and Habitat: Aragon, Benjamin, Céline," *Romance Studies*, 22 (1): 17–26.
Snell-Hornby, M. (2006), *The Turns of Translation Studies. New Paradigms or Shifting Viewpoints?* Amsterdam: John Benjamins.
Snell-Hornby, M., F. Pöchhacker, and K. Kaindl, eds. (1994), *Translation Studies: An Interdiscipline*, Amsterdam: John Benjamins.
Steiner, G. (1975), *After Babel: Aspects of Language and Translation*, London: Oxford University Press.
Sturge, K. (2009), "Cultural Translation," in M. Baker (ed.), *Routledge Encyclopedia of Translation Studies*, 67–70, London and New York: Routledge.
Toury, G. (1995), *Descriptive Translation Studies and Beyond*, Amsterdam: John Benjamins.
Trivedi, H. (2005), "Translating Culture vs. Cultural Translation," in P. St-Pierre and P. C. Kar (eds.), *In Translation – Reflections, Refractions, Transformations*, 277–87, Amsterdam: John Benjamins.
Tymoczko, M. (2010), "Forum: Cultural Translation. Response," *Translation Studies*, 3 (1): 106–10.
Venuti, L. (2004), *Translation Studies Reader*, London and New York: Routledge.
Venuti, L. (2008), *The Translator's Invisibility: A History of Translation*, 2nd ed., London: Routledge.

Vermeer, H. J. (1986), "Übersetzen als kultureller Transfer," in M. Snell-Hornby (ed.), *Übersetzungswissenschaft – eine Neuorientierung*, 30–53, Tübingen: Francke.

Vieira, E. (1994), "A Postmodern Translational Aesthetic in Brazil," in M. Snell-Hornby, F. Pöchhacker, and K. Kaindl (eds.), *Translation Studies: An Interdiscipline*, 65–72, Amsterdam: John Benjamins.

Vieira, E. (1999), "Liberating Calibans: Readings of Antropofagia and Haroldo de Campos' Poetics of Transcreation," in S. Bassnett and H. Trivedi (eds.), *Post-colonial Translation: Theory and Practice*, 95–113, London and New York: Routledge.

Wagner, B. (2009), "Kulturelle Übersetzung. Erkundungen über ein wanderndes Konzept," *Kakanien Revisited*, 23 July. Available online: www.kakanien-revisited.at/beitr/postcol/BWagner2.pdf (accessed April 29, 2023).

Weber, S. (2008), *Benjamin's-Abilities*, Cambridge, MA: Harvard University Press.

Weidner, D. (2011), "Fort-, Über-, Nachleben. Zu einer Denkfigur bei Benjamin," in D. Weidner and S. Weigel (eds.), *Benjamin-Studien 2*, 161–78, Paderborn: Wilhelm Fink.

Williams, R. (1958), *Culture and Society, 1780–1950*, New York: Columbia University Press.

Wohlfarth, I. (2001), "Das Medium der Übersetzung," in C. Hart-Nibbrig (ed.), *Übersetzen: Walter Benjamin*, 80–150, Frankfurt a.M.: Suhrkamp.

Young, R. J. C. (1996), *Colonial Desire: Hybridity in Theory, Culture and Race*, London and New York: Routledge.

Young, R. J. C. (2010), "Forum: Cultural Translation. Response," *Translation Studies*, 3 (3): 357–60.

Young, R. J. C. (2012), "Cultural Translation as Hybridisation," *Trans-Humanities*, 5 (1): 155–75.

Young, R. J. C. (2017), "The Dislocations of Cultural Translation: On Bhabha's *The Location of Culture*," *PMLA*, 132 (1): 186–97.

Zenker, O. (2014), "Writing Culture," *Oxford Bibliographies*, May. Available online: www.oxfordbibliographies.com/view/document/obo-9780199766567/obo-9780199766567-0030.xml (accessed April 29, 2023).

Online Resources, Reference Works and Media:

Das Wortauskunftssystem zur deutschen Sprache in Geschichte und Gegenwart. Hosted by Berlin-Brandenburgische Akademie der Wissenschaften. Available online: http://www.dwds.de.

Deutsches Wörterbuch, eds. Grimm, Jacob and Wilhelm, Leipzig, 1845–1961. Hosted by Berlin-Brandenburgische Akademie der Wissenschaften, DFG, Akademie der Wissenschaften zu Göttingen. Available online: http://woerterbuchnetz.de/DWB/.

Encyclopaedia Britannica. Available online: https://www.britannica.com/.

Google Books Ngram Viewer. Visualization of word/phrase frequency searches. Available online: https://books.google.com/ngrams.

Internet Archive: Walter Benjamin's Collected Writings. Benjamin, W. (1972–1999), *Gesammelte Schriften*, eds. Rolf Tiedemann and Hermann Schweppenhäuser, VII vols., II supplements, Frankfurt a.M.: Suhrkamp. Available online: http://www.archive.org.

Lexico. Oxford Dictionaries. Online Dictionary hosted by the Oxford University Press. Available online: https://en.oxforddictionaries.com.

Index

Numbers followed by n. refer to note numbers

Adorno, Gretel   64
Adorno, T.W.   58, 64, 70, 75–7, 151
After Babel (Steiner)   40, 91
'Afterlife': A Productive (?) Mistranslation
    (Disler)   102–3
Agamben, Giorgio   77
Allegorese, allegorical interpretation   109
allegory, concept of   109–10, 112
Althusser, Louis   11–12
Angelus Novus (Benjamin)   27, 44
anthology   54–5, 154–5
Anthropophagie (Jarry)   152–3
anthropophagy   151–3, 158
anti-colonial cultural processes   8
Anzaldúa, Gloria   10
apocryphal   21, 151, 157–8, 162 n.21
Aragon, Louis   46, 77, 79
arcades, *see also The Arcades Project*
    (Benjamin)
  Babel, visual presentations   86
  Baudelaire complex   77
  in Benjamin's writings   82–90
  black briefcase   79
  and cultural translation (*see* cultural
    translation)
  in early travelogues   83–4
  function of   84–5
  painting (Konterfei)   85
  and passage   19, 79–82
    Arkade description   80–1
    Arkaden and stairways   87
    fidelity   80–1
    similarities and differences   88–9,
      102
  significance   78–9
  structure and description   83, 88
  transitory space   79
  Wörtlichkeit, strategy of   80–1
The Arcades of Paris (Benjamin)   87

The Arcades Project (Benjamin)   76–83,
    94, 99, 101, 114
Arendt, Hannah   75
*The artwork in an age of mechanical
    reproduction* (Benjamin)   61,
    69–70, 71, 123, 125–6
Asad, Talal   3–4, 7, 12–13, 120–1
aura   43, 65, 125
The Author as Producer (Benjamin)
  plagiarism   60–1
  processes of melting and
    re-casting   60–1
  technical factors, conditions or
    prerequisites   61
autoethnographic films, force of surfaces
    in   96–7

Balzac, Honoré de   46
Bassnett, Susan   5–6, 12
Bataille, Georges   71, 76–7
Baudelaire complex   77
Bertaux, Felix   46
Bery, Ashok   1
Bhabha, Homi   1, 8, 115
  agency   143
  blasphemy   120, 138
  critique of Jameson   140
  cultural diversity and cultural
    difference   11
  cultural translation   21, 120, 128, 136,
    140, 142–4, 159 n.4, 177 n.22
  cultures of survival   127
  element of resistance (*see* un/
    translatability)
  foreignness of language   138–40
  foreign relations   119
  formulation of culture   11
  Fortleben, concept of   115, 119–20,
    138

image of the border 118
liminality of migrant condition 137–8
(mis-)reading of Benjamin 145
notion of survival 147
postcolonial context 20
postmodern subjects 137
supplementarity 178 n.28
survivre 138
untranslatability and survival (*see* un/translatability)
biblical Apocrypha 157
biblical topoi 33
bibliography 52–3, 145
Bibliothèque Nationale in Paris 76–7, 88–9
Boas, Franz 6, 160 n.14
Brill, Hans Klaus 69–70
Brodersen, Momme 87
Bruegel, Pieter 86
Buden, Boris 15

cannibalism 152–5, 179 n.5
Chamoiseau, Patrick 144
Chaudhuri, Amit 90
Chomsky, Noam 4
Chow, Rey 19–20, 95–100
Christoph Martin Wieland (Benjamin) 112
The Concept of Cultural Translation in British Social Anthropology (Asad) 3, 121
conservatism 21, 158
Contemporary Translation Theories (Gentzler) 9
Cornelius, Hans 46
correspondence 106
criticism 9, 15–18, 20–1, 26, 28, 31, 32, 38–41, 43–5, 51–4, 108, 154–5
Criticism as the Fundamental Discipline of Literary History (Benjamin) 111
Critic's Technique in Thirteen Theses (Benjamin) 151
cultural cannibalism 152
cultural diversity 11, 119, 137
cultural translation
and arcade
Arkade and *Passage*, architectural proximity 91–2

colonnade 91
mass media 98
in *My Paris* 100–1
postcolonial translation 92–3
primitive passions 95–6
Wörtlichkeit-as-an-arcade 94–5, 98
art-selfies 126
Bhabha's formulation of 19, 21, 120, 128, 136, 140, 142–4, 159 n.4, 177 n.22
concept of 2–4, 13–14, 149
cross-disciplinary developments 12–13
culture-as-text 14–15, 122
formulations of 16
genealogies of 13
metaphorized concept of 141–2
methodological validity 122
original and translation, relation 124
perspective of cultures of survival 127
process of 123
transformative quality 126
transgressive moment of 138
Cultural Translation and Postcolonial Poetry (Bery) 1–2
Cultural Translation. Explorations on a Travelling Concept (Wagner) 141
Cultural Turns: Neuorientierungen in den Kulturwissenschaften (Bachmann-Medick) 14
culture
cultural studies 12
culture-as-text 6–7, 13–15, 122
diversity and difference 11
home discipline 13, 15
language, culture, and nation 66, 92, 95
media and mass culture 98–100
migrant 142
popular 8, 12
self-representation 97
of survival 127
target and source 6
as transformational 11, 118–19 (*see also The Location of Culture* (Bhaba))

translation of   3, 93, 121
untranslatable aspect of   142
Williams' formulation of culture   12
working-class   12
Writing Culture-debate   7
Customs and Cultures (Nida)   4

d'Annunzio, Gabriele   46
de Andrade, Oswald   151–4, 156
De Campos, Haroldo   151–3
de Chirico, Giorgio   84–5
De Man, Paul   4, 75, 80, 91–3, 95, 97–8, 149
de Montaigne, Michel   152
Der Anfang (magazine)   31
Der Deutsche in der Landschaft (Borchardt)   55–6
Derrida, Jacques
  borderline of translatability   117
  criticism   90
  The Ear of the Other   149
  The Eyes of Language   116
  Fortleben, concept of   116, 120, 138, 147
  logocentrism   9
  survivre, concept of   91, 116, 118–19, 138, 147
Des Tours de Babel (Derrida)   91, 115, 117
Deubel, Léon   50–1
Die Aufgabe des Übersetzers (Benjamin)   19, 25, 75, 103–4, 128, 164 n.1, 166 n.25
Die Herzogin von Guermantes (Proust/Benjamin)   47
Die literarische Welt (Magazine)   52, 58
Disler, Caroline   102–5, 115
Doctrine of the Similar (Benjamin)   58–9
dogmatism   21, 158

The Ear of the Other (Derrida)   149
Einverleibung, imagery of   63, 154
ethnographers   7, 93, 121
Eurocentrism   15
Europäische Lyrik der Gegenwart (Kalmer)   54
Eysteinsson, A.   90

Fälschung, plagiarism   61–2, 154

Ficino letters, review of   51
fidelity, understanding of   80–1
First World War   32, 38
Fittko, Lisa   76
foreignness of languages   87, 117, 138–9
forgery   62, 154–5
Forget Culture: Replacement, Transcendence, Relexification (Brightman)   7
Fortleben, concept of   20, 54, 103–5, 115, 119–20, 125, 129, 138, 146–7
  allegorical figures   109–10
  artwork's   110
  Bhabha's reference to   119
  cognition, process of   108
  collections of letters   111
  correspondence   106
  Derrida's   116–17, 120
  Fourier's   113
  meaning of   105
  Nachleben   113–14
  perpetual preliminarity *vs.* eternal Fortleben   146
  renditions of   104
  transformative quality of   108
  Über-/Fort-/Nachleben   105–6, 114–15
  Wieland's   112
Forum: Cultural Translation   15
Fourier's *Nachleben*   20, 103, 105, 113–15
Frankfurter Zeitung (newspaper)   28, 58, 135
freedom and fidelity, concepts of   41–2
From Cultural Translation to Untranslatability (Baer)   15
Fuchs, Eduard   157
Fürnkäs, Josef   155

Gandillac, Maurice   115–16, 149
Geertz, Clifford   3, 6, 122, 161 n.15
geistiges Wesen and *sprachliches Wesen*   65
Gellner, Ernest   3
Gemeintes and *Arten des Meinens*, difference   41
Genesis, references to   33, 35, 40, 42, 59
Gentzler, Edwin   10
George, Stefan   25, 28–9
German Romantics   38, 108

knowledge and criticism 38
Novalis, Benjamin's comments 38–9
translation theory, radical criticism 17–18
German Youth Movement 31
Graham, Joseph 116–17
Gramsci, Antonio 11–12
The Great Tower of Babel (Bruegel) 86

Ha, Kien Nghi 17
Habilitation 39, 44–6, 49
Hein, Claudia 152
Heinle, Fritz 32
Hellingrath, Norbert von 32
Hessel, Franz 46, 47, 49, 56, 87
Hofmannsthal, Hugo von 28–9, 62–3, 81, 154–5, 157
  Augurenlächeln 28–9
Hölderlin, Friedrich
  reflections on 32
  Sophocles translations 133
Horkheimer, Max 58, 69, 77
Hulbert, James 117
hybridity 119, 136–7, 144
Hynd, James 90–1, 104, 132

Illuminations (Arendt) 75, 90
Im Schatten der jungen Mädchen (Proust) 47
interdisciplines 6, 12
interlingual interpretations 147–8
intersemiotic translation or transmutation 9
intralingual translation 9
Italy, educational journey to 30–1, 83

Jacobs, Carol 91
Jäger, Ludwig 101
Jakobson, Roman 8–9
Janmohamed, Abdul 140
Jarry, Alfred 152
Jean Christophe (Rolland) 68
joint translation process 70
Jouhandeau, Marcel 46

Kalmer, Josef 54–5, 154
kinship
  criticism and translation 52, 56–7, 61, 108
  of languages 40, 108, 129, 135
Klee, Paul 27
Klossowski, Pierre 69–71
Kracauer, Siegfried 28
Krause, Karl Christian Friedrich 56, 68–9, 155–6
Krausism 68–9
Kulturnation 65

Language(s)
  concept of 33–5, 37, 59, 66, 140
  harmony of 43, 133
  natural 143
  philosophy and epistemology 37–8, 59, 142
À la recherche du temps perdu (Proust) 47–8
Leben-compounds 103–5
Lefevere, André 4–6
Le Paysan de Paris (Aragon) 77–8
letters 58, 68–70, 151, 164 n.1
Licht vom Licht: Hymnen (Symeon) 54
Lienhardt, Godfrey 3
limitations of translation 50, 67–8
Lindner, Burkhardt 155–6
linguistic being 35, 66, 143
Literary History and the Study of Literature (Benjamin) 56–7, 111
Lloyd, David 140
The Location of Culture (Bhabha) 1, 3, 11, 115, 118–19, 127, 136, 147
logocentrism 9, 93

Maitland, Sarah 20, 120–7
Manifeste Cannibale Dada (Picabia) 153
Manifesto Antropofago (de Andrade) 151–3
The Manipulation of Literature: Studies in Literary Translation (Hermans) 5
Man Ray's collection of rayographs 46
Mattenklott, Gert 106
metaphorization 15, 141–3, 157–8, 162 n.23
mistranslation 20, 102–3, 149, 160 n.7
A Modest Proposal (Swift) 152, 180 n.16
Monnier, Adrienne 46, 70–1
The Monstrosity of Translation (Jacobs) 91

Moscow Diary (Benjamin)   113
multiculturalism   11, 136
music, translation of   67–8, 136
mutual non-recognition, situation of   65
My Paris (Scott)   101
Mythologies (Barthes)   96–7

Nachleben   20, 103, 105, 113–15
Namensprache   36
new barbarism   156
Nida, Eugene A.   4–5, 13, 160 n.9, 162 n.21
Nietzsche   65–6
Niranjana, Tejaswini   19–20, 92–6, 98–100, 173 n.24, 173 n.26
Nowotny, Stefan   15–17, 164 n.28

On Empiricism and Bad Philosophy in Translation Studies (Pym)   15, 141, 145
One-Way Street and Other Writings (Benjamin)   90, 152
On Language as Such and on the Language of Man (Benjamin)   33
On Some Motifs in Baudelaire (Benjamin)   65
On the Concept of History (Benjamin)   63
On the Mimetic Faculty (Benjamin)   58–60
On the Trail of Old Letters (Benjamin)   111–12
The Origin of German Tragic Drama (Benjamin)   109
Ostermann, Dr. Christian   51

Pannwitz, Rudolf   127, 159 n.6
Paris, the Capital of the Nineteenth Century (Benjamin)   79
Paris arcades   88, *see also* arcades
Pariser Passagen II (The Arcades of Paris) (Benjamin)   87
Peirce, Charles Sanders   8
Pensieri (Leopardi)   52–3
Perse, Saint-John   46
Peters, Dr. Richard   52–3, 67
physiognomy   65, 110, 135
Picabia, Francis   153
Pindar-translations   32
Pollock, Friedrich   63

postcolonial translation   14, 92–3, 95, 151
poststructuralism   8, 10–11, 16, 18, 92, 100, 120
power relations, inequality of   15, 93, 122, 173 n.24
Primitive Passions: Visuality, Sexuality, Ethnography, and Contemporary Chinese Cinema (Chow)   95–8
Proust, Marcel   46–9, 54, 56, 63, 154–5
pure language, elements of   41–2, 75
Pym, Anthony   15, 17, 122, 141, 145–9, 164 n.28

Radt, Jula   47
real humanism   156
Rendall, Steven   90, 104, 124–5
Rexroth, Franz von   49–51
Rilke, Rainer Maria   32, 48
Rimbaud, Arthur   49
The Ring of Saturn (Benjamin)   87
The Role of Language in Trauerspiel and Tragedy (Benjamin)   45
Rolland, Romain   68
Romantic critics   41
Romanticism   38
The Rule of Anthropophagy (de Andrade)   151, 153
Rushdie, Salman   3, 119–20, 136, 138

Said, Edward   8
The Satanic Verses (Rushdie)   3, 119, 136–7, 159 n.4
Scholem, Gershom   26, 33, 39, 45, 47, 58–9, 77, 151
Schottlaender, Rudolf   46, 47
Schulte, Christian   156
Schultz, Franz   45–6
Scott, Gail   100
Selected Writings (Benjamin)   91, 104, 128, 166 n.34, 177 n.23, 180 n.12
Sewell, William H.   6–7
Sodome et Gomorrhe (Proust)   46–7
Specters of Marx (Derrida)   10
Spivak, Gayatri Chakravorty   8
Steiner, George   91
Stern-Anders, Günther   64
Stilübung   31–2, 51, 164 n.2
The Storyteller: Tales Out of Loneliness (Benjamin)   71

Surrealism: The Last Snapshot of European Intelligentsia (Benjamin) 56, 84, 87
survival 41, 62, 104–5, 109–10, 116–21, 124–5, 127, 138, 145–7
survivre, Derrida's 91, 116–20, 138, 147
Swift, Jonathan 152, 180 n.16

Tableaux Parisiens (Baudelaire) 25, 27, 30, 39, 75, 84
  bilingual Baudelaire translations 28
  translation and publication of 25–6
target language 43, 50, 55, 80, 123
The Task of the Critic (Benjamin) 56, 110
The Task of the Translator (Benjamin) 20, 29, 30, 39–40, 43–5, 49–50, 60, 79–80, 82, 86–7, 90–4, 98–9, 101–3, 106, 109–10, 116, 127, 129, 131–8, 140, 142, 145–7, 149
Teaching and Valuation (Benjamin) 31, 44, 51, 55
Tiedemann, Rolf 64, 77
Toury, Gideon 5
transformation 19, 35, 39, 41, 48, 52, 54, 59, 95, 97, 104, 108, 114–15, 119, 122–3, 125, 134, 136–7, 153
translatability 35, 37, 40, 60, 106–7, 114, 117, 125, 131–7, 147, 155, 176 n.8
translating a translation 130, 133, 146–8
Translating Culture vs. Cultural Translation (Trivedi) 15
translation
  act of knowing 38
  additive quality of 52
  of cultures 3, 93, 121
  deconstructive perspective on 10
  healing power of 44
  interlingual 9, 15, 40–1, 64, 92, 122–3
  intralingual 9
  limitations 50, 67–8
  metaphorical extension of 16
  original and 40
  and poetry 41
  re-theorized concept of 100
  science of 4
  as temporal movement 32
  transformative 58–9

translational conflict 20
  types of 9
Translation, History and Culture (Bassnett and Lefevere) 6
Translation-For and Against (Benjamin) 64–5
Translation Studies Forum 141, 148
Translation Studies Reader (Venuti) 90
Translation-Theory and Practice (Weissbort and Eysteinsson) 90
Translation Trinity 92, 95
The Translator's Task (Rendall) 90, 104
Trauerspiel 45–6, 109
Trauerspiel and Tragedy (Benjamin) 45
Trivedi, Harish 15
TTR: traduction, terminologie, redaction (Journal) 90
Two Poems by Friedrich Hölderlin (Benjamin) 32
Tzara, Tristan 46, 153

Überleben 104–5, 107, 116, 125, 147, 174 n.3
übersetzen 31, 47, 142–3
Übersetzung 30–3, 35–8, 40, 43, 45, 48, 56, 60–2, 64, 69, 81, 102, 111, 132, 134, 136, 144
Underwood, J. A. 90, 104
un/translatability 20, 117, 131–6, 142, 145, 149–50
  biblical act of naming 134
  blasphemy 138
  continua of transformation 134–5
  foreignness of languages 138–9
  Fortleben 138
  gradations of translatability 133
  liminality 137
  limits of translation 136
  literalness and freedom 134
  resistance, element of 136–41, 148
  sense and language, relation 133
  translation and *Sinn*, relation 132–3
  value and dignity 132

Valk, E. M. 90–1, 104, 132
Vermeer/Reiss skopos theory 4, 160 n.10
Vermittlung 44, 27 n.178

Wagner, Birgit   141–5, 149
Weißbach, Richard   25–7
Weissbort, D.   90
What Is Cultural Translation?
   (Maitland)   120–1, 163 n.27
Williams, Raymond   12
Wolfenstein, Alfred   49–50
The Work of Art in the Age of Its
   Technological Reproducibility
   (Benjamin)   63
Wörtlichkeit   42–3, 51–2, 75, 80–2, 87,
   91, 94–5, 98–9, 133–4
Writing Culture: The Poetics and Politics
   of Ethnography (Clifford and
   Marcus)   3, 7–8, 13, 121

Writing Culture-debate   93
Wyneken, Gustav   31

Young, Robert J. C.   16–17, 136

Zement (Gladkov)   50
Zeugnis   105–6
Zhang Yimou   96, 98
Zohn, Harry   20, 75, 90–1, 98, 102–4,
   107, 124, 128–32, 137, 145, 166
   n.25, 176 n.8, 177 n.24, 177
   n.25, 178 n.27
   misrepresentation of *Fortleben*   104–5
   translation of *Die Aufgabe des*
      Übersetzers   128

www.ingramcontent.com/pod-product-compliance
Lightning Source LLC
Chambersburg PA
CBHW052117300426
44116CB00010B/1692